FROM CLASSICAL ECONOMICS TO DEVELOPMENT ECONOMICS

Also by Gerald M. Meier

ASIAN DEVELOPMENT (*co-author*)
ECONOMIC DEVELOPMENT
EMERGING FROM POVERTY: The Economics that Really Matters
EMPLOYMENT, TRADE, AND DEVELOPMENT
FINANCING ASIAN DEVELOPMENT
INDUSTRIAL ADJUSTMENT IN SUB-SAHARAN AFRICA (*co-editor*)
INTERNATIONAL ECONOMIC REFORM: Collected Papers of Emile Despres (*editor*)
INTERNATIONAL ECONOMICS: Theory of Policy
INTERNATIONAL TRADE AND DEVELOPMENT
LEADING ISSUES IN ECONOMIC DEVELOPMENT
PIONEERS IN DEVELOPMENT (*editor*)
POLITICS AND POLICYMAKING IN DEVELOPING COUNTRIES: Perspectives on the New Political Economy (*editor*)
PRICING POLICY FOR DEVELOPMENT MANAGEMENT
PROBLEMS OF COOPERATION FOR DEVELOPMENT
PROBLEMS OF TRADE POLICY
PROBLEMS OF A WORLD MONETARY ORDER
THE INTERNATIONAL ECONOMICS OF DEVELOPMENT

From Classical Economics to Development Economics

Edited by

Gerald M. Meier
Konosuke Matsushita Professor of International Economics and Policy Analysis, Emeritus
Stanford University

M

St. Martin's Press

First published in Great Britain 1994 by
THE MACMILLAN PRESS LTD
Houndmills, Basingstoke, Hampshire RG21 2XS
and London
Companies and representatives
throughout the world

A catalogue record for this book is available
from the British Library.

ISBN 0–333–60414–8

Printed in Great Britain by
Antony Rowe Ltd
Chippenham, Wiltshire

First published in the United States of America 1994 by
Scholarly and Reference Division,
ST. MARTIN'S PRESS, INC.,
175 Fifth Avenue,
New York, N.Y. 10010

ISBN 0–312–12033–8

Library of Congress Cataloging-in-Publication Data
From classical economics to development economics / edited by Gerald M. Meier.
p. cm.
Includes index.
ISBN 0–312–12033–8
1. Economic history. 2. Economic development—History.
3. Classical school of economics. 4. Asia—Economic conditions.
5. Asia—History. 6. Development economics. I. Meier, Gerald M.
HC51.F76 1994
330'.09—dc20 93–37497
CIP

To **Hla Myint** — a leader on the development frontier who for more than four decades has enriched the subject with his reinterpretation of the dynamics of classical economics, welfare economics, and the history of economic thought.

Generations of students, professional economists, and development practitioners have benefited from the breadth and quality of his insights.

In his honor, former students, colleagues, and friends now contribute these essays.

Contents

Preface

Most development economists are versed only in the post-World War II period of their subject. But economic growth was a major concern in the eighteenth century, and colonial economics and policy commanded much attention in the nineteenth and first half of the twentieth centuries. A return to these earlier concerns can now provide present-day development economists with a greater appreciation of the intellectual history of their subject. Even more, such a return might strengthen the conceptual and empirical foundations of the subject. These are this book's objectives.

The contents range from a general exposition of the relevance of classical economics for development issues to specific studies of countries and periods in terms of export-led development, colonial policy, colonial economic thought, and the role of government. Taken as a whole, the volume may widen the perspective of development economics and encourage fresh thinking for the future in light of the past.

Special appreciation is extended to all the contributors. As a warm personal tribute to Hla Myint, each contributor undertook his assignment most generously and enthusiastically. And their essays have been contributed with the highest professional care.

Ronald Findlay, Deepak Lal, and Heinz Arndt have been most helpful in advising me on the volume's contents and contributors.

Support from the Economic Development Institute of the World Bank is also gratefully acknowledged. David Davies of the World Bank was especially encouraging, and it is satisfying to know that development practitioners recognize the value of the larger and longer perspective, as represented in this book.

GERALD M. MEIER

Notes on the Contributors

H. W. Arndt is Emeritus Professor of Economics at the Australian National University and Visiting Fellow in its Development Studies Centre. In the last thirty years he has worked largely on Indonesia and other parts of the Asian-Pacific region. He is editor of *Asian-Pacific Economic Literature* and author of *Economic Development: The History of an Idea* (1987), among other works.

William J. Barber is Andrews Professor of Economics at Wesleyan University. His degrees are from Harvard University (AB) and University of Oxford (BA, DPhil). He is author of numerous studies in economic development and the history of economic thought. These interests are combined in his *British Economic Thought and India, 1600–1858* (1975).

Lord (Peter) Bauer is a Fellow of Gonville and Caius College, Cambridge, Professor of Economics, Emeritus, at the London School of Economics, and a Fellow of the British Academy. As a pioneer in development, he published *The Rubber Industry* (1948) and *West African Trade* (1954), and since then has written extensively on major issues in the field of economic development.

P. J. Drake is Vice-Chancellor of Australian Catholic University. His previous academic appointments were in The University of New England, where he was Deputy Vice-Chancellor and Head of the Department of Economics, The University of Melbourne and The Australian National University. He has held visiting fellowships in the University of Manchester and the University of London, Institute of Commonwealth Studies. He has been an adviser to the World Bank, the Australian International Development Assistance Bureau and various governments in the Pacific region. Professor Drake has pub`lished many journal articles and several books, including *Money, Finance and Development.*

Ronald Findlay is Ragnar Nurkse Professor of Economics at Columbia University. His degrees are from Rangoon University and MIT. Specializing in international trade and economic development, he has written numerous books and articles, as well as being a consultant to international organizations.

Yujiro Hayami is Professor of International Economics at Aoyama Gakuin University in Tokyo. His previous appointments were Professor of Economics at the Tokyo Metropolitan University and economist at the International Rice Research Institute. He has held research awards from the Japanese Society of Agricultural Economics and the American Agricultural Economic Association, and is author of *Japanese Agriculture under Siege* and *Agricultural Development: An International Perspective* (with V. W. Ruttan).

Shigeru Ishikawa is Professor of Economics at Aoyama Gakuin University, Tokyo and Professor Emeritus, Hitotsubashi University. He is an authority on Asian economic development, particularly People's Republic of China. He is the author of *Economic Development in Asian Perspective* (1967) and numerous other publications on agriculture, technology and employment in development.

Deepak Lal is the James Coleman Professor of International Development Studies at UCLA, and Professor of Political Economy at University College London. He is the author of numerous articles and books on development, including *The Poverty of Development Economics* and *The Hindu Equilibrium*. He has advised a number of governments in developing countries and has worked for various international organizations including the World Bank.

Mats Lundahl is Professor of International Economics at the Stockholm School of Economics. He is the author of many books on international trade and development, with special application to the Caribbean and Africa.

Gerald M. Meier is Konosuke Matsushita Professor of International Economics and Policy Analysis, Emeritus at Stanford University. His degrees are from Reed College (BA), University of Oxford (BLitt), Harvard University (PhD). Meier is the author of a number of books in international economics and economic development. Now in its 6th edition is his *Leading Issues in Economic Development*. He was also editor of the World Bank's *Pioneers in Development* (1984) and *Pioneers in Development, Second Series* (1986).

Lloyd G. Reynolds was born in Canada and received his BA from the University of Alberta, MA from McGill University, and his PhD degree from Harvard University. He is an applied comparative micro-economist, who has made contributions to industrial organization and public control, wage theory, comparative economics, and development economics. In 1985, he published *Economic Growth in the Third World, 1850–1980*. In addition to a dozen or so research monographs, he is the author of texts on principles of economics and on labor economics and industrial relations. He was the Founder and first Director of the Economic Growth Center at Yale University, and is Sterling Professor of Economics Emeritus at Yale.

W. W. Rostow is Rex G. Baker Jr Professor Emeritus of Political Economy at the University of Texas at Austin. As a pioneer in development, he published *The Process of Economic Growth* (1952) and *The Stages of Economic Growth* (1960). Among his many books in economic history and development is his *Theorists of Economic Growth from David Hume to the Present* (1990).

R. M. Sundrum was educated in economics at Rangoon University and had his first academic appointment there. Since then, he has been with UNESCO, ESCAP and the World Bank. He has been a visiting professor at Columbia University, Delhi University, the University of Kerala and Dalhousie University, and has been a consultant to the IMF and ILO. He was a Professorial Fellow in Economics at the Australian National University, 1970–89. His most recent book is *Economic Growth in Theory and Practice* (1991).

"Our interpretation of the classical outlook on the economic problem, if accepted, seems to cast a serious doubt on the practice of taking it for granted that the central problem of the classical economists was to demonstrate the 'allocative efficiency' of the equilibrium adjustments to consumers' demand in the free market. ...The central principle, which successfully unifies the various classical economic doctrines from Adam Smith to J.S. Mill, embodies the following fundamental proposition: viz. the economic welfare of society can be more effectively promoted (i) by increasing the physical productivity of labour, and (ii) by increasing the total volume of economic activity, rather than by tamely accepting the given quantity of productive resources and making refined adjustments in allocating them among different industries. From this follow the two major canons of classical economic policy, (i) free trade which extends the scope of division of labour and brings fresh resources into the productive framework, and (ii) capital accumulation which enables society to maintain a greater quantity of labour....

"After all, even when the economic welfare of society is regarded as consisting in the satisfaction of individuals' wants, it cannot be denied that this subjective economic welfare is as much quantitatively affected by the techno-institutional factors as by the equilibrium process of the market. Or perhaps even more. Therefore, it is not surprising that after decades of work on the 'allocative' problem many modern economists should have turned their attention to such problems as output per man hour, the extent of unused capacity, the socially desirable rate of investment, etc., problems having a distinctly classical flavour."

— Hla Myint, *Theories of Welfare Economics* (1948), pp. 12, 14.

1 Introduction

Gerald M. Meier

The essays in this volume examine the influence of classical economics in the evolution of development thought and policy. They focus on facets of the classical analysis of economic growth, aspects of colonial policy, and the classical roots in development economics. Of prime concern is the relevance of the classical heritage for contemporary research in development problems. To this end, the essays emphasize the macro-dynamics of the classical view of growth, the role of exports in the development process, the structural transformation process between agriculture and industry, and the political economy of development policy making.

The first essay on "The 'Progressive State' in Classical Economics" surveys the grand theme of classical economics — the development of the "progressive state" — as analyzed by Adam Smith and other classicists. Emphasis is on the forces contributing to economic development, the relation between international trade and development, and the roles of the market and state in promoting development — issues that will be re-examined in subsequent essays.

The essay "In Praise of the Classics" examines the relevance of the classical approach to the study of economic development in three areas: (a) the scope of the subject — in particular, the relevance of the "why" questions rather than the "how" questions that are the major concern of current theorizing on economic development; (b) the analytical framework for policy analysis, in which unlike the contemporary "public economics" school, the polity is not subsumed into a committee of Platonic Guardians; and (c) an empirical research methodology that meets many of the epistemological objections against the currently fashionable positivist methodology based on Popperian falsificationism.

Chapter 4, "British Classical Economists and Underdevelopment in India", presents themes and variations on Arthur Lewis's classically-inspired dual-sector model of development. It does so in the context of analyses offered by the classicists when they grappled with problems of underdevelopment in their own time. They assigned special attention to British India, and their various models of development are examined in this chapter. When Lewis's resurrected classical model is juxtaposed against the thinking of nineteenth-century classicists, an ironical result emerges.

The next three chapters (5–7) relate to the classical "vent-for-surplus" theory of international trade and the experience with export-led development. Chapter 5 on "Natural Resources, Vent-for-Surplus and the Staples Theory" unifies the Smithian "vent-for-surplus" approach to trade and development with the "staples theory" of growth and the factor proportions theory of comparative advantage. The concept of an endogenous land frontier is the basis for the unification. The model is applied to some case studies of export-oriented growth during the period 1870–1914 in "regions of recent settlement", "plantation economies," and "peasant export economies".

Chapter 6 on "Vent for Surplus, the Subsistence Fund, and the Evolution of Money" recognizes that in the colonial economies much investment was in the classical form of circulating capital or advances to labor, as distinct from fixed capital. One of the uses given to surplus-venting trade from colonial economies was the creation of a wages or subsistence fund in the form of both consumables and a stock of money. Money constitutes not merely the most versatile store of the subsistence fund, working or circulating capital, but also the most efficient means of accumulation towards long-term capital investment. The accumulation of internationally acceptable money in the colonial export economies depended upon a surplus in the autonomous balance of international payments, arising from the net transfer of merchandise, services, or property rights to foreigners. Thus, surplus-venting, money acquisition, and the accumulation of capital funds went hand in hand in colonial economic development.

Chapter 7 on "Exports and Economic Growth" summarizes both historical and recent statistical evidence that the growth of exports is one of the most significant influences on the growth of national income in most countries. This relationship is so strong that it cannot be fully explained in terms of only the neoclassical-classical concept of improved allocative efficiency. An alternative explanation is offered in terms of demand factors, as discussed in Smith's vent-for-surplus theory and in Keynesian macro-economics, both by themselves and in interaction with supply factors.

The essay on "Peasant and Plantation in Asia" (8) aims to provide a proper perspective on the roles of peasant and plantation in tropical economies. A traditional view developed under colonialism had been to identify "plantation" as a modern enclave in underdeveloped economies geared for the international market, and "peasant" as dominated by subsistence orientation and unresponsive to profit incentives created by changes in market demands and technological opportunities. It is shown that this old paradigm has been undermined as peasants' dynamic responses to profit opportunities have been duly recognized.

The next essay, "Traders and Development," emphasizes the critical role of trading and marketing in the advance from subsistence activity to production for wider exchange. The dynamic effects of trade contribute significantly to the early phases of the development process. This is common ground between market-oriented economists and advocates of state economic control. The contribution of wider exchange should not be ignored in development thought or policy.

Turning to broader issues, the next essay, "Development as a Societal Problem in a Colonial Society", illuminates social and political aspects of colonialism and development. It does so by focusing on the pre-1945 writings of Vera Anstey (India), R. H. Tawney (China), and Joyce Cary (Africa). They recognized that massive poverty could not be permanently alleviated without profound political and social as well as economic change, including escape from colonialism or quasi-colonialism. Three questions are posed: How did these authors introduce a dynamic historical perspective into their analyses; how did they link economic analysis to broader societal variables, politics in particular; and how did they relate colonial or neocolonial relationships to economic development?

During the heyday of the marginal revolution and neoclassical economics, problems of growth and development were neglected. With decolonization in the post-World War II period, however, came a rebirth of interest in economic development. Chapter 11, "From Colonial Economics to Development Economics", summarizes the early development thought of the 1950s and the initial period of teaching the subject when colonial economics gave way to development economics. The evolution of the subject at the University of Oxford is taken as a microcosm illustrative of a general change in the academic approach to the subject.

In the early post-war period, import substitution versus export promotion became a major policy issue for newly developing countries. The essay "Gamagori: In Retrospect" refers to the International Economic Association's conference in 1960 at Gamagori, Japan. Now re-reading the proceedings of the conference, three facts stand out: East Asia was interpreted to mean Japan and India; and there were only passing references to the three Chinas, the ASEAN countries, and South Korea. A pervasive endorsement of planning, import substitution, and export pessimism was qualified by only a few participants at the conference. For economists, a review of the conference is now at once humbling and exhilarating in view of how times have changed.

Chapter 13, "Structural Adjustment Policy: Asian Experience", illuminates the changes in policy that are needed as a developing economy moves from a *dirigiste* regime to a liberalized economy. Difficulties with the structural adjustment policy are noted for countries of East and Southeast Asia in particular. Proposals are made for the "adaptation" of adjustment policy to a country's initial conditions and for the "reconfiguration" of socioeconomic forces so that adaptation becomes possible. In Asia, the effectiveness of a structural adjustment policy often requires power reconfiguration such that coalitions between patrimonial bureaucratic and landowning elites give ground to a coalition of bureaucratic nationalists, technocrats, and industrialists.

The essay on "Government and Economic Growth" (14) returns to the classical issue of governmental intervention in the growth process. The desirable limits of government in economic affairs was outlined long ago by John Stuart Mill. As amended by Arthur Lewis with respect to the special problems of developing economies, Mill's principles still stand as received wisdom. In the development enthusiasm of the 1950s and 1960s, this view was temporarily overridden by advocates of autarkic development, economic planning, and extensive government intervention in private markets. As the weaknesses of this approach have become evident, most recently in the collapse of the socialist economies of Eastern Europe, there has been a strong reversion to neoclassical principles, in theory and practice.

Finally, by way of summary, the last chapter, "The Future in Perspective", offers some conclusions on the influence of classical thought, reviews the present state of the subject of economic development, and suggests a research agenda for the future.

2 The "Progressive State" in Classical Economics

Gerald M. Meier

Nobel Laureate W. A. Lewis (1988) has traced the roots of the subject of economic development to Britain in the century and a half running from about 1650 to Adam Smith's *Wealth of Nations* (1776). Lewis indicates that much of the development theory of today is already to be found in the writings of the eighteenth century, especially in those of Hume (1748), Steuart (1767), and Smith.[1] The essays in this volume build upon that classical heritage. Focusing on both the history of thought and development policy, they illuminate the evolution from classical economics to development economics. As such, they are prompted by the grand theme of classical economics — the development of the "progressive state".

2.1 SMITH'S "PROGRESSIVE STATE"

Smith argued that in a closed economy the size of the non-farm population depends on the size of the agricultural surplus. In an open economy, however, the towns are no longer limited by the size of the domestic agricultural surplus; they can import and export instead, leaving it to the agricultural community to do the same (Lewis, 1988, p. 29). This opportunity, "though it forms no exception from the general rule, has occasioned considerable variations in the progress of opulence in different ages and nations" (Smith, 1776, bk III, ch. 1). The constraint on a country's growth is thus shifted from the size of its agricultural surplus to its potential foreign exchange earnings.

Policies to promote production transformation and to relax the foreign exchange constraint are a prominent concern of modern development economists. So too is their emphasis on the gains from trade and the capacity for export-led development. Several of the essays in this volume reflect these concerns historically — both in the history of ideas and in historical experience.

But why the very early interest in economic development?[2] Smith answers that the central focus of political economy should be on the "progressive state":

> It is in the progressive state, while the society is advancing to the further acquisition, rather than when it has acquired its full complement of riches, that the condition of the labouring poor, of the great body of the people, seems to be the happiest and the most comfortable. It is hard in the stationary, and miserable in the declining state. The progressive state is in reality the cheerful and the hearty state for all the different orders of society. The stationary is dull; the declining melancholy. (Smith, 1776, bk I, ch. 8)

Smith denotes more specific objectives of development when he states that the objects of "Political Economy, considered as a branch of the science of a statesman or legislator" are "first, to provide a plentiful revenue or subsistence for the people, or more properly to enable them to provide such a revenue or subsistence for themselves; and secondly, to supply the state or commonwealth with a revenue sufficient for the public services" (Smith, 1776, bk IV, Introduction).

With his emphasis on the "progressive state", Smith — for the first time in the history of economic thought — adopts production per head, as distinct from aggregate production, as the central criterion of development. "According ..., as this produce, or what is purchased with it, bears a greater or smaller proportion to the number of those who are to consume it, the nation will be better or worse supplied with all the necessaries and conveniences for which it has occasion" (Smith, 1776, vol. I, p. 1).

Smith maintained an optimistic outlook on the progressive state. Not only would it be for the Professor of Moral Philosophy "the cheerful and hearty state", but one could identify and promote various sources of growth that would support the "progress of opulence". According to Smith, the level of output per head, together with its growth,

> must in every nation be regulated by two different circumstances: first, by the skill, dexterity, and judgment with which its labour is generally applied; and secondly, by the proportion between the number of those who are employed in useful labor, and that of those who are not so employed. (Smith, 1776, vol. I, p. 1)

Smith's concern with rising *per capita* income was partly for its own benefit and partly as a means of encouraging population expansion and consequently the extension of the productive or capitalist sector of the economy. As Hollander comments (1973, p. 254), expansion of the productive sector, in turn, was recommended in part because of the productivity advantages of large scale, and in part because of the desirable social and personal characteristics engendered in the capitalist sector.

It is a misreading of classical economics to believe that the central problem of the classicists was to demonstrate the conditions of "allocative efficiency". As Myint (1948, p. 87) explained:

> The nature and significance of the classical welfare analysis cannot be fully appreciated except by considering it against its proper background of the man-against-nature conception of the central economic problem.... It now becomes clear that the principal welfare objective of classical economics is to attain a continuous state of economic expansion, rather than to "tighten" up the equilibrium allocation of resources within a given static framework. This of course follows from the view that the welfare of society, as measured by the measuring rod of labour, may be regarded as being roughly proportional to the volume of output and economic activity. The allocative approach accepts given labour supply, capital equipment, and technique as data and tries to make the best of them to satisfy given consumers' preferences. The classical economists, on the other hand, accepted Land as given; they believed that instead of accepting the rest of the data as given, far-reaching additions to the welfare of society can be made by changing these data into component parts of an expanding framework, even if it entails interfering with the given time preferences of individuals. ... Hence the entire classical economic policy was primarily directed towards the attainment of the ideal 'balance of production and consumption".

In a similar vein, Hicks (1966, p. 258) observes that

> The "static" state of mind ... was not original to economics. It was itself the product of an evolution ... The modern growth theorist does find stuff that interests him in Adam Smith and Ricardo, such as he does not find in Marshall and Marshall's contemporaries. It is fair to say that classical economics is actually, from one aspect, an Old Growth Economics, which has something of the same relation to modern Growth Economics as Greek geometry to modern mathematics. In the neoclassical epoch, it was just put to bed.

According to Smith, the major sources of growth are (1) growth in the labor force and stock of capital (machinery and equipment), (2) improvements in the efficiency with which capital is applied to labor through greater division of labor and technological progress, and (3) foreign trade that widens the market and reinforces the other two sources of growth.

Smith assigned a major role to capital accumulation or investment in the growth process. For capital is the main determinant of "the number of useful and productive laborers" that can be set to work. Labor is "put into motion" by capital. Capital accumulation allows population and the labor force to increase, provides workers with better equipment, and, most important, makes possible a more extensive division of labor. Capital accumulation therefore serves to increase both total output and output per worker (labor productivity). An economy's rate of progress is proportional to its rate of investment: more investment leads to more employment and output, and faster growth in living standards.

> When we compare, therefore, the state of a nation at two different periods, and find, that the annual produce of its land and labor is evidently greater at the latter than the former, that its lands are better cultivated, its manufactures more extensive, we may be assured that its capital must have increased during the interval between those two periods.

Underlying the process of capital accumulation is thrift or saving — Smith's stipulation that "the exchangeable value of the annual produce" must exceed "that of the annual consumption." "Capitals", he says, "are increased by parsimony and diminished by prodigality and misconduct. Whatever a person saves from his revenue he adds to his capital, and either employs it himself in maintaining an additional number of productive hands, or enables some other person to do so, by lending it to him for an interest, that is, for a share of the profits. As the capital of an individual can be increased only by what he saves from his annual revenue or his annual gains, so the capital of a society, which is the same with that of all the individuals who compose it, can be increased only in the same manner" (Smith, 1776, bk II, ch. 3).

What is saved is then invested, provided that a "neat or clear profit" can be earned: "[E]very prodigal appears to be a public enemy, and every frugal man a public benefactor." But even though wages exceed subsistence in a progressive state, the margin is hardly sufficient to allow saving by laborers. Most of the addition to a nation's capital stock must therefore originate with "undertakers" (businessmen) or with landlords. In the Smithian trade-off between growth and equity, the national product could not be raised while at the same time giving the poor a larger share.[3] A rise in the share of profits was the key to increasing the saving rate.

As for the policy of forcing savings through taxation by the state, Smith gave no support to this. Indeed, public prodigality was considered the enemy of private parsimony, and "The whole, or almost the whole public revenue, is in most countries employed in maintaining unproductive hands." In contrast, Smith believed that capital accumulation would proceed most rapidly when capital was "employed in the way that affords the greatest revenue to all the inhabitants of the country, as they will thus be enabled to make the greatest savings". Such employment would result when investors were left free to invest according to their self-interest in seeking the best attainable returns. It was "the highest impertinence and presumption, therefore, in kings and ministers ... the greatest spendthrifts in the society ... to pretend to watch over the economy of private people" (Smith, 1776, bk II, ch. 3).

Considering "the different employments of capitals", Smith emphasized the differential employment-generating capacities of investment in agriculture, manufacturing, and trade of various kinds:

> When the capital of any country is not sufficient for all those three purposes, in proportion as a greater share of it is employed in agriculture, the greater will be the quantity of productive labour which it puts into motion within the country; as will likewise be the value which its employment adds to the annual produce of the land and labour of the society. After agriculture, the capital employed in manufactures puts into motion the greatest quantity of productive labour, and adds the greatest value to the annual produce. That which is employed in the trade of exportation has the least effect of any of the three. (Smith, 1776, bk II, ch. 5)

Classical economists also viewed education and the growth of knowledge as a form of investment.[4] Smith classified "the acquired and useful abilities of all the "inhabitants or members of society" as one of the forms of fixed capital.

> The acquisition of such talents by the maintenance of the acquirer during his education, study, or apprenticeship, always costs a real expense, which is a capital fixed and realized, as it were, in his person. Those talents, as they make part of his fortune, so do they likewise of that of the society of which he belongs. The improved dexterity of a workman may be considered in the same light as a machine or instrument of trade which facilitates and abridges labour, and which, though it costs a certain expense, repays that expense with a profit. (Smith, 1776, bk II, ch. 1)

Once begun, the growth process becomes self-reinforcing in the progressive state. As long as the growth in wealth (GNP) favors profits, there are savings and additional capital accumulation, and hence further growth. And with capital accumulation, the demand for labor rises, and the growing labor force is absorbed in productive employment.

Smith attributed overwhelming importance to the division of labor, in the broad sense of technical progress: "It is the great multiplication of the productions of all the different arts, in consequence of division of labour, which occasions, in a well-governed society, that universal opulence which extends itself to the lowest ranks of the people." The division of labor entails improved efficiency of labor, and increasing specialization leads to rising *per capita* income. By increasing the division of labor, improvements in production would reduce the amount of input per unit of output.

> This great increase of the quantity of work, which, in consequence of the division of labour, the same number of people are capable of performing, is owing to three different circumstance; first, to the increase of dexterity in every particular workman; secondly, to the saving of the time which is commonly lost in passing from one species of work to another; and lastly, to the invention of a great number of machines which facilitate and abridge labour, and enable one man to do the work of many. (Smith, 1776, bk I, ch. 1)

Smith also emphasized that the extent of the division of labor is limited by the extent of the market. "When the market is very small, no person can have any encouragement to dedicate himself entirely to one employment, for want of the power to exchange all that surplus part of the produce for his own labour, which is over and above his own consumption, for such parts of the produce of other men's labour as he has occasion for" (Smith, 1776, bk I, ch. 3).

The division of labor increases wealth, and this in turn widens the market, which enables the division of labor to be carried further forward. An increase in buying power through a rise in average income and numbers would enlarge the division of labor, and this enlargement would further expand buying power. This view of the progressive and cumulative changes associated with increasing division of labor is the basis for Smith's optimism with regard to economic growth.

Smith's analysis became dynamic when he recognized that "the annual produce of the land and labour of any nation can be increased in its value by no other means, but by increasing either the number of its productive labourers, or the productive powers of those labourers who had before been employed" — and this, in turn, depends not only on the extent of the market but also the supply of capital (Smith, 1776, bk II, ch. 3). Because an inadequate supply of capital limited the division of labor, Smith's distinction between "productive" and "unproductive" labor led him to conclude that growth of capital depended on the most extensive use of funds in the employment of productive labor.

Accordingly, he based his encouragement of agriculture on the superior productivity of capital when combined with land. This conformed to his contemporary mid-18th century experience of agriculture being the main source of Britain's growth. Smith did recognize, however, that at a later stage of development when "there is either no uncultivated land, or none that can be had upon easy terms, every artificer who has acquired more stock than he can employ in the occasional jobs of the neighborhood, endeavours to prepare work for more distant sale" (Smith, 1776, p. 359). That is, the profit rate in manufactures for foreign trade would then exceed that in agriculture or manufactures for the home market.[5]

Some passages in the *Wealth of Nations* may be interpreted as suggesting that agriculture is in some absolute sense "advantageous". But the agricultural emphasis should not be exaggerated: Smith recognized that there can be too much agricultural investment as well as too little, as his discussion of the interdependence between country and town indicates.[6] Moreover, Smith certainly did not exclude industrialization in favor of agriculture but recommended that while industrialization should proceed in landed states, it should do so only in "due time" and not by artificial government interventions (Hollander, 1973, p. 291).

Recent expositors of 'urban bias' in developing countries (that is, the protection and subsidization of the urban sector at the expense of the rural sector) may also find in both Steuart (1767, bk I, ch. 10) and Smith (1776, bk 2, ch. 5) a rural agricultural versus urban manufacturing dichotomy.[7] Michael Lipton (1977, pp. 92–97), for instance, detects incipient 'urban bias' in (a) Smith's stage theory of economic growth and the claim that the role of agriculture is to provide 'surpluses' for urban manufacturing development; and (b) in Smith's view that the potential for the division of labor and thus for technical progress and output growth is larger in manufacturing than in agriculture.[8]

In contrast to Lipton's interpretation, one could contend that Smith claims that rural-urban economic conflict arises only in periods of general economic stagnation but that in the process of economic growth the interests of town and country are mutual and harmonious (Smith 1776, bk III, ch. 1). It is also significant, as Myint (1976, p. 157) has noted, that Smith emphasized in Bk III of the *Wealth of Nations* the doctrine of "balanced growth" that was to be prominent in the development literature of the 1950s:[9]

> It is the surplus produce of the country only, or what is over and above the maintenance of the cultivators, that constitutes the subsistence of the town, which can therefore increase only with the increase of this surplus produce.
>
> The town is a continual fair or market to which the inhabitants of the country resort, in order to exchange their rude for manufactured produce. It is this commerce which supplies the inhabitants of the town both with the materials of their work and the means of their subsistence. The quantity of their finished work which they sell to the inhabitants of the country necessarily regulates the quantity of the materials and provisions which they buy. Neither their employment nor subsistence, therefore, can augment but in proportion to the augmentation of the demand from the country for finished work; and this demand can augment only in proportion to the extension of improvement and cultivation. (Smith, 1776, bk III, ch. 1)

The classicists' concern with the changing relationship between agriculture and industry continues in the modern models of a dual economy undergoing production transformation.[10] To the classicists, the relation to the means of production defined the classes of society — capitalists, laborers, and landlords. The task of political economy was not only to illuminate the process of national economic development but also to explain how in the course of a country's development its national income is distributed in the form of profit for capital, wages for labor, and rent for landlords. If capital accumulation was the fundamental force in development, profit was the key to capital accumulation. How do the relative income shares change as development proceeds? And why can the dynamic process of development terminate in a stationary state?

Considering first a recently settled region, rich in natural resources, Smith postulates a high rate of profit because the capital stock is small in relation to resource opportunities. Furthermore, because the rate of capital accumulation is then high, wage rates are also relatively high. But, as more capital is accumulated, the rate of profit falls. Finally, as the population grows, and the capital stock becomes very large, the economy attains "that full complement of riches which the nature of its soil and climate, and its situation with respect to other countries, allowed it to acquire" (Smith, 1776, pp. 94–95). When the economy reaches this state, the rate of capital accumulation slackens, and, therefore, wages decline, but rents have become relatively high as more land has been brought into use. A stationary state is ultimately reached in which investment ceases.

In the Ricardian analysis, capitalists also play the major dynamic role. In undertaking production, they rent land from the landlords, provide the laborers with fixed capital, and advance as wages the circulating capital consumed by the workers during the production period. A rate of profit above zero encourages capitalists to save a portion of their income and to hire additional workers in order to expand production. If the wage rate is assumed to be initially at its "natural" price, the addition of the savings to the wages fund causes the wage rate to be bid up above its "natural" price. Population then increases, the price of food rises, rents rise, and the real wage rate eventually returns to its customary, near-subsistence level. But in money terms, the wage rate is higher because the prices of agricultural commodities are higher, and this implies that the rate of profit is lower. Ricardo recognizes that technological improvements can mitigate the downward pressure on the rate of profit. But he contends that in mature economies, the profit rate is eventually squeezed in agriculture and manufacturing. Again, as in Smith, the lower profit rate curtails investment, and the rate of growth in national income declines. Finally, when the rate of profit is too low to afford adequate compensation for the trouble and risk involved in capital accumulation, the economy becomes stationary. Rents are then high, the real wage rate is at its minimum, and the profit rate is near zero.

Samuelson (1978, p. 1416) has formalized the classical long run theory by noting that just as the classicists had a long-run horizontal supply curve for the subsistence wage, so they had a long-run horizontal supply curve for capital at the minimum-effective rate of accumulation, that profit rate just low enough and just high enough to cause capital to be maintained with zero net algebraic saving.

The pessimistic outcome of the stationary state in classical economics depends, however, on two assumptions: historical diminishing returns and the Malthusian principle of population. Fortunately, subsequent history has belied both assumptions, and the dismal science has had to defer to the classicists' initial optimism of the progressive state.

2.2 TRADE AND DEVELOPMENT

Classical economists gave special attention to how the gains from trade contribute to growth. The gains from trade take several forms. As an extension of the division of labor on an international scale, Smith viewed overseas trade as a way to allow a country to purchase goods more cheaply:

> It is the maxim of every prudent master of a family, never to attempt to make at home what it will cost him more to make than to buy … What is

> prudence in the conduct of every private family, can scarce be folly in that of a great kingdom. If a foreign country can supply us with a commodity cheaper than we ourselves can make it, better buy it of them with some part of the produce of our own industry, employed in a way in which we have some advantage. (Smith, 1776, bk IV, ch. 2)

Smith also viewed foreign trade as providing a "vent-for-surplus":

> When the produce of any particular branch of industry exceeds what the demand of the country requires, the surplus must be sent abroad, and exchanged for something for which there is a demand at home. Without such exportation, a part of the productive labour of the country must cease, and the value of its annual produce diminish. The land and labour of Great Britain produce generally more corn, woollens, and hardware, than the demand of the home-market requires. The surplus part of them, therefore, must be sent abroad, and exchanged for something for which there is a demand at home. It is only by means of such exportation, that this surplus can acquire a value sufficient to compensate the labour and expence of producing it. (Smith, 1776, bk II, ch. 5)

> In every period, indeed, of every society, the surplus part both of the rude and manufactured produce, or that for which there is no demand at home, must be sent abroad in order to be exchanged for something for which there is some demand at home. (Smith, 1776, bk III, ch. 1)

In another passage, Smith relates the vent-for-surplus phenomenon to the gains from trading on a wider market:

> Between whatever places foreign trade is carried on, they all of them derive two distinct benefits from it. It carries out that surplus part of the produce of their land and labour for which there is no demand among them, and brings back in return for it something else for which there is a demand. It gives a value to their superfluities, by exchanging them for something else, which may satisfy a part of their wants, and increase their enjoyments. By means of it, the narrowness of the home market does not hinder the division of labour in any particular branch of art or manufacture from being carried to the highest perfection. By opening a more extensive market for whatever part of the produce of their labour may exceed the home consumption, it encourages them to improve its productive powers, and to augment its annual produce to the utmost, and thereby to increase the real revenue and wealth of the society. (Smith, 1776, bk IV, ch. 1)[11]

In recognizing the significance of the width of the market, Smith also presents a productivity theory of trade. If growth in productivity is due to the division of labor, which, in turn, is limited by the extent of the market, then trade on world markets has the advantage of enabling a small country to overcome the diseconomies of small size.

Smith's vent-for-surplus theory of international trade differs from Ricardo's comparative cost theory. In his 2-country 2-commodity 1-factor (labor) model, Ricardo demonstrated that under conditions of free trade, a country will specialize in the production and export of those commodities for which its costs are comparatively lowest, and will import commodities it can produce only at high relative cost. The cost of "indirectly producing" imports through specialization on exports is less than if the country directly produced the importables at home. In following its comparative advantage, each country maximizes output (imports) per unit of input (exports). The welfare result, according to Ricardo, is that "the extension of foreign trade ... will very powerfully contribute to increase the mass of commodities, and therefore, the sum of enjoyments." And these gains from trade will accrue to each trading nation: trade is symmetrically beneficial.

Smith's vent-for-surplus theory contrasts with the Ricardian analysis in two ways (Myint, 1958): (1) the comparative cost theory assumes that a nation's resources are given and fully employed before the nation enters international trade. After being opened to trade, the country faces a new set of relative prices on world markets and reallocates its given resources more efficiently between expansion of export production and contraction of domestic production. In contrast, according to the vent-for-surplus theory, the country enters into international trade with surplus productive capacity over domestic consumption requirements. The function of international trade then is not to reallocate given resources but rather to provide the new effective demand for the output of surplus resources that would have remained unutilised without trade. Export production can thus be increased without reducing domestic production; exports become a virtually costless means of acquiring imports and expanding domestic activity. This was how Smith used the theory to support free trade.

J. S. Mill thought this theory crude and "a surviving relic of the mercantile theory". Modern economists may also consider it crude for its deficiencies in technical analysis. The theory, however, has helped to illuminate some historical episodes of nineteenth century development. Myint, for instance, has applied the theory to the opening up of the primary exporting countries in Southeast Asia, Latin America, and Africa during the nineteenth century. When brought into world markets in the nineteenth century, these underdeveloped countries began with a sparse population in relation to natural resources. At this time, the economies were essentially subsistence economies, and a well-developed price mechanism and high degree of factor mobility did not exist to equilibrate away the disproportion between land and labor. As Myint observes, given the genuine historical setting of an isolated economy, the initial disproportion between its resources, techniques, tastes, and population showed itself in the form of surplus productive capacity.

Once the opening up process got into its stride, the export production of these countries expanded very rapidly along a typical growth curve, rising very sharply to begin with and tapering off afterwards. Peasant export production of a traditional crop (for example, rice in Southeast Asia) expanded by using underemployed labor and by bringing more land under cultivation with the same traditional methods of cultivation. Even where new peasant export crops were introduced (for example, palm oil and ground nut exports in West Africa), they could be produced by fairly simple methods that involved no radical change from the traditional techniques of agricultural production. While peasant export crops expanded by extension of cultivation using the traditional methods of production, the mining and plantation sectors of the economy expanded through the inflow of large movements of cheap labor from India and China and by western enterprise improving transport and communications and discovering new mineral resources (the "unlocking of the tropics" in Professor L. C. A. Knowles's phrase). Rather than making a given volume of resources more productive, these external influences increased the total volume of resources that could be drawn into export production.

Myint concludes that

> instead of a process of economic growth based on continuous improvements in skills, more productive recombinations of factors and increasing returns, the nineteenth century expansion of international trade in the underdeveloped countries seems to approximate to a simpler process based on constant returns and fairly rigid combinations of factors. Such a process of expansion could continue smoothly only if it could feed on additional supplies of factors in the required proportions. (Myint, 1958, pp. 317–20)

A more extended interpretation of Ricardo's comparative advantage model may actually relate it to Lewis's dual sector model (1954) insofar as Ricardo formulated his model to provide a persuasive case for free trade in order to secure repeal of the Corn laws. He wanted this policy outcome not simply because it would reduce the price of food so as to increase "the mass of commodities and sum of enjoyments" — the static gains from trade — but because it would also redistribute income from landowners who absorb their rents in luxury consumption to capitalists who save and invest.[12] If the wage good (food) could be kept low through free trade, profits could be high, savings and investment increase, and economic growth in Britain could accelerate as the capitalist sector expanded.[13]

Regardless of their various interpretations of the gains from trade, the classical economists agreed that all the trading countries benefit from free trade. And the gains are not only the static gains of efficiency as in the Ricardian model, but also dynamic gains of growth.

Smith's productivity theory of trade — based on his dictum that "the division of labor is limited by the extent of the market" — links development to international trade by interpreting trade as a dynamic force based on economies of scale. By widening the extent of the market and the scope of the division of labor, trade may raise the skill and dexterity of labor, encourage technical innovations, overcome technical indivisibilities, and generally enable the trading country to enjoy increasing returns and economic development.[14]

John Stuart Mill noted that trade according to comparative advantage results in a "more efficient employment of the productive forces of the world," and this is to be considered the "direct economical advantage of foreign trade. But there are, besides, indirect effects, which must be counted as benefits of a high order" (Mill, vol. II, bk III, ch. 17, sec. 5). One of the most significant "indirect" benefits, according to Mill, is "the tendency of every extension of the market to improve the processes of production. A country which produces for a larger market than its own, can introduce a more extended division of labour, can make greater use of machinery, and is more likely to make inventions and improvements in the processes of production."

Further, Mill observed that another result "principally applicable to an early state of industrial advancement", is that "the opening of a foreign trade, by making [people] acquainted with new objects, or tempting them by the easier acquisition of things which they had not previously thought attainable, sometimes works a sort of industrial revolution in a country whose resources were previously undeveloped for want of energy and ambition in the people: inducing those who were satisfied with scanty comforts and little work, to work harder for the gratification of their new tastes, and even to save, and accumulate capital, for the still more complete satisfaction of those tastes at a future time".[15]

Or again, "It is hardly possible to overrate the value in the present low state of human improvement, of placing human beings in contact with persons dissimilar to themselves, and with modes of thought and action unlike those with which they are familiar .... Such communication has always been and is peculiarly in the present age, one of the primary sources of progress."[16]

Mill also emphasized that trade benefits the less developed countries through "the introduction of foreign arts, which raises the returns derivable from additional capital to a rate corresponding to the low strength of accumulation; and the importation of foreign capital which renders the increase of production no longer exclusively dependent on the thrift or providence of the inhabitants themselves, while it places before them a stimulating example, and by instilling new ideas and breaking the chain of habit, if not by improving the actual condition of the population, tends to create in them new wants, increased ambition, and greater thought for the future".[17]

The dynamic benefits of trade on development are therefore of three kinds: (1) those that widen the extent of the market, induce innovations, and increase productivity; (2) those that increase savings and capital accumulation; and (3) those that have an educative effect in instilling new wants and tastes and in transferring technology, skills, and entrepreneurship (Ricardo's "trade in ideas"). This emphasis is on the supply side of the development process — the opportunity that trade gives a poor country to remove domestic shortages, to overcome the diseconomies of the small size of its domestic market, and to accelerate the "learning rate" of its economy. In modern terminology, the dynamic gains from trade raise total factor productivity and hence the rate of growth in national income.

Given the gains from trade, any restriction on free trade should therefore be generally opposed. As Smith argued, the "mean and malignant" trade regulations of the earlier mercantilist system should be disbanded in favor of trade liberalization that would widen the extent of the market and promote growth.

Only a few exceptions to free trade — under limited conditions — were recognized. Smith acknowledged "defence before opulence". But while the infant industry case for protection had appeal for some, Smith rejected it on grounds that it would retard capital accumulation and fail to maximize current national income: "But the immediate effect of every such regulation is to diminish its revenue, and what diminishes its revenue is certainly not very likely to augment its capital faster than it would have augmented of its own accord, had both capital and industry been left to find out their natural employments" (Smith, 1776, bk IV, ch. 2). And again: "No regulation of commerce can increase the quantity of industry in any society beyond what its capital can maintain. It can only divert a part of it into a direction into which it might not otherwise have gone; and it is by no means certain that this artificial direction is likely to be more advantageous to the society than that into which it would have gone of its own accord" (Smith, 1776, bk IV, ch. 2).

In answer to Smith, however, John Rae argued that

> individuals, as well as nations, acquired wealth from other sources than mere saving from revenue ... skill is as necessary, and consequently as valuable a co-operator with the industry of both as either capital or parsimony". Nonetheless, Rae cautions that the legislator "is never justified in attempting to transfer arts ... from foreign countries to his own, unless he have sufficient reason to conclude that they will ultimately lessen the cost of the commodities they produce, or are of such a nature, that the risk of waste to the stock of the community from a sudden interruption to their importation from abroad, is sufficiently great to warrant the probable expense both of the transfer and of maintaining the manufacture at home". (Rae, 1834, pp. 61, 367).

Mill also recognized the infant industry exception.

> The superiority of one country over another in a branch of production often arises only from having begun sooner ... A country which has ... skill and experience yet to acquire may in other respects be better adapted to the production than those which were earlier in the field ... But it cannot be expected that individuals should, at their own risk, or rather to their certain loss, introduce a new manufacture, and bear the burden of carrying it until the producers have been educated up to the level of those with whom the processes are traditional. A protecting duty, continued for a reasonable time, might sometimes be the least inconvenient mode in which the nation can tax itself for the support of such an experiment.

But after witnessing the abuses of protection, Mill stated that "I am inclined to believe that it is safer to make it [infant industry support] by an annual grant from the public treasury, which is not nearly so likely to be continued indefinitely, to prop up an industry which has not so thriven as to be able to dispense with it".[18]

The classical view of the complementarity between foreign trade and the promotion of domestic economic development is now a fundamental tenet of mainstream development economics. Many have verified the power of export-led development.[19] And even if it is debatable whether foreign trade is "the engine of growth," trade is at least the "handmaiden" of growth

(Kravis, 1970), serving as a check on the appropriateness of new industries by keeping prices and costs in touch with external prices and costs (Myint, 1976, p. 159).

A special feature of classical economics was the debate on colonization among the classicists.[20] Smith, Bentham, Ricardo, James Mill, McCulloch, J. S. Mill, Torrens, and to a lesser extent, Malthus, Senior, and Cairnes all contributed to this debate. As the historian of this debate, Donald Winch (1965, p. 2) observes: "The economic problems raised by colonies and colonization went straight to the root of classical inquiry: free trade, capital accumulation, population pressure, economic growth and the role of the state."

Between 1776 and 1830, the classical "economists and their Benthamite associates figured mainly as opponents of the concept of empire implied in the old colonial system. But after 1830 we find many of them associated with a movement dedicated to the erection of a new imperial edifice." Winch's study is definitive in tracing the development of the classical attitude to colonies in its shift from skepticism to enthusiasm.

In the early phase, "members of the classical school were chiefly concerned with exposing the burdens of empire and with presenting the free trade case against colonial trade restrictions". After 1830 the case for "systematic colonization" was advanced by the Colonial Reform movement under the leadership of Edward Gibbon Wakefield. While it could be argued that the role of new markets would stimulate the British economy, it also had to be demonstrated that, once established, colonies could be made economically and politically viable communities, without the characteristics criticized earlier by members of the classical school.[21] Robert Torrens was one of Wakefield's first converts among economists, and J. S. Mill also became a strong supporter.[22]

Herman Merivale, Drummond Professor of Political Economy at Oxford, devoted a series of lectures to the subject in the years 1839–41.[23] Merivale viewed favorably Wakefield's analysis of the export of capital associated with colonization and the new export markets thereby acquired. Like Wakefield, Merivale regarded the essential part of the subject to be that dealing with "the economical development of the colonies". He recognized that colonies might face special problems in their early stages, but distinguished different types of colonies. First, there are those colonies which possess "no peculiar advantages for the production, by agricultural or mining labour, of articles of value in the foreign market". The chief object of settlers of such colonies is to provide "a sufficient maintenance for a population of moderate wants"; production for world markets was a subsidiary end. Secondly, there are those colonies "in which the industry of the settlers has been principally turned towards raising the staple articles of produce for the European market". Systematic colonization was believed applicable only to this latter category.

2.3 MARKET AND STATE

If for the classicists the market was to determine a free trade strategy, so too were the domestic forces of competition and the virtues of the capitalist sector to limit the role of government in national development policy.[24] To Smith, the system of natural liberty permits change and development, while government intervention would handicap the positive forces of growth. Individuals should be free to act on "their propensity to truck, barter, and exchange one thing for another" and to pursue self-interest. Competition and market forces would act as an invisible hand to bring self-interest into harmony with public interest.

> As every individual, therefore, endeavors as much as he can both to employ his capital in the support of domestic industry, and so to direct that industry that its produce may be of the greatest value; every individual necessarily labours to render the annual revenue of society as great as he can … He generally, indeed, neither intends to promote the public interest, nor knows how much he is promoting it … he intends only his own gain, and he is in this, as in many other cases, led by an invisible hand to promote an end which was no part of his intention. (Smith, 1776, bk IV, ch. 2)

Yet Smith did not simply assume a 'spontaneous' identity of interest and did not rely merely on 'competition' in the abstract, but instead went beyond this to evaluate the effectiveness of different institutional forms in enforcing the identity of self interest and public interest (Rosenberg, 1960, p. 559). Recognizing that individuals are also influenced by certain impulses, motivations, and behavior patterns that could thwart, rather than reinforce, the beneficent operation of market forces, Smith gave considerable attention to specifying the institutional conditions under which a competitive market system would operate most effectively.

Robbins (1952, p. 56) puts it well: in the classical system of economic freedom,

> the invisible hand which guides men to promote ends which were no part of their intention, is not the hand of some god or some natural agency

> independent of human effort; it is the hand of the lawgiver, the hand which withdraws from the sphere of the pursuit of self-interest those possibilities which do not harmonize with the public good. There is absolutely no suggestion that the market can furnish everything; on the contrary, it can only begin to furnish anything when a whole host of other things have been furnished another way.

The ideal institutional order would allow the individual to behave with maximum industry and efficiency when the reward for effort is neither too low nor too great (monopolists, large landowners). Further, institutional arrangements should not allow income to be pursued without contributing to the public interest. This principle underlay Smith's attack on mercantilism. What would now be criticized as 'rent seeking' was condemned as the result of the dispensation of monopoly grants, the arbitrary bestowal of "extraordinary privileges", and "extraordinary restraints" upon different sectors of industry through government policies.

Smith therefore sought the establishment of appropriate institutions that would increase both the motivation and the capacity of the human agent (Rosenberg, 1960, pp. 560–61). For example, he opposed apprenticeship laws that diminished the incentive to industry and hard work, advocated certain systems of land tenure, argued that the ideal unit of agricultural organization is the small proprietorship, and opposed the joint-stock company.

The Smithian analysis is a perceptive point of departure for modern research on the relation of institutions to incentives and the behavior of agents. Thus, through his study of institutions and institutional change, North (1990) seeks to achieve an understanding of the differential performance of economies through time.[25]

Given his critique of mercantilism, Smith therefore advocated that individuals should be freed from governmental policy that had the distortionary effects of limiting capital formation, using capital unproductively, conferring monopoly privileges, and sapping the vitality of competitive forces. Public spending should be kept to a minimum, and production in the public sector should be limited to that small share that could not be supplied by private enterprise. Narrowly restricting the activities of government, Smith declared that the sovereign's duties were limited to defense, administration of justice, and the maintenance of certain public institutions and certain public works (bk IV, ch. 9). According to Smith, "Little else is requisite to carry a state to the highest degree of opulence from the lowest barbarism, but peace, easy taxes, and a tolerable administration of justice."[26]

Smith was especially emphatic in criticising any state allocation of investment:

> What is the species of domestic industry which his capital can employ, and of which the produce is likely to be of the greatest value, every individual, it is evident, can, in his local situation, judge much better than any statesman or lawgiver can do for him. The statesman, who should attempt to direct private people in what manner they ought to employ their capitals, would not only load himself with a most unnecessary attention, but assume an authority which could safely be trusted, not only to no single person, but to no council or senate whatever, and which would nowhere be so dangerous as in the hands of a man who had folly and presumption enough to fancy himself fit to exercise it. (1776, bk IV, ch. 2)

Hume, however, had argued in *A Treatise on Human Nature* that a large number of individuals might find it impossible to agree to execute a project of public interest, but "political societies" may accomplish what individuals cannot:

> Thus, bridges are built, harbours opened, ramparts raised, canals formed, fleets equipped, and armies disciplined, everywhere, by the care of government, which, though composed of men subject to all human infirmities, becomes, by one of the finest and most subtle inventions imaginable, a composition which is in some measure exempted from all these infirmities. (Rostow, 1990, p. 49)

Smith too saw as a major responsibility of government the provision of certain public works of such a nature that "the profit could never repay the expense to any individual or small number of individuals, and which it therefore cannot be expected that any individual or small number of individuals should erect or maintain" although "they might be in the highest degree advantageous to a great society" (1776, bk V, ch. 1, pt III). His examples are of transport infrastructure — roads, bridges, canals, and harbors.

Not only did Smith limit governmental activities, but he also promulgated a strong principle for the guidance of public administrators: "Public services are never better performed than when their reward comes only in consequence of their being performed, and is proportioned to the diligence employed in performing them" (Smith, 1776, bk V, ch. 1, pt II). The diligence, of course, was to be directed to only a restricted set of public duties that met Smith's criteria for the proper role of the state.

As for agriculture, this too should be free of government policies except insofar as the provision of public works might benefit agricultural development. Selective forms of taxation on the rents of landlords were also advocated to encourage landlords to take a more "active part in agriculture".

To appreciate *The Wealth of Nations'* emphasis on the market, it is important to recognize that the market was not a static conception for the analysis of value and distribution: instead it was to be conceived in a dynamic sense (Robbins, 1968, p. 101). In supporting the division of labor, free markets also promote invention and improvement; and, if economic freedom allows opportunities to be pursued, the force of self-interest disturbs existing equilibria and promotes progress.

Slight, if any, attention, however, was given to the process by which markets actually arise. The classicists focused their main attention on the spontaneous elements in economic society — on the way in which the private interests of individuals guided by the impersonal mechanisms of the market achieved an orderly system of social cooperation and some of the prerequisites of economic growth. "They saw markets and the organization of production arising, like language itself, without any act of conscious collective choice. They saw the main influences which bring about economic development operating without central initiative" (Robbins, 1968, p. 161).

With the coming of the "marginal revolution" in the 1870s, economists' interest in development gave way to problems of resource allocation. Britain had by then become "the workshop of the world". Moreover, the concern with economic growth was less acute if population could be controlled. Static analysis of the market price system and equations of general economic equilibrium claimed economists' attention instead of problems of the "progressive state". And while problems of colonization merited some notice, the interest in international development disappeared. Only with the emergence of new nations in the postwar decade of the 1950s was extensive analysis of the "progressive state" to be revived and the discipline of "development economics" to be established.

Notes

1. Also for an elaboration of the classical tradition, see W. W. Rostow (1990, Part I); "Development, Efficiency, and Equity in Historical Perspective", in *Equity and Efficiency in Economic Development*, edited by Donald J. Savoie and Irving Brecher (Montreal: McGill-Queen's University Press, 1992); Lionel Robbins, *The Theory of Economic Development in the History of Economic Thought* (London: Macmillan, 1968).

2. Illuminating analyses of the growth aspects of classical economics are presented by Hicks (1966), Samuelson (1978), Eltis (1984), Rostow (1990).
3. Confronting the historical evidence in the British and American industrial revolutions of the nineteenth century, Jeffrey Williamson (1991, pp. 101–13) has submitted that "an old lesson dating back to Adam Smith should be unlearned. American history suggests that more inequality did not raise conventional accumulation by much. British history suggests that more inequality did not raise conventional accumulation at all. When human capital is added to the accumulation story, the Smithian trade-off receives an even sounder rejection by history."
4. For an extended discussion, see Robbins (1968), ch. IV).
5. Cf. the models of Ch. V below.
6. For a more extended discussion of this issue, see Hollander (1973, ch. 10).
7. Mick Moore, "Political Economy and the Rural-Urban Divide, 1767–1981", *Journal of Development Studies,* 1986, 1–27.
8. Lipton (1977, p. 99) observes that "In the developments and distortions of Smith's ideas, we see in embryo almost all the arguments advanced for urban bias in the Third World today: the worship of intersectoral trade; the fear that the cities will get too little surplus or pay 'too much' for it; the wish to move capital along with rural workers to the cities. Then as now, all this produces a preference for big farms, selective deprotection of agriculture, cheap food, and manufactured exports."
9. See the discussion of "balanced growth" in ch. XV below.
10. See Hollis Chenery and T. N. Srinivasan (eds), *Handbook of Development Economics,* vol. I (Amsterdam, North-Holland, 1988).
11. The vent for surplus theory is also referred to in Smith (1776), bk I, ch. 11; bk IV, ch. 3. See also, Heinz D. Kurz, "Adam Smith on Foreign Trade: A Note on the 'Vent-for-Surplus' Argument", *Economica* 59 (1992) pp. 475–81; Myint (1977).
12. Ricardo, *Essay on the Influence of a Low Price of Corn Upon the Profits of Stock* (1815). For a modern restatement, see Ronald Findlay, "Growth and Development in Trade Models", in R. W. Jones and P. B. Kenen (eds), *Handbook of International Economics*, vol. I (Elsevier Science Publishers, 1948); pp. 185–91.

    For a more general analysis of the relation of Lewis's dual sector model to classical economics, see Gustav Ranis and John C. H. Fei, "Lewis and the Classicists", in Mark Gersovitz (ed.), *The Theory and Experience of Economic Development* (London: Allen & Unwin, 1982).
13. Jeffrey Williamson (1991, pp. 62–66) provides a quantitative analysis of what would have been the impact on Britain's distribution of income if the Corn Laws had been repealed in the mid-1830s. As predicted in the Ricardian model, an early repeal would have served to augment the supply of labor to manufacturing, raise manufacturing profits, stimulate exports, and boost the rate of industrialization.
14. Smith (1776), bk I, chs. II and III. See also Myint (1958). This aspect of Smith's theory was elaborated in Allyn Young's celebrated article, "Increasing Returns and Economic Progress", *Economic Journal*, December 1928, pp. 527–42.

15. J. S. Mill, *Principles of Political Economy* (London, 1848) vol. II, bk III, ch. XVII, sec. 5. See the relation to the "aspiration to consume" in ch. VIII, below.
16. Mill, *op. cit.*, vol. II, bk III, chap XVII, sec. 5. See for the "educative effect" of an open economy, H. Myint, *Economic Theory and the Underdeveloped Countries,* (New York: Oxford University Press, 1971) p. 255; also the illuminating section on "Trade as a Highway of Learning", in W. W. Lockwood, *Economic Development of Japan* (Princeton: Princeton University Press, 1963) pp. 320–334.
17. *Ibid.*, vol. I, sec. I, ch. 13.
18. Quotations in this section are from Robbins (1968) pp. 112–15.
19. For a survey of empirical studies, see Jagdish N. Bhagwati, "Export-Promoting Strategy: Issues and Evidence", *World Bank Research Observer,* vol. 3, no. 1, January 1988.
20. On colonial theory and practice, see also H. W. Arndt, *Economic Development: The History of an Idea* (Chicago: University of Chicago Press, 1987) pp. 22–29.
21. Winch (1965, chs. VII–IX).
22. For Mill's views, see Winch (1965), pp. 135–43.
23. Cf. ch. XIII below.
24. For illuminating discussions of the classical conception of the functions of the state and market, see Lionel Robbins, *The Theory of Economic Policy in English Classical Political Economy* (London: Macmillan, 1952) chs 1–3; Joseph Spengler, "Adam Smith and Society's Decision-makers," in Andrew S. Skinner and Thomas Wilson (eds.) *Essays on Adam Smith* (Oxford: Clarendon Press, 1975), ch. VII; George J. Stigler, "Smith's Travels on the Ship of State", *ibid.*, ch. XII.
25. See also R. C. O. Matthews, "The Economics of Institutions and the Sources of Growth", *Economic Journal,* 96, December 1986, pp. 903–18.
26. However, for an informative essay on Smith's many departures from *laissez faire* doctrine, see Jacob Viner, "Adam Smith and Laissez Faire", in John Maurice Clark *et al.*, *Adam Smith 1776–1926* (New York: Augustus M. Kelly, reprint, 1966, original edition 1928) pp. 116–55. Viner concludes that Smith "saw a wide and elastic range of activity for government, and he was prepared to extend it even farther if government, by improving its standards of competence, honesty, and public spirit, showed itself entitled to wider responsibilities".

References

Eltis, Walter (1984) *The Classical Theory of Economic Growth* (New York: St. Martin's Press).

Hicks, J. R. (1966) "Growth and Anti-Growth," *Oxford Economic Papers*, (November), 257–69.

Hollander, Samuel (1973) *The Economics of Adam Smith* (Toronto: University of Toronto Press).

Hume, David (1748) *Essays Moral and Political*, ed. Eugene Rotwein (London: Nelson, 1955).

Kravis, I. B (1970) "Trade as a Handmaiden of Growth: Similarities between the Nineteenth and Twentieth Centuries," *Economic Journal*, vol. 80, no. 32 (December).

Lewis, W. A. (1954) "Economic Development with Unlimited Supplies of Labour," *Manchester School*, 22, pp. 139–91.

Lewis,W. A. (1988) "The Roots of Development Theory," in Hollis Chenery and T. N. Srinivasan, (eds), *Handbook of Development Economics*, vol. I, (Amsterdam: North-Holland).

Lipton, Michael (1977) *Why Poor People Stay Poor* (Cambridge, Mass.: Harvard University Press).

Myint, Hla (1948) *Theories of Welfare Economics* (Cambridge, Mass.: Harvard University Press).

Myint, Hla (1976) "Comment on the Diffusion of Development," in Thomas Wilson and Andrew S. Skinner (eds), *The Market and the State* (Oxford: Clarendon Press).

Myint, Hla (1977) "Adam Smith's Theory of International Trade in the Perspective of Economic Development," *Economica*, 44, pp. 231–48.

North, Douglas C. (1990) *Institutions, Institutional Change and Economic Performance* (Cambridge: Cambridge University Press).

Rae, John (1834) *Statement of Some New Principles of Political Economy* (Boston: Hilliard, Gray).

Robbins, Lionel (1952) *The Theory of Economic Policy in English Classical Political Economy* (London: Macmillan).

Robbins, Lionel (1968) *The Theory of Economic Development in the History of Economic Thought* (London: Macmillan).

Rosenberg, Nathan (1960) "Some Institutional Aspects of the Wealth of Nations," *Journal of Political Economy* (December 1960), pp. 557–570.

Rostow, W. W. (1990) *Theories of Economic Growth from David Hume to the Present* (New York: Oxford University Press).

Samuelson, Paul A. (1978) "The Canonical Classical Model of Political Economy," *Journal of Economics Literature* (December), 1415–34.

Smith, Adam (1776) *An Inquiry into the Nature and Causes of the Wealth of Nations* (London: W. Stratham; Cannan edition, New York: Modern Library, 1937).

Steuart, James (1767) *An Enquiry into the Principles of Political Economy*, ed. Andrew S. Skinner (Edinburgh: Oliver & Boyd, 1966, reprinted).

Williamson, Jeffrey G. (1991) *Inequality, Poverty, and History* (Oxford: Basil Blackwell).

Winch, Donald (1965) *Classical Political Economy and Colonies* (London: G. Bell).

3 In Praise of the Classics

Deepak Lal

'As civilized human beings, we are the inheritors, neither of an enquiry about ourselves and the world, nor of an accumulating body of information, but of a conversation, begun in the primeval forests and made more articulate in the course of centuries. It is a conversation which goes on both in public and within each of ourselves. Of course there is argument and enquiry and information, but wherever these are profitable they are to be recognized as passages in this conversation, and perhaps they are not the most captivating of the passages. It is the ability to participate in this conversation, and not the ability to reason cogently, to make discoveries about the world, or to contrive a better world, which distinguishes the human being from the animal and the civilized man from the barbarian. Indeed, it seems not improbable that it was the engagement in this conversation (where talk is without a conclusion) that gave us our present appearance, man being descended from a race of apes who sat in talk so long and so late that they wore our their tails.' — M. Oakeshott, *The Voice of Poetry in the Conversation of Mankind* (London: Bowes & Bowes, 1959) p. 11

3.1 INTRODUCTION

This essay provides a defense of the relevance of classical political economy for development policy and research. As the above quotation from Oakeshott pinpoints, a good education requires us to continue age old conversations. With the current "scientistic" pretensions of technocratic economics, there is an increasing danger that many economists will come to believe that the only conversations worthy of their notice are those taking place in the latest issues of well-known journals. The past masters having been superseded by their modern descendants, the former's views are then considered to be of only antiquarian interest for students of the history of economic thought. This attitude fails to take account of the policy and analytical relevance of classical thought for the economics of developing countries.[1]

In this paper, therefore, I will briefly outline three aspects of the classical tradition that (no doubt, refurbished by modern techniques) need to be revived in the study of economic development. The first concerns the scope of the subject, the second the framework for policy analysis, and the third, research methodology for country comparisons of differential rates and patterns of development.

3.2 CLASSICAL CONCERNS

In his Chichele lectures for 1966, Lord Robbins notes that:

> The theory of economic development addresses itself to two types of questions. It asks what are the fundamental causes or conditions of economic development and it asks what path development will take, given any particular configuration of these factors or fundamental conditions. If you like to put things this way, we can say it asks *why* development takes place and *how* it happens. (Robbins, 1968, p. 1)

He then goes on to show that the classics by and large were concerned with the *why* questions. By contrast the modern neoclassical theory of growth and its offshoots such as the theory of the dual economy, which has been developed as particularly relevant for developing countries, are concerned with the "how" questions. The basic answer provided to the "why" question by the classics was that economic development was dependent upon thrift, productivity, and entrepreneurship. Government consumption was regarded as "unproductive," and (in modern terminology) could crowd out investment. Eltis (1984, p. 319) in a masterly translation of the classical theory of economic growth into modern language (including formalism) notes:

> there was far less to prevent growth in *The Wealth of Nations* than in the Physiocratic models. Only excess government expenditure which absorbed more than the surplus of the productive sector, and so rendered accumulation impossible, or government regulation, or a failure to sustain property rights could prevent the market from solving one or more of the many problems it was required to solve. Smith's simple statement that, all that was profitable was productive and that too much government expenditure or interference could prevent the conversion of the potential surpluses of the productive into the extra capital that was necessary for growth, were comprehensible to all, and sufficiently plausible to the economically literate to remain utterly orthodox until 1936.

Bacon and Eltis (1976) based their influential study of the British economy on a distinction between the "productive" surplus producing sector (agriculture, industry and the entire private sector) and the "unproductive" surplus using sector (provision of unmarketed government services). This as Eltis notes was clearly an echo of classical growth theory. As was the model that Lal and van Wijnbergen (1985) produced of the global crowding out of investment by the activities of national public sectors, increasingly linked through a globally integrated capital market. However, many of the other aspects of the classical theory of development seem to be obsolete. These include the assumption that wages were too low to be taxed or to provide an investible surplus, which must then come from profits and rents, seem to be obsolete. Nor does the Malthusian population analysis appear persuasive any longer (see Birdsall, 1988, for a review). Nor the belief in aggregate diminishing returns to capital accumulation that have been taken to be a hallmark of the classics. But as Eltis notes, these were later glosses on Smith's model of development, in which increasing returns from the division of labor and the widening of the market are central. These were supposed to characterize the new "industrial" sector. By contrast in agriculture Smith assumed constant costs (Eltis, 1976, p. 100). It would go too far beyond the remit of this paper to outline the mechanics of the resulting model of growth. The interested reader is referred to Eltis, particularly how he shows that Smith arrived at the conclusion that despite increasing returns to industry, it would be misguided to help industry *at the expense* of agriculture (Eltis, 1976, p. 104).

The diminishing returns assumption which underlay classical economics has not been borne out by the subsequent economic history of the developed or developing world (see Scott 1989). The classics believed that technical progress could hold the stationary state at bay, and in our day this avenue of escape has become the *deus ex machina* in the neoclassical theory of economic growth — on which more below.

However, as Wrigley (1988) argues in a brilliant book, the classics were concerned in explaining development in the economic conditions they believe prevailed at that time. Though these were changing with the rolling industrial revolution, the classics still saw their concern as the development of what had been for centuries an organic economy, which Wrigley defines as "an economy bounded by the productivity of land" (p. 5). In such an economy — and historically this has been the dominant type — there is a universal dependence on organic raw materials for food, clothing, housing, and fuel. Their supply is in the long run inevitably constrained by the fixed factor — land. This was also true of traditional industry and transport. Most metal working industries were dependent upon the supply of charcoal (a vegetable substance) for providing the heat to smelt and work the crude ores.

> A recognition of the significance of the productivity of land to the whole range of the productive activities of society is both implicit and explicit in the writings of the classical economists, and the leverage which the application of the principle of declining marginal returns thus exacted was very powerful. (Wrigley, 1980, pp. 18–19)

The industrial revolution according to Wrigley essentially led to the substitution of this organic economy by a mineral based energy economy. But this fundamental change was becoming apparent only towards the mid 19th century in England, and it was not till Marx was writing that it had become manifest. This new economic regime "escaped from the problem of the fixed supply of land and of its organic products by using mineral raw materials". Moreover, the:

> organic economy was necessarily severely inhibited by its energy budget. Just as raw materials were all organic, both heat and mechanical energy were obtained from organic sources, the heat energy from burning wood (or its derivative charcoal); the mechanical energy from human or animal muscle.... Moreover, since animals need the same "fuel" as men, they compete with men for the same scarce resource, fertile land. When, therefore, a mineral source, coal, began to supply more and more of the heat energy needed by industry and later, following the development of an effective device for turning heat into mechanical energy in the form of the steam engine, also provided a solution to the problem of securing a virtually unlimited supply of such power, the prospects for growth both in aggregate output and in output per head were entirely transformed from those which had always previously detained. (Wrigley, 1988, pp. 5–6]

Thus the industrial revolution in England was based on two forms of "capitalism", one institutional, namely that defended and described by Adam Smith — because of its productivity enhancing effects, even in an organic economy — and the other physical: the capital stock of stored energy represented by the fossil fuels which allowed mankind to create a

> world that no longer follows the rhythm of the sun and the seasons; a world in which the fortunes of man depend largely upon how he himself regulates the economy and not upon the vagaries of weather and harvest;

> a world in which poverty has become an optional state rather than a reflection of the necessary limitations of human productive powers. (Wrigley, 1988, p. 6)

The classical insights therefore that still remain valid for the contemporary process of economic development concern the institutional aspects, their mechanics of growth (though logically consistent) have been overtaken by an historical change in mankind's economic base. Though those who believe in the limits to growth because the stock of fossil fuels too is finite would argue that the final denoument — the stationary state — has merely been postponed!

It is time to turn to the answers to the "how" question. The growth theories developed in the 1950s and 1960s were the descendants of the Harrod–Domar (HD) model. In particular the Solow–Swan model of steady state (equilibrium) growth repaired the worrying knife-edge problems of the HD model by substituting a neoclassical production function for the fixed coefficients technology implicit in the famous HD growth equation. But the relevance of the subsequent neoclassical equilibrium growth theory for answering the "how" question of economic development has been questioned (for instance by Hicks, 1965, p. 3). Nevertheless, as Arthur Lewis in his more directly relevant and famous work *The Theory of Economic Growth,* (1955) accepted, the proximate determinants of growth remain technical progress and the *per capita* investment rate — the basic building blocks of the Solow–Swan model. Moreover, even though the steady state features of the model may not be of direct relevance, developing country growth outcomes might still be explicable in terms of the so-called "traverse" in the model; that is, the movement of an economy from one steady state equilibrium to the next (as, say, the rate of investment is increased or the exogenously determined rate of technical progress alters). However, one prediction of the model is that in the long run, growth is entirely exogenous — dependent only on the rate of labor-augmenting technical progress and the rate of growth of population, the so-called natural rate of growth.

This exogeneity of growth within the neoclassical framework has troubled theorists. Attempts by Kaldor (1957) and Arrow (1962) to repair this lacuna by essentially making technical progress endogenous were unsuccessful. After a lapse of nearly two decades there is a recent flurry of interest in developing endogenous equilibrium growth models. The pioneers of this "new" growth theory are Romer (1986, 1989) and Lucas (1988). However, as for instance Stern (1991) has shown, these models which build on the earlier models by Arrow and Uzawa (1965), make growth endogenous by essentially making arbitrary assumptions — the value of a key parameter in determining the level of knowledge in Romer's model,[2] and by an unexplained externality to human capital formation in Lucas. Like so much of modern growth theory their relevance in explaining developing country growth outcomes is limited (see Stern, *op. cit.*, and Lal and Myint, 1991).

A more fruitful approach to the "how" question that yields endogenous steady state growth is a model developed by Scott (1989). It is relevant for our purposes because it harks back to an approach to growth — what Harry Johnson labeled the "generalized capital-theoretic" approach, stemming from Irving Fisher (1930). On this approach, investment is defined broadly to include all forms of investment (consumption foregone) that yield a stream of income (and consumption) over time. This wider notion of investment includes

> such diverse activities as adding to material capital, increasing the health, discipline, skill and education of the human population, moving labor into more productive occupations and locations, and applying existing knowledge or discovering and applying new knowledge to increase the efficiency of the productive processes. (Johnson in Meier, 1989, p. 461)

This notion of investment as the prime mover of the growth process also makes growth endogenous (as is explicitly shown by Scott) and "facilitates the discussion of problems of growth policy by emphasizing the relative returns from alternative investments of currently available resources" (Johnson in Meier, 1989, p. 462). Technical progress is *not* an independent determinant of growth. It is subsumed in investment.

Moreover, as Scott shows, the relevant notion of investment is *gross* investment,[3] whose rate, together with the growth of the quality adjusted labor force are the only sources of growth in the Scott model. In Lal and Myint (1991) this model also provided a good statistical explanation for the proximate causes of growth in the 21 countries studied over the 1950–85 period. Moreover, the qualitative evidence (on whose status more below) from the comparative country studies, which were the building blocks for the Lal–Myint synthesis, also supported Scott's model.

Thus unlike the Solow–Swan model, which says "no technical change no growth," Scott's model asserts (as did Fisher) the importance of conventional economic factors as the proximate causes of growth. "The determinants of the volume and efficiency of investment are restored to the centre of attention and both have long been the concern of economists" (Scott, 1989, p. 100).

How long? This takes us back to the classics. For as Robbins emphasizes, and as Fisher recognized explicitly in the dedication of his great book

The Rate of Interest, there was a classical precursor to his "capital-theoretic approach" to growth and development. This was John Rae, whose *New Principles of Political Economy* (1834), though outside the main classical tradition dealing with the "why" question, did provide an answer to the "how" question in terms of the interaction of productivity and thrift (or as Fisher called it, "opportunity" and "impatience") in determining *per capita* growth rates of income and consumption. This, as the above highly-condensed summary of subsequent developments shows, is still, in my judgment, the only sensible way to examine the proximate causes of growth. But as has become increasingly obvious, this only leads us to dig deeper into the reasons for differences amongst nations in these factors, by in effect asking the classical "why" questions. For the volume of investment (savings) depends upon preferences and its efficiency upon policy. Both depend also upon "entrepreneurship".

Differences in preferences ultimately require explanations in terms of what can broadly be called "culture" and its determinants — a sorely neglected subject to this date, despite popular assertions in the media about such things as the culturally determined high savings rates of the Confucian societies, for example, Japan! The policy determinants of the efficiency of investment requires explanations in terms of what the classicals called political economy. The evidence from the Lal–Myint country studies show that these differences in public policy are crucial in explaining the inter-country growth and poverty alleviation outcomes. The classical perspective on political economy along with differences in factor endowments, within a three factor, multiproduct, open economy model due to Krueger (1978) and extended by others was found most useful in both explaining these differences and in providing prescriptions for the future. We therefore turn to these public policy aspects of economic development in the next section.

3.3 POLITICAL ECONOMY

As Robbins (1976) notes, classical

> political economy, in the sense of the contents of [Adam] Smith's book, not only described how the economic system actually worked, or could work, but also how, according to the assumptions of the author, it ought to be made, or allowed to work. This usage was followed in general by the majority of classical economists. Thus description and prescription enjoyed a common title. (p. 3)

But Robbins prefers to limit the term explicitly

> to a discussion of principles of public policy in the economic field: and while it makes appeal to the finding of economic science, it also involves assumptions which, in the nature of things, lie outside positive science and which are essentially normative in character. (p. 3)

The ethical objective was the greatest happiness, where each man's capacity for happiness was to be counted as equal. But this "individualist utilitarianism" derived from Hume did not (emphasizes Robbins) imply any belief in interpersonal comparisons of utility or adherence to a quantitative felicific calculus. It was for Bentham "nothing more than a working rule of legislation" (Robbins, 1952, p. 180). Robbins notes:

> There is much talk in the Benthamite literature of a felicific calculus; and the term naturally suggests a most pretentious apparatus of measurement and computation. But, in fact, this is all shop window — the use of the felicific calculus lay in quite another direction — in rough judgments of the expediency of particular items of the penal law, in general estimates of the suitability of existing institutions or the desirability of other institutions to take their place. There can be no doubt that their practice was in the sphere of broad appraisals rather than quantitative computations. (Robbins, 1952, p. 187)

Moreover, the classics did not assume that the state consisted of a committee of Platonic Guardians. Following Hume, they were aware of the divergence between the interests of public agents and the general public they were meant to serve. This is a theme that has been revived by the "new" political economy.

The greatest happiness principle was best served according to classical liberalism by Adam Smith's system of natural liberty. "This liberty in the field of individual choice and liberty in the organization of production became the innovating doctrines of the classical political economy" (Robbins, 1976, p. 6). As Myint (1948, p. 52) emphasized, the resulting system of free enterprise was not seen by the classics as desirable merely for the static advantages of allocative efficiency:

> It is only when free competition is further interpreted as an auxiliary instrument of dynamic economic progress that it fits in with the fundamental classical outlook on the economic problem .... Thus a free economy was thought to encourage thrift, enterprise and initiative which

> promote a greater division of labor, expansion of markets, accumulation of capital ....

As he notes, the "allocative" interpretation of free competition became current with the development of the Walrasian theory of perfect competition. The subsequent incorporation of an explicit utilitarian social welfare function with an implicit egalitarian bias, then led on to the famous development of what is today called public economics (see Atkinson and Stiglitz, 1980, for a coherent treatment and Newbery and Stern, 1987, for applications to developing countries). This has become the modern "welfare economics" school of public policy analysis. The danger with this, as Myint noted in his Pioneers lecture, is that: "welfare economics with its emphasis on market failures, externalities, and the divergences between social and private costs, has for many decades been a powerful intellectual force behind interventionist policies" (Myint, 1987, p. 108). This *dirigisme* fostered by modern technocracy leads to a new form of mercantilism (see Lal, 1987, 1990), and then to its demise because of the "disorder" it engenders.

The basic argument against this form of enlightened *dirigisme* flowing from the "market failure" literature, is that the public agents charged with its implementation cannot be expected to have the requisite information as emphasized by both the classics (see Robbins, 1952), and neo-Austrians (see Hayek, 1948), nor character (they need to be "economic eunuchs" in Buchanan's apt phrase), as emphasized by the classics and the new political economists (see Lal, 1987a).

The classical policy prescriptions have been caricatured "by Carlisle's phrase anarchy plus the constable, or by Lasalle's simile of the nightwatchman" (Robbins, 1952, p. 37). As Myint (1948) and Robbins (1952) amongst others have noted, "to identify such doctrines with the declared and easily accessible views of the classical economists is a sure sign of ignorance or malice" (Robbins, 1952, p. 37). As Robbins indicates, Adam Smith's famous statement of the three functions of the state,[4] is almost identical with Keynes's famous formulation in *The End of Laissez-Faire*. The ensuing principles of economic liberalism were clearly set out in Mill's *Principles*, and their clearest modern reformulation is in Hayek's (1960) great work *The Constitution of Liberty*. But the most succinct restatement is by David Henderson (1986):

> The objections to economic liberalism and the market economy centre round the role of governments and states, both nationally and internationally. For many people liberalism goes with *laissez-faire*, which in turn is viewed as outdated, negative, unconcerned with what happens to

> weaker members of society and *de facto* favouring the stronger, and uncompromisingly negative in its attitude to the state. This rests on a double misconception. First, it distorts the message of *laissez-faire*. Second, it wrongly identifies belief in a market economy with an extreme interpretation of the laissez faire principle....
>
> Liberalism is not to be identified with hostility to the state, nor with a doctrinaire presumption that governments have only a minor role in economic life. On the contrary, the liberal view of the role of the state, both internal and external, is strongly positive. (pp. 98–99)

At a time of widespread neo-mercantilist predatoriness, engendered in part by the contemporary "welfare economics" school of public policy, the importance and validity of the prescriptions of classical liberalism remain as important as ever for economic development in all three worlds.

3.4 THE CLASSICAL METHOD

3.4.1 Introduction

In the study of developing countries, one of the most fruitful methods has been the use of comparative historical analysis or what I prefer to call the method of analytical economic history. The famous Little–Scitovsky–Scott (1970) study of *Industry and Trade in Some Developing Countries*, the NBER studies of Krueger (1978) and Bhagwati (1979) on trade liberalization, by Krueger (1983) on employment and trade, and the more recent comparative studies sponsored by the World Bank[5] are all examples — as is the well-known study by Sargent (1982) of five big inflations. This type of analysis has a distinguished pedigree in social science, though more technocratic economists may claim that it does not meet current standards of rigorous testing.

J. S. Mill sets out the logic of the method explicitly in his *A System of Logic* (bk III, ch. VIII), and this comparative method was applied with great skill by de Tocqueville in his *Democracy in America*, and by Marc Bloch in *Feudal Society*.

The method is particularly suited to the empirical study of problems of growth and development as J. N. Keynes (1890) noted at the turn of the century:

> There are in fact few departments of political or social science in which the a priori method avails less than in economic development.... In more

> general problems relating to economic growth and progress the part played by abstract reasoning is reduced to a minimum, and the economist's dependence upon historical generalizations is at a maximum .... For only by the direct comparison of successive stages of society can we reasonably hope to discover the laws, in accordance with which economic states tend to succeed one another or to become changed in character. (J. N. Keynes, 1890, pp. 283–84)

It is increasingly being realized that the evolution of institutions is likely to be central in explanations on differences in growth performance. For the present decisions of economic agents which impinge on the development process are constrained in part by their past — through various cultural and ideological norms and organizational structures. We need to understand the different "rules of the game" and the different incentive structures relating to alternative organizational forms, and how they evolve. Also we need to know how people react to changes in the set of choices facing them when either the informational constraints or "cultural" norms or the more purposive ones embodied in particular organizational structures alter. In short, we need to understand dynamic institutional change if we are ultimately to find deeper answers to the question of why some countries have grown and developed and others have not. However, there is no rigorous model defining dynamic institutional change; even if there were, it is unlikely that it would be amenable to econometric analysis, so our approach must be ecletic. It must also connect the present with the past. This is one major aim of the historical comparative studies method.

A major difference between the comparative study method and statistical (econometric) analysis can be seen in terms of the two forms of induction distinguished by J. N. Keynes (1890, p. 334), namely quantitative induction and "qualitative induction". Quantitative induction is based purely on statistical analysis; qualitative on the historical or comparative method. The latter concerns us.

The logical status of this experimental method was clearly set out by J. S. Mill. He distinguished between what he called the "Method of Agreement" and the "Method of Difference" (as two of his five methods of experimental inquiry). The method of difference is the normal method used in the experimental sciences. By this method "one can try to establish that several cases have in common a set of causal factors, although they vary in other ways that might have seemed causally relevant" (Skocpol, 1979, p. 36). The method of agreement by contrast deals with "cases in which the phenomenon to be explained and the hypothesized cause are both present to other cases in which the phenomenon and the causes are both absent, but which are otherwise as similar as possible to the positive cases" (Skocpol, 1979, p. 36).[6] Mill emphasized that the method of difference is by itself a more powerful method for establishing valid causal connections. But that

> on those subjects where artificial experimentation is impossible ... our only records of a directly productive nature [is the method of Agreement], while in the phenomena which we can produce at pleasure, the method of difference generally affords a more efficacious process which will ascertain causes as well as mere laws. (Mill, 1843, p. 219)

In practice, on the comparative historical method, it is possible to combine both types of comparative methods. "This is done by using at once several positive cases along with suitable negative cases as contrasts." (Skopcol, 1979, p. 36).

The method like any other method of multivariate analysis must depend upon some prior theoretical structure. It also has the usual problem concerning the selection of the relevant sample, the appropriate *ceteris paribus* conditions used in the identification of relevant causal links, as well as in drawing robust inferences about the relative strength of various "causes" leading to the "effects" that are of interest. If statistical analysis is broadly defined as the arrangement of quantitative data into patterns, together with the attachment of some measures of the confidence that can be attached to the "correctness" of the pattern that is inferred, it is clear that statistical analysis, whenever it is feasible, is not only complementary but can form an important part of the comparative method. However, as Keynes emphasized, this comparative method is wider than the purely statistical inquiry by which "social science and political economy are spoken of as branches or departments of the science of statistics, a science which studies social and economic phenomena in the only satisfactory way, namely, by the accumulation of facts and generalizations from them" (Keynes, 1890, p. 334). He rightly argues that this view is too narrow, as the economic methods used in practice by economists embody not only this form of quantitative induction, but also qualitative induction and, of course, deduction.

The comparative studies method is thus by and large the classical method of economic analysis applied to comparative history. As such it is best termed "analytical economic history", which combines the deductive analysis of economic theory with both the quantitative inductive analysis of statistics (to the extent this is possible) and the qualitative inductive analysis of comparative history.

3.4.2 Three Schools of Thought on Method

This method of "analytical economic history" can be looked upon as part of what Stewart (1979)[7] calls the "analytical school" and Hausman (1989)[8] the "deductivist" school in economics. This is to be distinguished from those economists who subscribe to either an "aprioristic method" (notably von Mises and some other members of the Austrian school) or to some form of positivism (which at its most cogent, is based on Popperian Falsificationism).

As the major practitioners of the "analytical" or "deductivist" school were the classical English economists (particularly Mill) and their modern day successors (particularly Keynes and Robbins), we prefer to refer to this method as the classical English method in economics. As both Stewart and Hausman emphasize, economists' actual practice is based on, and most of the existing body of economic knowledge has been obtained through this method. The official methodological rhetoric is positivist.[9] Thus there are three broad schools of thought, one *a priori*, and two empirical — the classical and positivist.

The epistomological difference between the "*apriorism*" of the Austrian school and the empiricism of the classical English and positivist schools is best seen in terms of Hume's distinction between analytic (*a priori*, deductive) and synthetic (factual, inductive) statements.[10]

It is usually held that deduction leads to logical truths, induction to material truths. But some philosophers have argued that there may be some propositions that are materially true *a priori*. Amongst these are the Austrians. Von Mises (1962) argued that all the deductions of economics followed from an axiom concerning human agents' calculus of choice, which was materially true *a priori*. For it was impossible to make sense of a world in which this axiom — whereby human agents sought to substitute a "better" for a "worst" situation — was not true. All the theorems of economics followed from this and any "testing" of economic theories was superfluous. We need not go into the cogency of this viewpoint. Suffice it to say that it has not been accepted by most economists.[11]

The *classical* view was refurbished and put in modern garb by Robbins. Caldwell summarizes this as follows:

> The fundamental generalizations of economics are self-evident propositions about reality: ends are multiple and can be ordered; means and time are limited and capable of alternative application; knowledge of present and future opportunities may be incomplete or uncertain, so that expectations are important. To handle this last difficulty, the expository

devices of rationality (consistency in choice) and perfect foresight are usually invoked as simplifying assumptions which are first approximations to reality. Finally, these basic postulates are combined with subsidiary postulates which reflect the actual conditions of the world to yield the applications of economic theory. Empirical studies are used to suggest plausible subsidiary postulates, and to check on the applicability of the theoretical framework to given situations. The collection of data to predict future constellations of valuations on the basis of past valuations may be of limited use in the short run, but it should not be imagined that such efforts will ever yield empirical "laws" which share the necessity of the basic postulates. (Caldwell, 1982, p. 103)

The *positivist* views are better known. There are three broad positivist methodological stances, in "scientific" economics. The first two have been called "confirmationism" and "instrumentalism". The former is associated with early Hutchinson and Samuelson,[12] and the latter with Friedman[13] and the Chicago school. The third is "falsificationism" associated with Karl Popper[14] whose most thorough going recent proponents have been Blaug and Hutchinson.[15]

Most economists have come to believe that a form of positivist methodology is the valid form of scientific activity. This is ironical when the philosophers have resoundingly rejected the naive positivism espoused by most economists as the hallmark of the scientific method.[16]

Moreover, as both Stewart and Hausman (and others, for example, McCloskey) argue, in fact most of our existing corpus of economic knowledge was developed by some variant of the classical method (production theory, consumption theory, Keynesian theory, etc.) rather than that recommended by positivists whether of the confirmationist, instrumentalist, or Popperian variety.[17]

3.4.3 Forensic Story Telling

The comparative studies method which is largely based on the classical method can also be looked upon as a form of story telling. Moreover, as a story teller tries to tell a story which is both interesting and persuasive, the method is attuned to the multifaceted aspects of persuasion. These concern the selection of facts, the crafting of the story, and choosing from amongst a number of competing stories, the one which fits the "facts" better than another.

In our stories of comparative development, we are attempting to establish plausible casual links. Two different forms of causation are distinguished by philosophers. One is based on statistical regularities, the other on counterfactual analysis. It is the latter form of causal analysis which underlies analytical economic history.

This analysis of causation in terms of counterfactuals has been most ably outlined and defended by Sir John Hicks.[18] He distinguishes among three types of causality in relationship to time: "Sequential (in which cause precedes effect), contemporaneous (in which both relate to the same period), and static (in which both are permanencies)" (Hicks, 1979). Much economic analysis is concerned with contemporaneous and static causation. Although this is useful and illuminating in many areas — demand analysis, welfare economics, international trade theory — it is not of much use in answering the type of questions concerning the *processes* of development that are concerned with sequential causation. As Hicks notes:

> The more characteristic economic problems are problems of change, of growth and retrogression, and of fluctuation. The extent to which these can be reduced into scientific terms is rather limited; for at every stage in an economic process new things are happening, things which have not happened before — at the most they are rather like what has happened before. We need a theory that will help us with these problems; but it is impossible to believe that it can ever be a complete theory. It is bound, by its nature, to be fragmentary. It is commonly called "dynamic" in contrast to "static"; but that is a name which now seems to me to be better avoided. For "dynamics", in its original sense, is a branch of mechanics; and *the problem to which the economic counterpart (if it is a counterpart) refers, are not mechanical.* As economics pushes on beyond "static" it becomes less like science, and more like history. (Hicks, 1979, p. xi, emphasis added)

But the resulting "historical" method is different from that conventionally used by historians, largely because in economics it must include the application of the theoretical apparatus (the "tool kit", in Joan Robinson's felicitous phrase) of the economist.[19] As Hicks (1979, p. IX) notes: "When theory is applied it is being used as a means of explanation: we ask not merely what happened, but why it happened. That is causation; exhibiting the story, so far as we can, as a logical process."

The resulting method of analytical economic history is then a composite of the characteristics of two different types of economic history.

According to Hicks (1965, p. 11):

> One of the standard ways of writing economic history (much practiced by political historians in their economic chapters) survey the state of the economy under consideration, as it was in various historical periods comparing one state with another. This is comparative statics. It is when the economic historian tries to throw his work into the form of a narrative that it becomes in our sense, dynamic.

Moreover, the method is essentially forensic. As Hicks (1979, p. 5) notes:[20]

> Take the field which is common to economics and history; the study of the past, with the object of finding out, not only what happened, but why it happened. That is causality; if the study is successful, it should enable us to state a cause; we should be able to say that A caused B.... There is clearly an analogy with the proceedings of a court of law. Someone was murdered; who was the murderer?

The resulting answer will not be infallible, but should still meet the requirement that the jury arrives at a conclusion that is "beyond reasonable doubt". But, of course, there will always be debate about what is "reasonable doubt", and in that sense it is unlikely that any important empirical issue in economics will ever be finally settled. This applies to the method of analytical economic history in explaining differential rates of development as to any of the other methods of empirical social science.

3.5 CONCLUSION

In summary, the method of analytical economic history to illuminate the forces of economic development involves using theoretical constructs to order whatever evidence is available to tell as plausible a "story" as the facts will bear, using Mill's principles of agreement and difference in a comparative analysis of different countries' historical experience. The theoretical constructs required to order the "facts" are Joan Robinson's economist's "box of tools". They are

> economic theory in its verbal and mathematical forms, statistical theory and practice, familiarity with certain accounting conventions, statistical sources, and a background of stylized historical fact and worldly experience. The use of such tools to fashion sturdy little arguments is the metier of the economist, the economists' "method". (McCloskey, 1985, p. 24)

Finally, the classical comparative studies method is essentially forensic. We need to persuade the jury of our professional peers. And, because the method recognizes the importance of persuading a sceptical jury, if successfully applied, it *is* persuasive!

Notes

1. Thus, as Hicks (1975, p. 320) notes, unlike the natural sciences there are no real scientific revolutions in economics. One cannot then say that modern theory has superseded the old. Most revolutions in economic thought are more in the nature of a "change of attention". Economic theories underpinning beliefs about the workings of an economy, which at particular times are fairly appropriate, are subsequently rejected in the light of changing circumstances. Whereas in the natural sciences "the facts" to be explained are in a sense immutable, in economics "the facts" are thrown up by a constantly changing world.
2. Stern (1991) rightly concludes: "That such important conclusions turn on such a fine distinction (which is unlikely to be settled empirically) should make us uneasy about relying on the Romer model as a basis for explaining the role of policy in determining the rate of growth" (p. 127).
3. This echoes an old debate about the measurement of capital, and the validity of the neoclassical production function. The latter is concerned with the change in the net stock of capital — gross investment minus depreciation. This depreciation has either been taken to be due to a physical process or as a result of scrapping. Scott says neither notion of depreciation makes sense, as machines which are well maintained can go on producing output well past the date they disappear from the production function, while scrapping is an economic process which depends on the date they cease adding to net output. When machines which are profitless are scrapped no productive capital is lost. Hence, gross investment is the best measure of the change in the capital stock. But there is no way in which a measure of this stock can be obtained, say by summing up all past gross investments. So the idea of the production function that links the *level* of output to the *level* of capital has to be abandoned, and all one can do is explain *changes* in output by changes in capital —that is gross investment. The difficulty contemporary theorists bred on the neoclassical growth theory have in accepting these ideas is shown by the exchanges between Scott and eminent economists in the *Journal of Economic Literature* (Sept. 1990) and *Oxford Economic papers* (1991) .
4. For Adam Smith (Cannan edition, vol. ii, pp. 184–85) these were (i) to protect society from foreign invaders, and (ii) every member, as far as feasible from oppression and injustice, by other members of society and (iii) provide and maintain various public works and public institutions which provided public goods. For Keynes: "The important thing for government is not to do things which individuals are doing already; but to do those things which at present are not done at all" (Keynes 1926, pp. 46–47).

5. Besides the comparative studies on the political economy of poverty equity and growth co-directed by Lal and Myint (1991), there are three others on liberalizing foreign trade regimes co-directed by D. Papageorgiou, M. Michaely, and A. Choksi; on the political economy of agricultural pricing co-directed by Anne Krueger, A. Valdez and M. Schiff, and on macroeconomic adjustment co-directed by I. M. D. Little, W. M. Corden, R. Cooper, and S. Rajapatirana.
6. Skopcol (1979) provides a good account and justification of this method.
7. Stewart (1979). This book provides the best available account of the epistomological bases of different viewpoints on economic methodology.
8. D. M. Hausman (1989). Also see Redman (1991), and de Marchi (ed.) (1988).
9. As Caldwell (1984) puts it: It may reasonably be conjectured that a majority of economists would consider the construction of theoretical models which are capable of generating testable predictions to be the hallmark of scientific activity. And it seems that the converse is also a widely held sentiment; a proposed theory which is not expressed in testable (preferable, falsifiable) form is not scientific (p. 124).
10. David Hume (1748), *An Enquiry Concerning Human Understanding*, Sec. IV, pt. I, pp. 25–6. Oxford, Clarendon Press, 1975.
11. For a critique of Mises' "apriorism" see Stewart *op. cit.* pp. 118–121. Also see Caldwell (1982, pp. 103–351).
12. See T. Hutchinson (1938), P. Samuelson: (1983), (1952) and (1963). Critiques of these views are in F. Machlup (1982) and B. Caldwell, *op. cit.*
13. M. Friedman (1953).
14. K. Popper (1959).
15. M. Blaug (1980) and Hutchinson (1938) (1977), (1978).
16. See for instance the devastating critique of Popper by the Harvard philosopher Hilary Putnam (1981), and by Ian Hacking (1981) of that other member of the LSE Popperian group, Imre Lakatos. For another devastating critique, in terms of the history of ideas, of the whole Popperian enterprise see D. C. Stove (1985). Also see the essays in P. Achinstein (ed.) (1983), E . Sosa (ed.) (1975), B. Caldwell (1982), D. N. McCloskey (1985), J. Elster (1983), A. Ryan (ed.) (1973), and Antony Flew (1985).
17. The rise and fall of "testing" in economics, has been valuably surveyed by de Marchi (1988), in terms of the revolt against the leading contemporary proponent of the classical viewpoint — both its methodology and prescriptions — Lionel Robbins, which was led at the L.S.E. by the group of Young Turks surrounding Richard Lipsey. Robbins and Keynes took the view that "in economics the parameters are themselves in the most important cases quickly changing variables" (Robbins, 1938), so that they were both sceptical about quantification. The above quotation was also cited by Popper (1957, p. 143) in his "nearly" exempting economics as a subject requiring testability.

    But as De Marchi notes, amongst Robbins' younger colleagues there was growing dissatisfaction that: "There must be something more to economic science than (as Steuer has nicely put it...) 'the discovery of irresistible truth through logical manipulation of a few self-evident postulates" (de Marchi, 1988, p. 144). De Marchi surveys their subsequent discovery of Popper and the twists and turns in their final disenchantment with Popperian falsificationism, epitomised by Lipsey's statement in the second edition of his famous textbook: "I have abandoned the Popperian notion of refutation" (Lipsey, 1966, p. XX).

Robert Solow (1985) has also recently questioned the belief amongst "the best and brightest in the profession ... [that] economics is the physics of society" (p. 330). He argues that, "the attempt to construct economics as an axiomatically based hard science is doomed to fail ... [as] the classical hard science devices for discriminating between competing hypotheses are closed to us. The main alternative device is the statistical analysis of historical time series. But then another difficulty arises." In order to distinguish between complex and subtle competing hypotheses, many of which "are capable of fitting the data in a gross sort of way... we need *long* time-series observed under *stationary* conditions ... [But] much of what we observe cannot be treated as the realization of a *stationary* stochastic process without straining credulity" (p. 328).

He then "recommends" marrying the tools of the economist with "the ability [of the economic historian] to imagine how things might have been before they became as they now are" (*ibid.* p. 331). This is close to the classical method of analytical economic history discussed here.

18. "Hicks (1979, Ch. 2) rests his whole analysis of causation on the purported counterfactual implications" (Elster, 1983, p. 240, n. 23).

19. Also Hayek has emphasized

> if our historical fact is such a complex as a language or a market, a social system or a method of land cultivation, what we call a fact is either a recurrent process or a complex pattern of persistent relationships which is not "given" to our observation but which we can only laboriously reconstruct — and which we can reconstruct only because the parts (the relations from which we build up the structure) are familiar and intelligible to us. To put it paradoxically, what we call historical facts are really theories which, in a methodological sense, are of precisely the same character as the more abstract or general models which the theoretical sciences of society construct. The situation is not that we first study the "given" historical facts and then perhaps can generalize about them. We rather use a theory when we select from the knowledge we have about a period certain parts as intelligibly connected and forming part of the same historical fact. (F. H. Hayek: "The Facts of Social Science," in his *Individualism and Economic Order*, Routledge, 1949, p. 71)

20. Also see McCloskey: "The Consequences of Rhetoric," in Klamer, McCloskey, Solow (eds.), *The Consequences of Economic Rhetoric*, *op. cit.*, p. 289.

References

Achinstein, P. (ed.) (1983) *The Concept of Evidence* (Oxford: Oxford University Press)

Arrow, K. J. (1962): "The Economic Implications of Learning by Doing," *Review of Economic Studies*, vol. 29.

Atkinson, A. B. and J. E. Stiglitz (1980) *Lectures on Public Economics* (London: McGraw-Hill).
Bacon, R. and W. Eltis (1976) *Britain's Economic Problems: Too Few Producers* (London: Macmillan).
Bhagwati, J. N. (1979) *Anatomy and Consequences of Trade Control Regimes* (New York: National Bureau of Economic Research).
Birdsall, N. (1988) "Economic Approaches to Population Growth," in H. Chenery and T. N. Srinivasan (eds.), *Handbook of Development Economics* (Amsterdam: North-Holland).
Blaug, M. (1980) *The Methodology of Economics* (Cambridge: Cambridge University Press).
Caldwell, B. (1982) *Beyond Positivism in Economics* (London: Allen & Unwin).
de Marchi, N. (ed.) (1988) *The Popperian Legacy in Economics* (Cambridge: Cambridge University Press).
Elster, J. (1983) *Explaining Technical Change* (Cambridge: Cambridge University Press).
Eltis, W. (1984) *The Classical Theory of Economic Growth* (London: Macmillan).
Fisher, I. (1930) *The Theory of Interest* (New York: Macmillan Co.).
Flew, A. (1985) *Thinking about Social Thinking — The Philosophy of the Social Sciences* (Oxford: Basil Blackwell).
Friedman, M. (1953) "The Methodology of Positive Economics," in his *Essays in Positive Economics* (Chicago: University of Chicago Press).
Hacking, I. (1981) "Lakatos' Philosophy of Science," in Hacking (ed.), *Scientific Revolutions* (Oxford: Oxford University Press).
Hacking, I. (1989) "Economic Methodology in a Nutshell," *Journal of Economic Perspectives*, 3(2) (Spring).
Hausman, Carl R. (1989) *Metaphor and Art* (Cambridge: Cambridge University Press).
Hausman, D. C. (ed.), (1984) *The Philosophy of Economics — An Anthology* (Cambridge: Cambridge University Press).
Hayek, F. (1948) "The Use of Knowledge in Society," in his *Individualism and Economic Order* (London: Routledge & Kegan Paul).
Hayek, F. (1960) *The Constitution of Liberty* (London: Routledge & Kegan Paul).
Henderson, P. D. (1986) *Innocence and Design — The Influence of Economic Ideas on Policy* (Oxford: Basil Blackwell).
Hicks, J. R. (1965) *Capital and Growth* (Oxford: Clarendon Press).
Hicks, J. R. (1975) "The Scope and Status of Welfare Economics," *Oxford Economic Papers*, Nov.
Hicks, J. R. (1979) *Causality in Economics* (Oxford: Basil Blackwell).
Hutchinson, T. (1938) *The Significance and Basic Postulates of Economic Theory* (London: Macmillan).
Hutchinson, T. (1977) *Knowledge and Ignorance in Economics* (Oxford: Basil Blackwell).
Hutchinson, T. and M. Blaug (1978) *On Revolution and Progress in Economic Knowledge* (Cambridge: Cambridge University Press).
Kaldor, N. (1957) "A Model of Economic Growth," *Economic Journal*, vol. 67.
Keynes, J. M. (1926) *The End of Laissez-Faire* (London: Hogarth Press).
Keynes, J. N. (1890) *The Scope and Method of Political Economy* (London: Macmillan).

Klamer, A., D. M. McCloskey and R. M. Solow (eds.) (1988) *The Consequences of Economic Rhetoric* (Cambridge: Cambridge University Press).

Krueger, A. O. (1978) *Liberalization Attempts and Consequences* (New York: National Bureau of Economic Research).

Krueger, A. O (1983) *Trade and Employment in Developing Countries 3 — Synthesis and Conclusion* (Chicago: National Bureau Economic Research).

Lal, D. (1983) *The Poverty of "Development Economics"* (London: Institute of Economic Affairs; American edition, Cambridge Mass.: Harvard University Press, 1985).

Lal, D. (1987a) "The Political Economy of Economic Liberalization," *World Bank Review*, vol. 1, January.

Lal, D. (1987b) "Markets, Mandarins and Mathematicians," *CATO Journal*, vol. 7, no. 1, Spring/Summer.

Lal, D. (1990) *Political Economy and Public Policy*, Occasional Paper #19, International Center for Economic Growth, San Francisco, ICS Press.

Lal, D. and S. van Wijnbergen (1985) "Government Deficits, the Real Interest Rate and LDC Debt: On Global Crowding Out," *European Economic Review*, vol. 29, no. 1.

Lal, D. and H. Myint (1991) *The Political Economy of Poverty, Equity and Growth*, processed (London: University College).

Lewis, W. A. (1955) *The Theory of Economic Growth* (London: Allen & Unwin).

Lipsey, R. E. (1966) *An Introduction to Positive Economics*, 2nd ed. (London: Weidenfeld & Nicolson).

Lipton, M. (1984) "Comment on P. Bauer, 'Remembrance of Studies Past: Retracing First Steps," in G. M. Meier and D. Seers (eds), *Pioneers in Development* (New York: Oxford University Press).

Little, I. M. D. (1982) *Economic Development: Theory, Policy and International Relations* (New York: Basic Books).

Little, I. M. D., M. F. Scott and T. Scitovsky (1970) *Industry and Trade in Some Developing Countries* (London: Oxford University Press).

Lucas, R. E. (1988) "On the Mechanics of Economic Development," *Journal of Monetary Economics*, vol. 22.

McCloskey, D. N. (1985) *The Rhetoric of Economics* (Madison, Wisconsin: University of Wisconsin Press).

McCloskey, D. N. (1988) "The Consequences of Rhetoric," in Kramer, McCloskey and Solow (1988).

Machlup, F. (1982) "Operationalism and Pure Theory in Economics," in his *Methodology of Economics and other Social Sciences* (New York: Academic Press).

Meier, Gerald M. (1989) *Leading Issues on Economic Development* (New York: Oxford University Press).

Mill, J. S. (1843) *A System of Logic* (London: J. W. Parker).

Mises, L. von (1962) *The Ultimate Foundation of Economic Sciences* (Princeton, van Nostrand).

Myint, H. (1948) *Theories of Welfare Economics* (Cambridge, Mass.: Harvard University Press).

Myint, H. (1958) "The 'Classical" Theory of International Trade and the Underdeveloped Countries," *Economic Journal*, vol. 68, June.

Myint, H. (1972) *South-East Asia's Economy: Development Policies in the 1970s* (London: Penguin).
Myint, H. (1985) "Organizational Dualism and Economic Development," *Asian Development Review*, March–April.
Myint, H. (1987) "Neoclassical Development Analysis: Its Strengths and Limitations," in Gerald. M. Meier (ed.), *Pioneers in Development*, 2nd series (New York: Oxford University Press).
Newbery, D. G. M. and N. H. Stern (eds.) (1987) *The Theory of Taxation for Developing Countries* (New York: Oxford University Press).
Popper, K. (1959) *The Logic of Scientific Discovery* (New York: Basic Books).
Putnam, H. (1981) "The 'Corroboration' of Theories", in Hacking (ed.), *Scientific Revolutions* (Oxford: Oxford University Press).
Rae, J. (1834) *Statement of Some New Principles of Political Economy* (Boston: Hilliard, Gray).
Redman, D. (1991) *Economics and the Philosophy of Science* (New York: Oxford University Press).
Robbins, L. (1935) *An Essay on the Nature and Significance of Economic Science* (London: Macmillan).
Robbins, L. (1938) "Live and Dead Issues in the Methodology of Economics," *Economica*, vol. 5.
Robbins, L. (1952) *The Theory of Economic Policy in English Classical Political Economy* (London: Macmillan).
Robbins, L. (1968) *The Theory of Economic Development in the History of Economic Thought* (London: Macmillan).
Robbins, L. (1976) *Political Economy: Past and Present, A Review of Leading Theories of Economic Policy* (London: Macmillan).
Romer, P. (1986) "Increasing Returns and Long Term Growth," *Journal of Political Economy*, vol. 94.
Romer, P. (1989) "Capital Accumulation in the Theory of Long-Run Growth," *Journal of Political Economy*, vol. 94.
Ryan, A. (ed.) (1973) *The Philosophy of Social Explanation* (Oxford: Oxford University Press).
Samuelson, P. (1952) "Economic Theory and Mathematics: An Appraisal," *American Economic Review*, 42 (May): 56–66.
Samuelson, P. (1963) "Discussion," *American Economic Review*, 53 (May): 231–36.
Samuelson, P. (1983) *Foundations of Economic Analysis*, enlarged edition (Cambridge, Mass.: Harvard University Press).
Sargent, T. (1982) "Four Big Inflations," in R. Hall (ed.), *Inflation, Causes and Effects* (Chicago: University of Chicago Press).
Scott, M. F. (1989) *A New View of Economic Growth* (Oxford: Clarendon Press).
Skocpol, T. (1979) *States and Social Revolutions* (Cambridge: Cambridge University Press).
Solow, R. M. (1985) "Economic History and Economics," *American Economic Review* (May).
Sosa, E. (ed.) (1975) *Causation and Conditionals* (London: Oxford University Press).
Stern, N. (1991) "The Determinants of Growth," *Economic Journal*, vol. 101, January.

Stewart, I. M. T. (1979) *Reasoning and Method in Economics — An Introduction to Economic Methodology* (London and New York: McGraw-Hill).

Stove, D. C. (1985) "Karl Popper and the Jazz Age," *Encounter* (June).

Uzawa, H. (1965) "Optimum Technical Change in an Aggregative Model of Economic Growth," *International Economic Review*, vol. 6.

Wrigley, E. A. (1988) *Continuity, Chance and Change: The Character of the Industrial Revolution in England* (Cambridge: Cambridge University Press).

4 British Classical Economists and Underdevelopment in India*

William J. Barber

At least since W. Arthur Lewis's pathbreaking contribution — "Economic Development with Unlimited Supplies of Labour" (1954) — modern students of development economics have required no reminder that economists in the classical tradition were fundamentally concerned with problems of long-term economic growth. The "composite" classical model he then presented drew on their insights to illuminate the dynamics of expansion in the setting of economic dualism.[1]

This line of argument insisted that the typical less developed economy could best be understood when decomposed into two distinct, though interacting, sectors. In a "capitalist" one, production and exchange were organized along the lines of an advanced money economy. The "subsistence" sector, on the other hand, embraced traditional (and primarily agrarian) economic activity in which households produced primarily for their own consumption. The driving force in the overall system was capital accumulation, fed by savings generated from the capitalist surplus. This widened the productive base and increased the demand for labor in wage employment. To meet this incremental demand, labor would be drawn out of the "subsistence" sector (where its productivity was low) into capitalist employment. Lewis held that the supply of labor available for wage employment would be perfectly elastic and would remain so until resources initially committed to traditional activities had been absorbed into capitalistic ones. At that point, labor would become genuinely scarce and, in Lewis's terms, the system would leave the world of classical economics and enter a neoclassical one.

*A number of the points treated in this essay have been elaborated at considerably greater length in William J. Barber, *British Economic Thought and India, 1600–1858* (Oxford: Clarendon Press, 1975).

Lewis ingeniously reformulated classical teaching on the linkages between income distribution and long-term expansion. Sectors replaced the classical distributional categories based on social classes (that is, capitalist, landowning, and laboring classes). His treatment of the "subsistence" sector as a labor reservoir assigned to it a role in wage determination analogous to the one played by the Malthusian population principle in the original classical system. The classical proposition that capital formation was a function of capitalist profit was also reincarnated.

Subsequent scholarship has found flaws in a number of the details in the Lewis model of 1954. Nevertheless, there can be no disputing its impact on a significant body of theorizing about the development process. Pre-Lewis, the dominant orientation of the first wave of post-World War II development economics had a post-Keynesian flavor. Within that framework, it was argued that attention should be focussed on the behavior of aggregative variables: for example, aggregate income, capital-output ratios, saving-income ratios. Implicitly, that analytic perspective presupposed that structural distinctions between developed and underdeveloped economies were of little consequence. The essential difference separating them was that the latter were poorer.

Lewis's classically-inspired plea for disaggregated dualism challenged such presuppositions of structural homogeneity. In addition, his line of argument brought to the fore a still broader methodological issue. Was it legitimate to conceptualize problems of development in the Third World around categories pertinent to the latest "master model" devised in the advanced economies? Lewis was skeptical about the validity of such transfers of analytic techniques.

The purpose of this paper is to revisit questions Lewis raised, but to do so in the context of analyses offered by a number of classical economists when they grappled with problems of underdevelopment in their own time. They shared a commitment to the overriding importance of economic growth as a desirable objective and they concurred in holding that analysis of the linkages between income distribution and capital formation was crucial to understanding its prospects. At that level of generality, all British classicists would find Lewis's "composite" characterization to be an acceptable interpretation of one of their messages. But, on a variety of other issues, major contributors to the original classical debate did not speak with one voice. They were certainly not at one, for example, in their views about structural continuity (or discontinuity) or on the validity of transferring intellectual constructs from one institutional environment to another.

4.1 CLASSICAL ECONOMISTS AND THE INDIAN CONNECTION

For the British classicists, economic growth was *the* central problem. But it did not follow that the particular circumstances of today's less developed countries were at the top of their agenda. Concern over economic expansion in their own country took precedence. Nevertheless, their intellectual orientation was still global in its aspirations. By contrast with the mercantilists (who had been pre-occupied with *the* nation), classicists united in endorsing Smith's insistence that inquiry should be directed to the nature and causes of the wealth of *nations* (in the plural).

British India was the part of today's less developed world to which the classicists assigned special attention. This was hardly surprising. Since the formation of the English East India Company — founded in 1600 as a chartered monopoly with exclusive rights to British trade with the whole of Asia — its affairs had been a lightning rod for public controversy. The Company had always claimed preferential treatment and had guarded jealously its monopoly privileges. Indeed the debates stimulated by the periodic renewals of its charter (called for about every two decades) inspired a voluminous pamphlet literature that had sharpened economic discourse about the significance of the balance of trade and the implications of alternative market structures. By the 1760s, the Company had acquired still greater public prominence. It had by then appropriated powers of tax collection in the territory of Bengal and had merged governance with its commercial monopoly over foreign trade.

For the new breed of political economists, this turn of events presented both intellectual challenges and professional opportunities. The East India Company's government over a steadily-enlarged domain in the Indian subcontinent continued until 1858, when the British Crown took over its functions. The lifespan of Company governance was thus roughly co-terminous with the heyday of classical political economy. Over those years, affairs in India touched the thinking of virtually all of its practitioners. Some of them were directly involved in the Company's activities — as a consultant, as a full-time employee, or as a shareholder — and those who were not so engaged usually put views of the "India question" on the record. Those who benefitted from Company sponsorship, it should be noted, still thought of themselves as intellectually detached commentators when analyzing economic problems in India. None of the front-rank contributors to classical economics, however, saw India at first hand: the Company was not given to subsidizing field missions for visiting experts. The authority they claimed for their insights stemmed from confidence that their "models" could explain India's economic circumstances and prescribe remedies that would enable its peoples to participate in the "progress of improvement."

4.2 PROBLEMS IN DIAGNOSING THE NATURE OF INDIA'S ECONOMIC PLIGHT

In the late eighteenth and early nineteenth centuries, events in the Indian sub-continent sparked an interpretive question of substantial dimensions. Europeans had long regarded pre-British India as one of the wealthier parts of the globe. This part of the world was thought to be richly endowed by nature. By contrast with the harshness of Northern Europe's agricultural conditions, the sub-continent enjoyed a climate with multiple growing seasons and produced exotic primary commodities that Europe could envy but not match. These natural blessings, it was widely believed, had been supplemented by man-made irrigation systems thought to be remarkable in their technical sophistication. The skill of India's craftsmen reinforced the image of an affluent society: their "finely-wrought" luxury textiles were superior in quality to anything Europeans could then make. Evidence supplied by the well-understood commodity composition of intercontinental trade was especially compelling. Importers in the Indian sub-continent seemed to be indifferent to products of European manufacture and wanted the trade accounts to be settled in silver. Surely, it could plausibly be argued, this was convincing demonstration that its peoples were opulent to the point of being saturated with goods.

How then could the easy territorial conquests of a handful of East India Company mercenaries be explained? The "reality" revealed by events in the mid-eighteenth century appeared to be one of economic stagnation, rather than wealth. Why then had the potential of the Indian economy for sustained development not been realized? Differing explanations were offered by economists operating within the classical framework. The diagnoses they came up with, in turn, shaped subsequent thinking on approaches to India's condition.

In *The Wealth of Nations*, Smith struggled hard with this conundrum. He ultimately concluded that pre-British India had not exploited its rich potential because it had failed to develop an independent capability to conduct long-distance seaborne trade. The alleged reason: the proscription of the "Gentoo" religion against lighting fires — and hence the preparation of foodstuffs — at sea. In consequence, the normal extension of markets had been constrained and efficiency gains attainable from a widened division of labor had not been forthcoming. This situation also meant that India's exporters had been placed at the mercy of foreign carriers in long-distance commerce — and foreigners had appropriated a disproportionate share of the gains from trade.[2]

Smith's argument about India's inability to keep pace in the international growth race was of a piece with his general position on the virtues of "export-led" growth, uninhibited by institutional constraints on freedom of trade. In the case of pre-British India, the institutional constraint stemmed from a presumed attribute of the indigenous culture, not from governmentally-imposed controls like those he had indicted when writing about Europe. But his argument was grounded on what he took (incorrectly) to be fact. The particulars of the case he made thus do not survive later scrutiny. Even so, the direction of his thinking suggested that peculiarities in the cultural and institutional environment of India deserved a position of prominence in interpretations of its economic performance. This theme — in mutated forms — reemerged in subsequent commentary.

Though Smith found it difficult to comprehend arrested development in pre-British India, his diagnosis of its latter-day decline came easily. His writing in 1776, it will be recalled, identified Bengal as the prime exhibit of the "declining state" (that is, one in which the capital stock was shrinking and income per head declining). He introduced no empirical data to support that conclusion: indeed, documentation on the pertinent quantitative magnitudes was not then available. But this did not matter — his model told him that his conclusions must necessarily be true. No other outcome could have been expected following the intervention of the East India Company. As a monopolist, the Company had a stake in suppressing competition (which self-evidently arrested growth) and it tolerated extraordinary waste and mismanagement. These evils were compounded when the monopolist also acted as sovereign. Smith saw this combination as a monstrous incongruity. The rational sovereign ought to support the well-being and economic uplift of the governed. In that spirit, government should insure that imports into India were made available at the lowest possible price and that the highest possible prices were paid to Indian producers of goods procured for export. Unfortunately, the interest of the Company as merchant was exactly the reverse. Given this contradiction, Smith maintained that the government administered by an "exclusive company of merchants" was the worst form of government conceivable. He continued to believe that India possessed vast productive potential. But it would never be activated unless the East India Company's commercial monopoly was extinguished and its powers of governance transferred to the British Crown.[3]

For British intellectuals, the mystery of arrested development in pre-British India was effectively put to rest by James Mill with the publication of his three-volume *History of British India* in 1817. He accepted Smith's argument that the behavior of the East India Company in the recent past had aggravated India's economic difficulties and he joined the chorus of those denouncing the iniquitous effects of its trading monopoly But the fundamental impediment to its development went much deeper. In his reading of matters, the root cause was the deficiency in traditional — and, more particularly, Hindu — society. He insisted that those who had searched for an explanation of transition from opulence to stagnation had, in effect, been jousting with windmills. For too long, the European mind had been bemused by a myth. The basic reality, he argued, was a prolonged chapter of economic decadence, centuries in length.

From his perspective, the "evidence" introduced to buttress the image of opulence supported the opposite conclusion. For example, the Hindu's much-admired skill in weaving reflected, not a high state of development, but a low one. This craft was a sedentary occupation and "thus in harmony with his predominant inclination"; moreover, it required little physical exertion, "of which he is always exceedingly sparing, and the finer the production, the more slender the force which he is called upon to apply." Similarly, the demand for precious metals in the East should be understood as a reflection, not of wealth, but of backwardness; their scarcity made them attractive objects for ostentatious and unproductive display. The essential truth, Mill insisted, was a long-standing "state of poverty and wretchedness, as far as the great body of people are concerned ..." The proper question to ask was quite different from the one around which so much inquiry had been organized. The real puzzle was why Europeans had for so long been blinded. Mill assigned a heavy responsibility to officials of the East India Company for perpetuation of this error: they had an obvious stake in promoting the view that "India overflowed with riches".[4]

At least to his own satisfaction, Mill disposed of the notion that India's economy had once achieved significant development. But it was still incumbent on him to explain why its ample resource base had not been more effectively used. "Even in the richest parts of India", he maintained, "one half of the soil [had] never been under cultivation".[5] How could such waste be comprehended?

For Mill, this unfortunate outcome could be traced to mis-rule in the traditional system. Exactions imposed on the farming population by its rulers had been so excessive that cultivators were left with only the barest compensation. This had blunted incentives to productive effort and suppressed extension of the cultivated area. Such an outcome was a natural consequence of a system in which "the fruits of labour were never secure".[6] The population did not lack natural ability to improve its condition. Bad government had imposed an artificially low ceiling on economic performance.

Argument along this line acquired sharper analytic bite when the theory of differential rent became part of the conceptual kit of mainstream classical political economy. Ricardo's formalization of this concept was being crystallized when Mill's *History* was in press. From his friendship and editorial collaboration with Ricardo, Mill was certainly exposed to this idea, but he did not introduce it explicitly when discussing Indian agriculture in 1817. Malthus — who shared honors with Ricardo in the discovery of differential rent — was the first to establish a direct connection with India's circumstances.[7] With the aid of this insight, massive poverty in pre-British India was readily explicable. The mistake of traditional rulers in claiming a proportion of agricultural output was now clear. Differential rent theory taught that exactions on cultivators should be adjusted to the natural fertility of the soil. The most fertile acreages could yield a surplus which the ruler could appropriate as a proxy for the economic rent and still provide cultivators with sufficient rewards. The least fertile plots, on the other hand, could produce only just enough to sustain the cultivator. If the ruler claimed a share of the product of the latter, they would not be tilled and total output would be held below its potential.

At one stroke, the theory of differential rent provided a diagnosis of India's poverty and an implicit prescription for remedial action. Even though India's economic situation had special characteristics, the root cause of its difficulties was traditional misrule. What was needed was good government of a type that its indigenous culture had not provided.

4.3 BROADER IMPLICATIONS OF DIFFERENTIAL RENT THEORY FOR THE CLASSICAL PERSPECTIVE

Classical political economy achieved its mature expression when the theory of differential rent was assimilated into the conceptual structure Smith had set out. Positioning an economy on a sustained growth path, it now appeared, was a more complex matter than had originally been thought. Smith presupposed that the "progress of improvement" (once initiated by capital accumulation) would be cumulative and would bring benefits to all groups in the community. After the implications of differential rent had been incorporated into the classical system, confidence in this outcome was no longer secure. Accumulation by capitalists would indeed swell the demand for labor and generate improvement in real wages for the laboring class. But this effect would, in turn, spark increases in labor supply through the Malthusian population mechanism. Reduction in real wages toward their long-run equilibrium at "subsistence" would not long be delayed. Even though workers might not experience any lasting gains, these adjustments would still leave the system with more mouths to feed. But additional food requirements (at least if they were to be met from home production) could be satisfied only by drawing lands of lower fertility into use. As production costs rose, so also would food prices.

This turn of events would impinge directly on the position of capitalist employers. They would then be obliged to pay higher money wages simply to sustain their work force at "subsistence". In a world in which competition in output markets was thought to be vigorous, capitalists could not fully recoup by passing through higher labor costs to consumers. Profit would thus be squeezed. Owners of high fertility land, on the other hand, would reap an unearned windfall when food prices were bid up. This redistribution of income — in favor of landlords and at the expense of capitalists — had disturbing implications for the system's longer-term prospects. In the classicists' view of the world, landlords were spendthrifts. The accumulation that fueled an economy's expansion was fed by profits of capitalists and they were now under threat. The "stationary state" (a situation in which net accumulation ceased and growth stopped) was no longer just a hypothetical possibility, but a real and present danger.

As the force of this analysis was absorbed into British public debate, two lines of policy to postpone that outcome entered the discussion. One proposed that the rent share of income — the surplus trapped by landlords — should be taxed away. An attractive theoretical case could be made for this position. In the first place, rent was "unearned." It accrued to the owners of richer soils but without any additional effort on their part; the lucky landlords had simply been the beneficiaries of a system that had driven food prices upward. Secondly, leaving rental windfalls in the hands of prodigals had no redeeming social merit. These funds, if put at the disposal of the state, could be channeled into capital formation.

A second approach to a growth-sustaining policy in Britain focussed on the question of agricultural protection. Under shelter of the Corn Laws, domestic farmers had been privileged with artificially high prices. Read through the lenses of the classical model (as modified to include differential rent), the irrationality of that practice was clearer than ever. Smith had articulated earlier the general case for commercial freedom. Now it could be shown that free trade in agricultural products was all the more urgent. Unless the Corn Laws were repealed, the onset of the stationary state would be hastened.

The theoretical justifications for these strategies notwithstanding, both were non-starters in the Britain of the 1820s. In the unreformed Parliament of that day, landlord interests were more than sufficiently represented and they had no enthusiasm for such recommendations. These ideas had no immediate practical impact in the country of their origin. But they helped to shape the contours of debate over policy in British India.

4.4 THE CLASSICAL MODEL AS A GUIDE TO DEVELOPMENT STRATEGY IN INDIA: VARIATION I

In the first two decades of the nineteenth century, the operations of the East India Company were subjected to a searching reappraisal. The changes which followed created a climate in which relationships between political economists and the Company became easier. The Company's decision to found a semi-professional school for recruits to its service in the East was a first step in reform. In the late eighteenth century, the Company's image had been badly tarnished by public exposure of flagrant corruption by its agents overseas. To polish it, the Directors created a new institution — Haileybury College — which was intended to equip its officers with some modicum of expertise and to instill in them a higher sense of integrity. Tuition in political economy was to be part of the curriculum. T. R. Malthus was invited to provide it and, in 1806, he joined the staff at Haileybury as Professor of Political Economy. His appointment marked the first use of that title in the English-speaking world.

A more fundamental shift in relationships between political economists and the East India Company was made possible by amendments to its Charter mandated by Parliament in 1813. The Company then surrendered its monopoly privileges in the trade with India — although it retained that position in the China trade. As far as India was concerned, the Company's activities thereafter were concentrated on its role as a sovereign. This was not the job the organization had originally been established to do. If the Company were to pass the test of public scrutiny when performing it, competencies were needed that it did not then possess. With a void to be filled, its Directors were increasingly receptive to engaging political economists in the work of its headquarters staff in London. James Mill made known his availability for such an assignment and requested Ricardo, a shareholder and a member of the Company's Court of Proprietors, to lobby on his behalf. The indictments Mill had levelled against the Company in his writings did not appear to be disabling: those criticisms had been largely aimed at its activities in an earlier incarnation. As far as Mill himself was concerned, the termination of the Company's monopoly of the India trade permitted him to contemplate this new career without compromise to his intellectual integrity.

Mill moved into an office at East India house in 1819 as an "Examiner of the India Correspondence". This nomenclature was not accurately descriptive: the Examiner's office amounted to an economic planning staff for British India. He remained there until his death in 1836. His son, John Stuart, later followed in his footsteps and carried out similar functions until the Crown put the Company out of business in 1858.

James Mill warmed to this challenge with enthusiasm. The task was no less than to create conditions under which the Indian economy could be elevated from centuries of backwardness. And he had a clear vision of how this should be done The key to the whole matter was the reconstruction of its revenue system around the teachings of differential rent. Partisan special interests in Britain had denied the home country the blessings that would flow from action informed by this theoretical innovation. But they could be made available to India where a reformer had much greater freedom of maneuver. From the perspective of a political economist influenced by Benthamite utilitarianism, a more attractive laboratory in which to work would have been hard to imagine. The sum of human happiness would be greatly magnified if India's masses could be uplifted from their misery.

To their own satisfaction, both Mill and Malthus had already established that a flawed revenue system bore the primary burden of responsibility for poverty and resource under-utilization in Indian agriculture. This followed from the failure of traditional rulers to recognize the differences in rent-paying capacities of grades of land of uneven fertility. The target of reform was to confine the claims of the new sovereign within the surpluses generated by the true economic rent. Under ideal arrangements, lands of first quality would carry a substantially higher assessment than those of lesser fertility, and acreages at the margin of cultivation would pay nothing. This scheme promised enormous advantages to India. Tax claims so specified would not impinge on the natural returns to labor and capital and would thus be "neutral" (in the sense that they would not distort costs of production). Assessments could no longer be arbitrary, but would be scientifically determined. With legitimate rewards to labor and capital thus protected from governmental appropriation, incentives to productive effort — formerly suppressed — would be liberated. Market stimuli could then perform their natural functions in spurring efficiency and growth. In addition, a rent-based tax structure would provide the state with an elastic revenue base. As population grew over time, the rent share of the social product could be expected to swell. Government would thus be provided with expanded resources to finance public improvements.

Mill had full confidence in the soundness of such arrangements. Once in place, they would mean that "the wants of the state are supplied really and truly without taxation. As far as this source goes, the people of the country remain untaxed. The wants of government are supplied without any drain either upon the produce of any man's labour, or the produce of any man's capital".[8] A strategy for Indian development was thus at hand. If it could be fully implemented — and Mill was "not aware of any impossibility of attaining it"— then, he believed, the Indian revenue system would be "the best in the world".[9] He was very much aware that the varieties of land tenure systems in India added to the complexity of the administrative task. With practical learning acquired through experience, the difficulties they presented could be surmounted. These were matters to be addressed with "fine-tuning".

All of this was obviously inspired by Mill's understanding of the classical model. Had he so chosen, its categories could have been adapted to India's circumstances in yet other ways. He might, for example, have recommended nationalization of land. As the landowner, the state could then capture the rent at source. On a limited basis, he called for action along such lines to correct a mistake that the Company's government had made in Bengal in 1793. Governor-General Cornwallis had then treated the traditional zemindars as landlords and assigned property titles to them which would be valid so long as tax obligations were paid; moreover, the tax claim was fixed in perpetuity and could never be revised upward. The terms of this "Permanent Settlement," from the point of view of differential rent, were clearly wrong. The theory taught that assessments should rise as the rent share of income grew through time. But government in Bengal was honor-bound by its contractual commitment. Some of the damage could be repaired, Mill held, if the state became the pre-emptive buyer of zemindari properties put on the market. Government would then be a landlord in its own right, though opportunities to become so were rare. Nevertheless, his support for this position suggested that he was prepared to allow government in India to perform economic functions that would be off-limits in Britain.

The domain of government in India could, in principle, have been stretched still further. Given the importance of capital accumulation and the absence of an indigenous capitalist class, might it not have been expedient to call upon the state to be the country's primary saver and investor? The proposition that government behave as a capitalist was, however, too much at odds with classical conceptions of the proper division of labor between the private and public sectors to be seriously entertainable.

4.5 THE CLASSICAL MODEL AS A GUIDE TO DEVELOPMENT STRATEGY IN INDIA: VARIATION II

After 1819, James Mill spoke as an establishment "insider" about economic policy toward India. His rival claimant to the mantle of Ricardo — J. R. McCulloch — was always an outsider. As a journalist and compiler of mini-encyclopedias for popular consumption, McCulloch wrote extensively about Indian affairs. In his view, Mill had gotten the emphasis wrong. For McCulloch, the crucial message of post-Ricardian classicism for India was the central importance of uninhibited play for market forces.

McCulloch accepted the analytic validity of differential rent doctrine. He took issue, however, with its appropriation to shape a fiscal program in British India. In the first instance, governmental intervention on the scale called for by Mill's plans was inherently dangerous. He acknowledged that this strategy was benevolently motivated. But, he wrote in 1827: "It seems as if there were some strange fatality attending the government of India; and that the greatest talents and the best intentions should, when applied to legislate for that country, produce only the most pernicious projects."[10]

The fundamental truth, McCulloch insisted, was that the population was poor and overburdened with taxation. The revenue system already drained off too much potential purchasing power. The proper course was to provide cultivators with access to land at reduced rates. Then "industry would revive, and the peasantry would become attached to government. But so long as we compel the *ryots* to cultivate land that is over assessed — so long, in short, as we compel them to raise the crops, not for their own advantage, but for the exclusive advantage of Government and the host of harpies it is obliged to employ, so long will the scourge of universal poverty continue to afflict the country...".[11] In short, the Company's government engaged far too many unproductive visible hands who pre-empted resources better left available for private spending.

McCulloch's faith in the creative power of *laissez-faire* was total — and he took that to be the over-riding lesson of classical political economy. In this vision, reduction in the claims of the state would spur healthy growth. The capacity of the cultivating population to accumulate productively would be enhanced. Expansion in effective demand for consumption goods would revitalize India's non-agricultural sectors. It would also widen the market for British exports — a result that would further spur

India's internal development. Consumption horizons would thereby be elevated and fresh incentives for productive efficiency would be activated. McCulloch had no tolerance for elasticity pessimists and he wrote scathingly about those who had promoted the view that "Hindoo habits" were immutable.

Though widened market space in India's domestic economy was essential, McCulloch also assigned an important role to inflows of foreign capital and skill in his overall growth strategy. He made a strong plea for colonizing the sub-continent with Britons in order to accelerate diffusion of technical knowledge to the local populace. Unfortunately, in his view, Company government had not promoted foreign investment aggressively, nor had it offered the kind of hospitality to expatriates which would encourage them to make long-term commitments in India. It was then widely held that prospects for foreign investment on a substantial scale were dim unless a resident English population had access to English courts, staffed by English judges who administered English law. As an official, Mill stood firmly against such concessions — largely on the grounds that they would provide foundations on which dualism in the social and economic structure could be built. McCulloch did not share fear of that prospect. The legal framework should be adapted, as needed, to maximize capital formation. If unimpeded market forces ultimately produced enclaves of economic activity dominated by foreigners, that outcome should be accepted.

The thinking of McCulloch and Mill sprang from common intellectual roots. They parted ways, however, over what classical political economy should mean in the context of India. Nevertheless, these variations on Ricardian themes shared significant attributes. Though each recognized contrasts between economic conditions in Britain and India, both prescribed for India by drawing on modes of analysis and types of policies that had been formulated against the backdrop of British conditions. McCulloch and Mill diverged in their predispositions toward interventionist versus market solutions. They still proceeded from the same methodological premise: that the path to economic salvation in a poor country could be charted with the conceptual apparatus constructed for a rich one.

4.6 INDIA'S DEVELOPMENT PROSPECTS FROM A PERSPECTIVE OF HETERODOX CLASSICISM: VARIATION III

In one form or another, disciples of Ricardo shaped the bulk of British economic discourse on India in the middle decades of the nineteenth century.

There was, however, a noteworthy exception. Richard Jones, who succeeded Malthus in 1835 as the occupant of the chair of political economy at Haileybury, launched a frontal attack on the relevance of orthodox classicism to India. As an employee of the East India Company, Jones had standing as an "insider". But the analytic posture he adopted placed him well outside the mainstream of intellectual currents then in high fashion.

Jones focussed attention on the classical question: that is, the implications of the distribution of income for economic development. The answers he supplied were sharply at odds with those of Mill and McCulloch. He indicted both for practicing what Schumpeter would later characterize as the "Ricardian vice" (the use of deductive reasoning to establish truths for all times and all circumstances). In Jones's judgment, those captivated by Ricardian method had "quitted too soon the duty of dwelling long and humbly among things" and had instead engaged in "the more fascinating employment of laying down those maxims of imposing generality, which seemed to elevate the enquirer at once into the legislator of his subject, and gift him, as if by some sudden manifestation of intellectual power, with an instant command over its remotest details".[12] Proper procedure called instead for painstaking inductive studies which were sensitive to the diversity and peculiarities of economic life in specific institutional settings.

From Jones's methodological point of view, the error perpetrated in the extension of differential rent doctrine to India could be readily identified. The theory informing this exercise maintained that the rental share of income was universally determined by the natural fertility of the soil. For Jones, this proposition was unacceptable. Rent instead should be studied in an operational setting: it was the share of the product claimed by those who controlled use of land. The way that claim was exercised was far from uniform throughout the world and depended on the particularities of diverse agricultural systems. As Jones saw matters, rent originated with "the appropriation of the soil, at a time when the bulk of the people must cultivate it on such terms as they can obtain, or starve.... A necessity which then, compels them to pay a rent...is wholly independent of any difference in the quality of the ground they occupy, and would not be removed were the soils all equalised."[13] In other words, the phenomenon of rent grew out of society, not out of the soil.

Jones had little quarrel with Ricardian rent theory when English agriculture was the subject of discussion. In that institutional environment, market forces tended to establish income shares which, apart from the case of the small owner-operator, generally coincided with the classical concepts of distributive shares: wages, profits, and rents. But this was possible because of two supporting conditions. In the first place, labor and capital were priced in competitive markets; secondly, the bulk of the outputs of land were exchanged for money. Rent could thus be calculated as the residual by deducting costs of labor and capital from the gross revenues of the farming enterprise. This, however, was the economics of a special case. The institutional prerequisites necessary for isolating rent (in the Ricardian sense) were to be found, Jones maintained, on only about one per cent of the earth's surface.

Agrarian conditions in India stood in marked contrast. In traditional agriculture, little of the total output was marketed and most of the inputs were supplied by unpaid family labor. In such circumstances, the income shares written about in standard classical doctrine could not be readily distinguished. Only the total physical product was visible. No market criteria were at hand to decompose real output into separate shares as rewards to providers of land, labor, and capital.

As a practical matter, James Mill had recognized this difficulty. But, he had insisted, the problem could be solved. The net rent could be approximated by direct inspection of the productive power of individual plots. Thus, revenue officers in the field were instructed to insure that tax assessments were adjusted to accord with the fertility of the soil. Jones saw this as an impossible administrative undertaking that could never be performed accurately. Nevertheless, his objection to this procedure was based primarily on its conceptual inadequacy. In fact, he maintained, this approach to tax strategy in India had distorted Ricardian doctrine beyond recognition. The theory held that rent was what remained after the costs of agricultural production had been covered. Mill's scheme, on the other hand, treated rent — as approximated by the tax demand — as the prior claim on the output of the peasantry. Wages and profits, rather than rent, thus became the residual. Policies guided by this bowdlerized version of rent theory, Jones argued, had perpetuated agrarian poverty in India.

If Mill's brand of classicism was a misfit in India, so also was McCulloch's. The latter was preoccupied with the monetized exchange. This orientation precluded a clear understanding of the nature of economic activity conducted within largely self-sufficient households. This too was unfortunate. Failure to look beneath the veil of the money economy invited misjudgments about the basic realities in agrarian systems. In McCulloch's version of classicism, enlargement of market activity was self-evidently desirable and, when it occurred, provided unambiguous testimony to economic improvement. Jones challenged the validity of such conclusions in peasant societies. British administration in India, for example, had obliged the cultivating peasantry to market crops by insisting that tax obligations be settled in cash. Jones doubted the capacity of "the most wise and honest government to impose a definite money payment that shall not be oppressive".[14] The problem arose because a tax obligation fixed in money terms did not make adequate allowance for seasonal fluctuations in yields and for volatility in market prices. A peasant family could never calculate confidently about how much of its real output would be needed to raise the cash required by the tax collector. Conceivably, forced marketing mandated by a monetized tax system might reduce the economic welfare of peasant households, even though market participation had increased.

Jones's insistence on structural discontinuities between advanced economies and less developed ones made little dent in mainstream classical thinking. Indeed it was generally ignored in his lifetime.

4.7 A CLOSING WORD

Lewis's 1954 adaptation of classical political economy to address issues of development in the twentieth century stands as an impressive intellectual achievement. This contribution did not do full justice to variations on the common theme worked out by the original classicists. Nor, for that matter, should it have done so. His purpose was not to uncover refinements of their doctrine, but to extract its central analytic nerve. In this he succeeded admirably.

The exercise Lewis performed invited a rethinking of the development process in the modern context. The importance of directing attention to structural distinctiveness in the less developed world was then demonstrated. When Lewis's resurrected classical model is juxtaposed against the thinking of nineteenth century contributors to classical debate, an arresting irony emerges. His interpretation of the interactions between "capitalist" and "subsistence" sectors was faithful to the spirit of the mainstream version of the original master model and its approach to the links between income distribution and growth. But, in his treatment of the structural discontinuities imbedded in dualistic economies, the mainstream classicists of the early nineteenth century would have consigned him to the camp of the heterodox.

Notes

1. W. Arthur Lewis, "Economic Development with Unlimited Supplies of Labour," *The Manchester School of Economic and Social Studies*, 1954.
2. Adam Smith, *An Inquiry into the Nature and Causes of the Wealth of Nations*, ed., Edwin Cannan, London, 1904, vol. 2, p. 180.
3. *Ibid.*, vol. 2, pp. 72, 137.
4. James Mill, *The History of British India, London*, 1817, vol. 1, pp. 342, 463; vol. 2, p. 260.
5. *Ibid.*, vol. 1, p. 191.
6. *Ibid.*, vol. 1, p. 314.
7. T. R. Malthus, *Principles of Political Economy*, London, 1820, especially p. 156.
8. James Mill, Minutes of Evidence before the Select Committee on the Affairs of the East India Company, 2 August 1831, *Parliamentary Papers*, 1831, vol. 5, p. 292.
9. *Ibid.*, 11 August 1831, p. 336.
10. J. R. McCulloch, "Revenue and Commerce of India," *Edinburgh Review*, March 1827, p. 354.
11. *Ibid.*, p. 358.
12. Richard Jones, *An Essay on the Distribution of Wealth and on the Sources of Taxation*, Cambridge, 1831, p. xxiii.
13. *Ibid.*, p. 11.
14. Jones, *A Short Tract on Political Economy, Including Some Account of the Anglo-Indian Revenue Systems* (as reprinted in *The Literary Remains ... of the Late Rev. Richard Jones*, ed. William Whewell), London, 1859, p. 282.

5 Natural Resources, "Vent-for-Surplus", and the Staples Theory

Ronald Findlay and Mats Lundahl

The "vent-for-surplus" approach to trade and development, which Hla Myint (1958) derived from the writings of Adam Smith, is a celebrated contribution to economics. The objective of our paper is to unify the "vent-for-surplus" approach with what Watkins (1963) has called the "staples" theory of economic growth and with the factor proportions theory of comparative advantage. The basis for the proposed unification will be the concept of an endogenous land frontier.

5.1 INTRODUCTION

The formal theory of international trade and specialization has developed majestically on its Ricardian foundations for almost two centuries, and its logic has been impregnable against the perennial critiques of assorted protectionists. As a tool for historical research on trade patterns in the course of economic development, however, both the original Ricardian model and its Heckscher–Ohlin offshoot have not, on the whole, proved very sharp or effective. Although this may have been due to the fact that capital accumulation and technological change have only recently been incorporated into the theory, the fact remains that economic historians and applied economists have not, up to now, found it very helpful in their own research.

Since an intellectual vacuum, like any other, cries out to be filled, recourse has had to be found somewhere. One popular candidate, for those of a radical persuasion, has been the "dependency" theory, with its machinations of a hegemonic center against a helpless periphery. Much more successful, in our view, has been the "staples" theory of the Canadian economic historian, Harold Adams Innis, in his classic series of works on the role of primary exports in the economic development of his native country (Innis, 1930, 1940). Innis' work was very influential within Canada itself and also inspired the important work of Douglass North

(1966) on the United States. The approach was also applied to Australia (Mclean, 1989).

In 1958, Myint published his now celebrated article on the "classical theory of international trade and the underdeveloped countries". By "classical" Myint definitely meant Adam Smith and *not* David Ricardo. Partly, this implied a difference of style, the historically based "realism and relevance" of the former as against the strict deductive reasoning from "unrealistic" premises of the other. Substantively, however, the main difference, as Myint saw it, was that in Ricardo, the gain from trade was associated with a reallocation of given and fully employed resources, whereas in Adam Smith, trade provided a "vent" for labor and natural resources that were in "surplus" before the opening of trade. Thus the expansion of exports did not have to come at the expense of import-competing production and so the gains from trade would be larger than in the case of initial full employment and utilization.

This "vent-for-surplus" theory was eagerly adopted by several writers on the development of the "export economies" of Asia, Africa and Latin America. Richard Caves (1965) examined the "staples" and the "vent-for-surplus" approaches as alternatives to the standard trade doctrine in relation to the experience of Canada and other "regions of recent settlement" and the tropical underdeveloped economics. Caves tended to associate the former cases with surplus land and the latter with surplus labor *à la* Lewis (1954) although Myint had taken the view that both land and labor were in surplus in the case of the tropical economies.

The "staples" approach was first formalized by Chambers and Gordon (1966). In their model the export staple is produced by fixed land specific to that sector and labor, which is also used to produce an importable good "gadget", together with capital specific to that sector, and a non-traded good "haircuts". Caves (1971) gave an extended critique, extension and application of this model in relation to the wheat boom of the first decade of this century in Canada. Interestingly, 1971 was the same year that Ronald Jones (1971) and Paul Samuelson (1971) both published their now classic papers on the "specific factors" or Ricardo-Viner model of international trade. As just noted, the essential features of this model were all contained explicitly in Chambers and Gordon, though not developed as fully and elegantly as by Jones and Samuelson. The relationships between these papers and other works on international trade and factor mobility are very thoroughly explored in an inexplicably unpublished paper by Easton and Reed (1980).

The simplest way in which natural resources have been introduced into international trade is the so-called "availability" theory of Irving Kravis (1956), where it is reduced to a matter of geography. The answer given to the question "why does Kuwait export oil?" is the same as the mountaineer Mallory gave to the question of why he wanted to climb Everest, "Because it is there". This of course begs the question of the opportunity cost of complementary, non-specific inputs needed to get the oil out of the ground, as is pointed out in Findlay (1970, pp. 76–81), so that there is really no escape from the necessity of the logic of comparative cost.

Myint (1958), however, also wanted to escape from the confines of Ricardian comparative cost by postulating the existence, presumably in equilibrium, of "surplus" resources, both land and labor. One or the other can of course be accommodated, with the other as the binding constraint, but how can we account for both? Findlay (1970, pp. 70–76) attempts to provide a possible explanation in terms of an endogenous supply of labor, with the initial price of manufactures (produced by a primitive handicraft sector) so high that it restricts the supply of labor, which expands once cheaper manufactures become available through imports, Thus initially permitting food exports to expand without any contraction in handicrafts. Over time, however, the latter would be slowly wiped out by competition with the cheaper imports.

We now believe, however, that a much more powerful and historically relevant interpretation of the "vent-for-surplus" approach is in terms of the concept of an endogenous land "frontier". Originally introduced in the famous work of the American historian Frederick Turner (1921), this concept has been used extensively by historians and geographers for a wide variety of times and places, but has been neglected by economists. An exception is a highly suggestive paper by Guido Di Tella (1982) on the role of natural resources in the development of Argentina, which has been formally developed into a general equilibrium model of the links through trade and factor mobility of a previously settled "Europe" and an effectively empty "America" in Findlay (1993).

In the present paper we will apply a restricted "small open economy" version of this model to the experience of the export economies of different types. Before we do that, however, we will briefly survey the historical record with respect to some selected cases that are illustrative of the general trends and patterns that were observed.

5.2 CASE STUDIES

This section examines some brief case studies of export-oriented growth, concentrating on the period 1870–1914, which was the "golden age" of the creation of the modern world economy. It will be useful to classify our cases into three groups. First, we have the so-called "regions of recent settlement." These are what were the almost "empty" lands in the temperate zones of the Americas and Australia, which attracted substantial inflows of capital and labor from Europe to produce and export primary commodities in great abundance in return for manufactured imports. Here we will look at the experience of Canada, the United States, Argentina, and Australia. Next we will consider a pair of what we might call "plantation economies." These are tropical countries in which cash crops were introduced into what were previously mostly subsistence economies by foreign capitalists and entrepreneurs who employed imported as well as indigenous labor on large estates. Our cases will be Malaya in South East Asia and Costa Rica in Central America. The third category will be "peasant export economies," cases where native peasants themselves turned from subsistence to export production of tropical commodities. Our examples here will be the Gold Coast (now Ghana) and Burma.

5.2.1 Regions of Recent Settlement

The studies of Innis and others have told the story of Canadian development in terms of the successive discoveries and exploitation of natural resources such as furs in connection with the Hudson's Bay company, the cod fisheries of Newfoundland and the moving frontier for wheat cultivation on the prairies, all against a background of growing world demand and rising prices for these products. This expansion induced very substantial inflows of capital and labor, particularly around the turn of the century and in the next two decades. Manufacturing production also increased, though not without tariff protection. Linkage effects from the primary export sectors to the rest of the economy were substantial, particularly because of the transportation networks required to bind the vast country together. Caves and Holton (1959) give a very detailed analysis of the development of the Canadian economy, explicitly within the framework of the "staples" theory. It is also interesting to note that Meier (1953) rightly amended the classic analysis of Viner (1924) on capital inflows into Canada to take into account the growth of primary exports and associated linkage, as emphasized in the "staples" theory.

Given the similarities in the resource base of the Canadian and United States economics, it comes as no surprise that the "staples" approach illuminates the pattern of United States growth as well. The approach was first applied extensively by North (1966) who emphasized that international demand for export products had been the "prime mover" of economic development in the United States since early colonial times. In particular,

North applies the "staples" approach to the case of cotton and the *antebellum* South. Not only did cotton lead to a spectacular development of the Southern "plantation economy" itself but it also generated strong linkage effects to other regions of the country. The North East supplied the South with finance, transportation, insurance and marketing facilities, and most importantly, manufactures. Simultaneously the West was developed to supply the South, highly specialized on cotton, with its grain requirements. Westward migration was induced and the transportation network, first canals and then railroads, had to be provided for the South to be adequately supplied. According to North it was this interlinked process of staple-based growth, involving the inflow of people and capital to extend the agricultural frontier, that generated the prosperity of the United States in the *antebellum* period.

The post Civil War period can, of course, also be described within the framework of the "staples" theory. The frontier continued to be extended westwards, but now it was wheat, livestock, and minerals that were the staples around which development was generated, along with a surge of industrialization in the East to supply a return flow of manufactures to the western regions. Massive inflows of capital and population from Europe also took place, particularly from about 1890 to 1920.

A particularly interesting case of staple exports was Argentina in the late nineteenth century and up to the depression in 1929 (Diaz-Alejandro, 1984; Cortés Condé, 1985). Argentina was a relatively "empty" country in the mid-nineteenth century. However, the expansion of foreign trade during the latter half of that century provided strong incentives for economic expansion and rising *per capita* income. A number of staples contributed to this expansion: wool, hides, and salted meat in the 1870s, wheat (a leading product in the 1890s), corn and linseed around the turn of the century, and frozen meat a decade later. On the eve of the depression, staples-led growth had raised real GDP *per capita* to over two and a half times the corresponding figure in 1880. During this period the land "frontier" had expanded continuously, though not at zero cost, and in the process the best Pampa land had been concentrated in the hands of a powerful landowner class that was to constitute the most important political group during the pre-1929 period. This expansion was complemented by massive immigration from southern Europe, fueled mainly by the attractive economic conditions in Argentina and supported by the interest of the landowners in peopling the "wilderness" and bringing it to economic use. The step from cattle raising for hide production to sheep raising, agriculture, and beef production represented a substantial increase in the man/land ratio — one which could not be achieved with the aid of only the domestic population. Also, the country could count on a substantial inflow of capital from Europe, notably Britain, and later also the United States, which brought foreign investment to a level almost comparable to that prevailing in Canada.

For the growth locomotive to function, a number of linkages had to be established. As it appears, export prices were falling in the 1880s but the fall in transport costs that took place with the construction of the railroad network increased the profitability of staples production even in the face of falling product prices, mainly by opening the road to the fertile lands of the interior. In this process capital raised abroad played a crucial role. Not until the turn of the century was a strong impulse received from overseas demand.

The development of the transport network was instrumental in extending the domestic market as well. The rising incomes were distributed across the national territory and this gave rise to increased domestic trade in consumer goods. Many of the items could be manufactured domestically with the result that demand, or consumption, linkages were quickly established. The share of such items as staple foods and textiles in total imports fell significantly from the 1880s or 1890s until World War I, because local producers were able to take over.

Backward and forward linkages were also established. Refrigerated ships, meat packing, marketing etc., with the aid of foreign technology, machinery and equipment were all necessary, and forward linkages to the processing of agricultural and livestock products developed (Diaz Alejandro, 1970).

Still Argentina remained a primary exporter. The reasons for this are easily discernible (Ferns, 1969, p. 125):

> In 1896 the terms of trade began to alter in a way favourable to producers of food products, and these terms of trade became progressively and even fantastically favourable to Argentina until 1929, except for a period after World War I in 1920–24. The production of foodstuffs, linseed, and wool was very profitable. Capital naturally flowed into these activities, and commercial and industrial activities were nourished by the agricultural sector. It was so patently economically advantageous to do what Argentina in fact did that it seems a waste of time and a profitless exercise to look for any other explanation of what happened. Argentina became a highly specialized producer because it was profitable to do so, and those who profited most had no motive to seek alternative policies.

The entire Argentine economy revolved around the staple exports, including the infrastructure, notably the transport network. However, in the middle of the *belle époque*, it was seen only as a matter of time before a more balanced structure would prevail in the economy (Ferns, 1969, p. 125):

> Looking at the evidence of the 1890s and taking account of the profitability of agriculture and ranching compared with industrial activity at that time, there was no reason to suppose that industry would not develop as it did in Canada or Australia or other states producing primary products.

Unfortunately, things did not turn out this way. The depression was to mark the end of export-induced prosperity in Argentina. Internationally, the political mood had turned increasingly in favor of protectionism during the 1920s, and in the 1930s Argentine exports were to be hit severely by the efforts of the industrialized countries to protect their own primary producers. As a result of this (and the generally negative effects of the depression on exports), Argentina decided to follow suit. A period of import substitution that aimed at fostering the growth of the domestic manufacturing sector followed.

Another case of staples-induced expansion combined with an extension of the open range and vast inflows of labor and capital is that of Australia from the 1830s to the 1890s (McLean, 1989; also Lougheed, 1968) for a critical view of the staples thesis as applied to Australia. As with Argentina, the expansion of the international economy over this period contributed many of the forces that propelled Australia on a path of rapid growth. From 1860 to 1890 the country experienced a real GDP growth of close to five percent per annum.

Again, the expansion process rested on increased employment of land, labor and capital — to a much larger extent than on technological change, which was to assume major importance only later. To what extent favorable price movements were responsible for the expansion process is uncertain. No reliable figures are available for the pre-1870 period, but it nevertheless appears likely that Australia's terms of trade improved from around 1850 to 1870, since world commodity prices rose. However, the 1870s displayed no clear trend and a decline set in from around 1880.

At any rate, the discoveries of gold that began in the 1850s brought a tremendous boom in mineral exploitation, one which was to repeat itself also after 1890 (Maddock and McLean, 1984). The demand for wool was also high enough to make the land frontier expand, even though sheep ranchers had problems obtaining clear title to their lands during much of the period — opposed as they were by the miners. Wool accounted for no less than 54 per cent of Australia's total exports in the 1880s (Diaz-Alejandro, 1984, p. 334).

Exports may not have led growth during the entire period. The ratio of exports to GDP declined from 1861 to 1890. However, this may be a bit beside the point. The ratio probably rose during the gold rush years, and even a declining ratio may be compatible with the staples approach (McLean, 1989, p. 27):

> All that is required is that activity in the non-export industries expands along with the export expansion and the export ratio (usually measured with annual data) will remain unchanged. In an historical inquiry, the role of exports in growth is more appropriately viewed in a dynamic and general equilibrium context.

The extension of mining and of the land frontier in Australia could not take place without complementary production factors. Again, immigration and capital inflow provided the solution. During the three decades following 1860, the share of immigration in the total population increase and that of the foreign capital inflow in total capital formation both exceeded one-third on average [McLean (1989), p. 16].

5.2.2 Plantation Economies

The rubber plant was introduced in Malaya in the late 1870s, during a period of rising European demand and increasing prices, and towards the end of the century large-scale planting was begun. The first exports took place in 1906 and in just a few years, Malaya became the leading rubber exporter in the world. The period between this year and the beginning of the 1920s represented "a period of expansion with few comparisons in the history of tropical agriculture…" (Gunnarsson, 1979, p. 6).

In this development, the estate sector (holdings of more than 100 acres) took the lead. Coffee plantations existed in Malaya already before the arrival of rubber in the country and when relative prices turned in favor of rubber, after 1896, a switch took place towards the latter crop. The organization of production was similar for the two crops which facilitated the process. The planters were also given support by the colonial government: loans, land leases at low rents, and assistance with labor immigration. The plantation sector expanded on virgin lands with the aid of European capital and mainly Indian (Tamil) labor (and to a lesser extent Chinese, Malays and Javanese). The necessary political stability was obtained in the 1890s as the British gained control over the Malacca peninsula and exports were greatly facilitated by the transportation network that had been developed when tin production expanded before the turn of the century.

The initial reluctance shown by the European capital markets to invest in Malaya was gradually overcome as prices and dividends increased after 1900. As British merchant firms moved in, a link was created between the London capital market and the planters. This flow of capital was later supplemented by plowback of profits, and it is possible that the latter source was more important than the former during the great expansion period.

Plantation production of rubber required a large labor force and this demand could not be met locally. Beginning in 1907 the colonial government moved to facilitate the immigration of Tamil workers from India. They were cheaper than Chinese, had a reputation of being excellent workers and easy to handle and the fact that the migration took place between two British colonies greatly facilitated the process, in particular since it also allowed for a reduction of the labor force in times of stagnation.

With time, the leading "plantation" segment had to face competition from a "smallholder" (less than 100 acres) sector. Between 1910 and the outbreak of World War II, the smallholder acreage and output grew at a rate very few people had thought possible. As a matter of fact the expansion was, with very few exceptions, unique in the history of tropical agriculture during the colonial era (Gunnarsson, 1979, p. 21). Most of this expansion took place in the 1910s.

The mechanisms behind the growth of the smallholder sector differed considerably from those that fueled plantation expansion. The smallholders hardly received any government support. Rather, smallholder expansion was discouraged by a colonial government intent on fostering "commercial" agriculture. Also, the sector had no direct access to the European capital markets. In spite of these handicaps, the smallholder sector turned out to be a competitor that very strongly threatened the profitability of the plantation sector.

The expansion of smallholder rubber production took place in a "vent-for-surplus" situation. The new crop could easily be fitted into the existing agricultural system without detrimental effects on food production. There was plenty of unused suitable land that could be cultivated with the aid of a domestic labor force which hitherto had preferred leisure. Alternatively, cultivation was undertaken by immigrant Chinese who were better connected with the commercially oriented economy than the Malays and who could hardly be classified as "peasants". Thus both domestic and foreign migration was involved.

Capital played a subordinate role. The exceedingly simple methods employed only required some initial investment plus credits to carry the farmers over the dead season. The latter was supplied by the European merchant firms, and it is possible to argue that even in this case there probably was an element of capital inflow from abroad. After 1910 seeds were freely available and could be gathered by any prospective grower.

The smallholder expansion was highly successful, so successful that the British authorities saw it fit to put into effect a series of restriction schemes during the depression years of the 1930s when rubber prices dropped, which favored the plantations over the smaller holdings.

Our next case, Costa Rica, represents a mixture between small-farm and plantation export production (Cardoso, 1977; Bulmer-Thomas, 1987). The first staple product, coffee, began to be exported to Chile in 1832, for processing there and re-exportation to Europe, and, more importantly, to Britain in 1843 — long before the coffee expansion in the rest of Central America. In 1890, coffee dominated the export trade completely, accounting for no less than 91 percent of Costa Rica's total export value. During the latter half of the nineteenth century, coffee drinking was becoming *à la mode* in Europe, and the rapidly increasing demand was translated into an increasing price trend, with the result that in Costa Rica, coffee was to rise to a leading position not only in terms of exports but in terms of the entire economic life of the country.

The second staple was bananas. Banana cultivation was established much as a result of forward linkage from the coffee industry, when in 1884 construction was begun on a railway from San José to Puerto Limón on the Atlantic coast to facilitate coffee exports. With this began the well-known story of how Minor Keith, the future founder of the United Fruit Company, began growing bananas along the railroad tracks to pay for some of the construction costs and how this with time would make Costa Rica the world's leading banana exporter with a world market share of 60 per cent in 1929.

When coffee production began, Costa Rica was a sparsely populated country. The population in 1840 was a mere 72,000 and 137,000 in 1870 (Woodward, 1985, p. 478). The pressure on the available land was low. Only the Meseta Central had any population density to speak of, but even there a considerable number of *terrenos baldios* (waste lands) existed. These were state property, and when coffee production began, the procedure for acquiring these lands free of charge was simplified considerably, and public lands (*tierras públicas*) were sold at a low price. As a result, the period of Costa Rican history between 1832 and the great depression following the crisis of 1929 was strongly marked by a "moving frontier" of internal colonization associated with the vigorous expansion of coffee cultivation (Cardoso, 1977, p. 177). Until the 1880s, coffee growing could be extended in the Meseta Central without encroaching on areas planted with other crops, before the land frontier was closed.

In the banana case, the expansion took place in a completely uninhabited part of the national territory — the swamps and jungles of the Atlantic coast that had no alternative use. After the railway construction in 1884, a "vent-for-surplus" phase was inaugurated that was to last until the 1920s, when banana production as well could go on expanding only at the expense of other crops (Bulmer-Thomas, 1987, p. 38).

Coffee producers faced a serious labor shortage problem. In relation to the needs of the expanding staple the Meseta population remained scant, and there was no large-scale immigration (Cardoso, 1977, p. 179). Only land, not labor, was in abundance in the central highlands. Coffee could expand only at increasing wages as the Meseta Central population moved outwards when the coffee *fincas* did.

The banana case was different. The unhealthy conditions prevailing on the Atlantic jungle coast made the population in the Meseta reluctant to move there. The only solution possible consisted in bringing in black laborers from the West Indies at wages that were comparatively high in the Costa Rican context, while prohibiting the new immigrants by law from moving to the interior.

The early period of coffee production was financed out of capital that had been accumulated during the colonial era and the first years of independence from the cultivation of cocoa and tobacco and from exports of *palo brasil*. Because processing techniques were simple at the time and land cheap (or free), little capital was needed. However, as more sophisticated processing procedures were substituted for the original primitive ones, the demand for finance grew. From the 1840s a pattern was established whereby commercial houses in Britain made advances to Costa Rican exporters against future delivery and the latter extended credits to the growers.

The banana venture differed from the coffee one insofar as it was dependent on external finance from the outset. Large investments were required to transform the jungle and swamp areas into areas suitable for humans, and housing, schooling and health care added to the sums required. With time, the banana industry became firmly concentrated and vertically integrated in the powerful American-owned United Fruit Company.

The export-led growth of the Costa Rican economy involved the creation of a number of linkages. The most obvious is in processing, which made Costa Rican coffee a high-quality one fetching a comparatively high price in the international market. Transport was another area, with coffee first being exported via the Pacific coast and then with the inauguration of the Atlantic Railway in 1890 coffee could easily be exported from the

Atlantic side of Costa Rica. This venture also constituted a forward linkage to banana production. Coffee exports also resulted in the creation of banking facilities in the mid-nineteenth century whereas in the case of bananas, dominated by an American company, the demand for banking facilities lay in the United States, not in Costa Rica.

Beyond activities that were directly connected with the two staples, however, few production linkages were created. The coffee interests did not diversify because the relative price structure did not favor such investment, social infrastructure was lacking, and so was energy. Banks catered almost exclusively to the export sector. The banana sector, in turn, was in foreign hands that concentrated on the vertical integration of the banana trade itself and furthermore employed mainly import-intensive inputs. As a result, "developments in manufacturing activity in general in the 1920s were minimal" (Bulmer-Thomas, 1987, p. 40).

Moreover, coffee production resulted in delinkage once the land frontier in the highlands had been closed. Food shortages emerged a number of times during the nineteenth century, and competition between export agriculture and domestic use agriculture was gradually intensified as the banana industry was also running out of empty lands.

The demand structure generated out of coffee and banana production was concentrated on imports. This was definitely the case with the American-owned banana industry, but the same was true for coffee, despite the dominance of smallholder family farms in the sector, since there was considerable concentration at the later stages of the commercialization and processing process.

Finally, the Costa Rican government failed to diversify the economy via the tax system. The taxes applied to the export sector were not elastic with respect to the value of production and the domestic market was believed to be too small to sustain any industry (Bulmer-Thomas, 1988, pp. 46–47).

Dependence on two main export products lasted a long time in Costa Rica until the late 1950s, and this dependence made for vulnerability. The failure to diversify the economy meant that when the Great Depression hit in 1929, the subsequent adjustment had to take place directly through a fall in real income and employment in the export sector. Nonetheless, the concentration on the primary sector continued during the next three decades.

5.2.3 Peasant Exporters

Our first example of a staple-exporting peasant economy is the Gold Coast (later Ghana), which became the world's leading exporter of cocoa in 1910 after a brief but remarkably rapid expansion over only two decades. Ghana continued to be the world's leading producer until she lost that position in the late 1970s, mainly as a result of the misconceived monopsonistic policies of its marketing board.

Cocoa is not indigenous to Africa but was introduced there from the New World by the Portuguese. Stimulated by the growing world demand for chocolate in the late nineteenth century, production of this crop was taken up by the Akwapim people of the Gold Coast around 1890. Seeds and the elementary planting techniques were provided by the colonial Department of Agriculture but all subsequent development was a strictly African affair. The Akwapim, who originally inhabited a very infertile hilly region, had displayed remarkable drive and adaptability in their economic pursuits, which ranged from working as porters for the British army during the Ashanti wars to the cultivation of oil palms. When prices for palm oil dropped sharply in the 1880s they took up the cultivation of cocoa on virgin forest lands that they acquired from another tribe. The dramatic story of these developments is well told by Hill (1963).

Exports rose from just over 500 tons in 1900 to 5000 tons by 1904 to over 50,000 tons in 1913 by which time the Gold Coast had become the world's leading producer with over half of the value of its exports accounted for by this commodity (see Holmes, 1970).

Szereszewski (1965) makes the very Myint-like argument that cocoa cultivation was simply added, by "interseeding" with food crops, and so there was no switching of activities involved as in the comparative cost doctrine. However, this needs to be modified to take account of the migration of farmers to areas that were better suited for cocoa. Capital requirements were initially modest and provided by the farmers themselves but once the export trade was well established European trading houses began to finance the farmers over the harvest cycle. Linkage effects to other sectors, apart from the transportation involved in getting the crop to market, were modest.

Equally remarkable is the story of the rapid expansion of rice exports from the Irrawaddy Delta Region of lower Burma in the second half of the nineteenth century. The essentials were told in the classic study by J. S. Furnivall (1957) but more recent work by Aye Hlaing (1964) and especially Michael Adas (1974) has rounded out the picture significantly.

In 1852, when the area was occupied by the British after the second Anglo-Burmese war, it was sparsely populated despite its potential fertility since the Burmese population was concentrated in its original heartland in Central Burma, still under the rule of the Burmese dynasty. Production and trade were restricted by the deliberately autarkic and restrictive policy of the dynasty. British rule opened the region to the forces of the expanding world economy, particularly after the Suez Canal was constructed in 1869, which brought European markets for rice as well as cheap imports of manufactures. A stable political and administrative framework was created, along with infrastructure such as roads, railways and canals to supplement the already abundant rivers and creeks.

With these incentives Burmese cultivators rapidly migrated into the region from central and upper Burma in large numbers, supplemented by a substantial inflow of Indian temporary migrant workers to work in the rice mills and docks that processed and shipped the rice to world markets. The steam-powered rice mills were mostly established by European trading houses. There are no estimates of how much capital was brought in, and it is likely that high initial profits from rice-milling and export were the main source of further investment.

The area under rice cultivation rose from a million acres in 1852 to 6 million by the turn of the century and 8 million by 1915, with rice exports having risen from nothing to over 2 million tons by the first decades of the twentieth century when Burma was the leading rice exporter in the world. Substantial exports of teak and of minerals, such as petroleum, were additional contributions of the primary sector to the development of the country.

Linkages, however, were largely confined to the milling of rice and the sawing of logs. Manufactured imports, particularly cotton piece goods and household items, displaced local handicrafts. Socially the system created what Furnivall termed a "plural society" in which the Burmese were the rural labor force that produced the rice, on credit extended over the year by Indian money lenders, while other Indians processed the paddy in the European-owned rice mills and loaded it on to ships at the main ports, while the British were the administrators and managers of the firms that handled most of the commerce, transport, banking, and insurance.

Hlaing (1964, p. 51) estimates that GDP grew between 1901 and 1931, the onset of the great depression, at 1.9 per cent *per annum* while population grew by 1.1 per cent *per annum*, so that there was a rate of *per capita* growth that was quite respectable for that time. Since then the Depression, World War II, and decades of mismanagement by the current military rulers of Burma have ruined the prosperity of what was once the world's leading rice exporter.

5.3 LAND FRONTIER

Despite their considerable differences, all three types of export economy that we examined in the previous section display a remarkable uniformity in the character and pattern of their development. In every case the stimulus to development comes from rising prices and expanding markets in the world economy that leads to an extension of the land frontier internally, accompanied by substantial inflows of foreign capital and labor immigration, either from outside the country or another region within the same political borders. This frontier might be on the prairies of North America, the *pampas* of Argentina or the "outback" of Australia, in the case of the regions of recent settlement, or on the malarial swamps and jungles in the tropical lands of the plantation and peasant export economies. But in every case it was extended substantially at a significant cost in terms of the resources required to clear the land and provide the necessary physical, social, and administrative infrastructure. The new activities associated with the production of the primary export products generated additional demands for capital and labor that were met partly from foreign sources in every case, so that international and inter-regional factor mobility is always an integral part of the story.

Thus, at least as far as the "opening up" process in the creation of the modern world economy is concerned, the geographical differences between temperate and tropical zones, the ethnic differences between European settlers on the one hand and Asian and African peasants and workers on the other, all do not seem to matter. The "stylized facts" in every case conform remarkably to a simple model that we hope will capture the underlying structural pattern in all these instances, and thereby serve to integrate the vision of both the "vent-for-surplus" and the "staples" theories.

Although the model we construct is sufficiently flexible to cover all three cases in essentials, it is nevertheless important to respect the differences among them. Accordingly we will present the basic model in two alternative forms. The first, or "basic" model, intended to apply to the regions of recent settlement, is closer to the "staples" theory. The second, or "modified" model, intended to apply to the plantation and peasant economies of the tropics, is closer to the "vent-for-surplus" theory. The common feature of both, however, will be an endogenous land frontier, which serves to unify the two theories.

5.3.1 The Basic Model

The core of our formalization of these two theories is the so-called Ricardo-Viner "specific factors" model, which was itself influenced by earlier work on the staples approach, in the case of Ronald Jones (1971).

The basic technology consists of the constant returns to scale production functions for Primary Products, designated A, and Manufactures, designated M, which are

$$A = A\,(N, L_A) \tag{1}$$

$$M = M\,(K_M, L_M) \tag{2}$$

where N is the specific natural resource input or "land" into A, and K_M is the input of "capital" specific to M. The total labor force is given and we have

$$L_A + L_M = \overline{L} \tag{3}$$

We shall now, however, depart from the Jones formulation in two crucial respects. First, we do not take K_M as exogenously given. Instead we regard it as in perfectly elastic supply in the long run, at an interest rate $\overline{\rho}$ determined by domestic time preference.

As in Solow (1956) we can think of the flow output of M as capable of being either consumed or invested, so that K_M consists of an accumulated stock of M. The marginal productivity of M with respect to K_M is therefore a pure number per unit time.

The other crucial difference with the Ricardo-Viner model is that we regard the natural resource input N as determined by an endogenous "frontier" as in Findlay (1990) instead of being simply given. N can be increased by incurring a rising marginal cost in terms of capital so that we have

$$K_A = \phi\,(N) \tag{4}$$

with

$$\phi'\,(N) > 0,\ \phi''\,(N) > 0$$

where $\phi'(N)$ is the marginal cost of "clearing" a unit of land, which is a "convex" function of the amount of land that is cleared.

It will be convenient to choose M as the *numeraire*, and so p is the relative price of A and w the real wage, both in terms of M.

If we define output per worker and capital per worker in the M sector as m and k respectively, we can then write the production function for M in intensive form as

$$m = m\,(k) \tag{2'}$$

Profit maximization under project competition must then result in

$$m'\,(k) = \overline{\rho} \tag{5}$$

The value $\bar{k}$ of k that satisfies (5) also determines the equilibrium real wage as

$$\bar{w} = m(\bar{k}) - m'(\bar{k})\,\bar{k} \tag{6}$$

The given value of the rate of interest $\bar{\rho}$ thus determines $\bar{k}$ and hence $\bar{w}$ because of constant returns to scale in the M sector.

Writing a and n for output per worker and "land" per worker in the A sector, perfect competition and free mobility between sectors for labor result in

$$p[a - a'(n)\,n] = \bar{w} \tag{7}$$

Thus to each value of p there corresponds a unique value of n, and hence of the marginal productivity of land $a'(n)$, that satisfies (7).

The extent of the frontier, and hence the amount of land N, is determined by the condition that the rate of return on clearing land must, in the long run, be equal to the rate of interest so that we have the crucial condition

$$\frac{pa'[n(p)]}{\phi'(N)} = \bar{\rho} \tag{8}$$

in which the numerator is determined by (7) and thus the amount of land N is determined by the value of the marginal cost of land, equal to the asset price of land, which is the denominator $\phi'(N)$, that satisfies (8).

From (7) and the fact that

$$a'(n) > 0,\ a''(n) < 0$$

it follows that a rise in p leads to a fall in n and therefore to a rise in the numerator of (8), since the marginal physical productivity of a unit of land $a'(n)$ rises in response to the rise in p. Thus since $\phi''(N) > 0$ there must be a rise in N for (8) to continue to hold. Thus we have proved that

$$N = N(p),\ N'(p) > 0 \tag{9}$$

that is, the extent of the frontier is an increasing function of p.

Since to each p there corresponds a unique $n(p)$ and $N(p)$ it follows that it also determines a unique L_A and hence A. Since $N'(p)$ is positive and $n'(p)$ is negative from (7) it follows that L_A as well as N is an increasing function of p and thus we obtain

$$A = A(p),\ A'(p) > 0 \tag{10}$$

as the positively sloped supply curve of A.

To each p there corresponds a unique value of L_A, as we have just shown, and therefore by (3) a unique value of L_M as well. Since $\bar{k}$ is determined uniquely by (5) we know K_M and hence M as well. Since L_M is a decreasing function of p we obtain

$$M = M\left(\frac{1}{p}\right),\ M'\left(\frac{1}{p}\right) > 0 \tag{11}$$

as the positively sloped supply curve for M as a function of its own relative price, the reciprocal of p.

National income, denoted Y, is also determined as a function of p since

$$Y \equiv w\,(L_A + L_M) + \rho K_M + qN \tag{12}$$

where

$$q \equiv p\,a'(n)$$

is the rental per unit of land.

Assuming that consumers have identical and homothetic indifference curves we can define demand functions

$$A_D = A_D\,(p, Y) \tag{13}$$

$$\frac{\delta A_D}{\delta p} < 0,\ \frac{\delta A_D}{\delta Y} > 0$$

and

$$M_D = M_D\left(\frac{1}{p}, Y\right) \tag{14}$$

$$\frac{\delta M_D}{\delta\left(\frac{1}{p}\right)} < 0,\ \frac{\delta M_D}{\delta Y} > 0$$

From (10) and (13) we obtain the excess supply function for A as

$$E_A(p) = A(p) - A_D(p),\ E'_A(p) > 0 \tag{15}$$

with a positive slope. The value $\bar{p}$ of p that makes

$$E_A(p) = 0 \tag{16}$$

determines the full general equilibrium of the closed economy.

5.3.2 Opening to Trade: Rise in the Relative Price of Primary Products

We now imagine the economy being opened to the rest of the world. The main impact, of course, will come through a rise in the relative price of primary products, so that p rises from $\bar{p}$ to an appreciably higher level p^*, determined by conditions in the world as a whole that the economy is too "small" to influence.

The effect on all the endogenous variables of the economy is easy to evaluate since we have already obtained each of them as a function of the relative price p. Basically the economy moves up the excess supply function $E_A(p)$ defined in (15). A compact summary of the main effects is provided below, with the bar above a variable denoting the closed economy value and an asterisk the free trade equilibrium after the opening to trade. Since p^* is greater than $\bar{p}$ it follows immediately that

$$N^* > \bar{N} \tag{17}$$

$$L_A^* > \bar{L}_A \tag{18}$$

$$A^* > \bar{A} \tag{19}$$

$$q^* > \bar{q} \tag{20}$$

$$L_M^* < \bar{L}_M \tag{21}$$

$$K_M^* < \bar{K}_M \tag{22}$$

$$M^* < \bar{M} \tag{23}$$

It is useful to begin by assuming that N and K_M remain initially fixed, as in the standard Ricardo-Viner model. Then A increases and M falls because the rise in p increases L_A and reduces L_M. But the rise in p and L_A raises the rental per unit of land q. This raises the numerator of (8) and so the rate of return on the extension of the frontier. To reduce this rate to equality with the interest rate $\bar{\rho}$, N has to increase to raise the marginal cost of a unit of land $\phi'(N)$ relative to the rental. The additional land pulls even more labor out of M and into A. Since the interest rate and wage rate remain constant at $\bar{\rho}$ and $\bar{w}$ the capital–labor ratio in M remains unchanged also at $\bar{k}$. The stock of capital K_M in M must contract proportionally to the decline in L_M caused by the rise in p and the induced rise in N.

Thus the effect of making N and K_M endogenous is to *enhance* the impact of the rise in p on the economy, since both the increase in A and the decline in M are larger than they would be in the pure Ricardo-Viner case.

5.3.3 Opening to the World Capital Market: Fall in the Rate of Interest

The process of opening up the export economies in the nineteenth century was not simply a matter of higher relative prices for primary products. There was also a fall in the real rate of interest, inducing further extension of the frontier, the building of infrastructure, and to some extent an expansion of manufacturing. We accordingly postulate a fall in the real rate of interest, from the $\bar{\rho}$ of the closed economy to $\tilde{\rho}$ in the new equilibrium. We shall ignore the balance of payments effects and the question of ownership (whether foreign or domestic) of the new equilibrium capital stock.

From (5) we see immediately that a fall in ρ from $\bar{\rho}$ to $\tilde{\rho}$ will raise the capital–labor ratio k in manufactures to a value $\tilde{k}$ greater than $\bar{k}$. From (6) the rise in k from $\bar{k}$ to $\tilde{k}$ will raise the real wage from $\bar{w}$ to $\tilde{w}$ in terms of manufactures. Since p remains unchanged at p^*, we note from (7) that the rise in the real wage from $\bar{w}$ to $\tilde{w}$ must raise the marginal physical productivity of labor in A, that is, the land–labor ratio must rise in the primary producing sector.

If N is held constant, the left-hand side of (8) will fall in proportion to the numerator q, the rental per unit of land, which declines because of the rise in the land–labor ratio. If q falls less than proportionately to ρ, however, it will be profitable to *extend* the frontier as a result of the decline in ρ, that is, the new equilibrium may require an increase in N to raise $\phi'(N)$ sufficiently for the rate of return on clearing land to equal the lower rate of interest $\tilde{\rho}$.

A plausible case therefore is one in which N is increased as a result of the fall in the rate of interest, but the rise in the land–labor ratio n results in L_A falling and L_M rising. Since the capital–labor ratio $\tilde{k}$ rises above $\bar{k}$ this means that K_M and hence M are both higher as well. Thus the lower rate of interest increases L_M, K_M, and M. The effect on A is ambiguous because even if N increases, the fall in L_A may result in lower output. It is possible, however, that if the increase in N is large and the decline in L_A small, the output of A as well as M will increase because of the decline in the rate of interest. The possibility of general expansion arises because the decline in the rate of interest produces both a deepening of capital, which tends to raise M, and an extension of the frontier, which tends to raise A.

5.3.4 Labor and Immigration

The opening to trade, as we have seen, leads to an increase in L_A and a reduction in L_M. What, however, if the increase in L_A is so large, and the initial L_M so small, that the former exceeds the latter? In this case the demand for labor will exceed the available supply at the wage $\overline{w}$, and so an inflow of foreign labor will be required even if the economy is to be completely specialized on A at the wage $\overline{w}$. Any inflow of labor beyond this, however, will leave the output of primary products unchanged at A^*, and serve only to increase L_M, K_M, and M in the same proportion. This situation — a rapid extension of the frontier requiring an influx of labor — was present in most of the historical cases considered.

Since all immigration in excess of L_A^* leads to an expansion only of M^* the rise in national income must cause a reduction in the export surplus of primary products and hence of imports of manufactures because the supply of A is constant while domestic demand for A increases. Thus, as we would expect, the degree to which the economy is "open", varies inversely with the size of the labor force.

The reason why immigration does not reduce the real wage, of course, is because that variable is determined by the production function for manufactures and the rate of interest $\overline{\rho}$.

5.3.5 The Modified Model

The main difference between the situation considered in the basic model and that of the tropical economies on the eve of the export expansion process is that labor was mostly engaged in traditional "subsistence" agriculture in the latter instance, supplemented by handicrafts during the slack periods of the year. Thus there was no specialized manufacturing sector as we have postulated for the basic model, designed to apply to the regions of recent settlement.

Within the subsistence sector, however, we can suppose along with Lewis (1954) and Hansen (1979), that peasants can obtain a real income $\overline{w}$, measured in terms of a composite "basket" of food and other household necessities. Land suitable for cultivation of food is not a scarce factor. Initially the entire economy consists of this subsistence sector.

Now we introduce international trade and the world market for specialized primary exports in return for imports of manufactures, together with the possibility of borrowing capital at a fixed rate of interest. The primary export commodity, however, such as cocoa or rubber, is best grown on forest land that is abundant but which takes time to clear, during which period the labor has to be provided with the means of subsistence, as in the "advances to labor" of the physiocrats and Ricardo. In terms of the notation of the basic model, p^* is the price of cocoa or rubber in terms of the subsistence basket, ρ^* is the rate of interest at which the peasant who wishes to enter the market economy can borrow, and $\phi'(N)$ is the marginal cost of clearing an acre of forest land in terms of the "wage fund" that has to be borrowed. With this interpretation it is easy to see that a "rational" peasant will obey equation (7), since the opportunity cost of his labor input into cash crops, at the world price p^*, must be equal at the margin to $\overline{w}$. The value n^* of the land-labor ratio that satisfies (7) determines the numerator of equation (8), which together with ρ^* on the right-hand side determines the value N^* of $\phi'(N)$ that satisfies this equation. The extent of the frontier N^* in turn determines the labor engaged in cash crops L_A^*, since the land–labor ratio n^* is already known.

Ostensibly the real income of a cash crop cultivator is greater than that of a peasant who remains in the subsistence sector, since in addition to w he enjoys the "rent" on his holding of the newly cleared land devoted to the cash crop. However, in equilibrium this rent is going to be just equal to the interest cost of the borrowed funds needed to tide him over the period while he was clearing his holding. Thus, in "net" terms, the two real incomes are equal, as they should be, since the peasants form a homogeneous group initially and the cash crop frontier is an open one.

Suppose, however, that the cash crop is coffee as in the case of Costa Rica or some other case where it is produced by large-scale foreign estates or plantations, instead of individual peasants. Here the "technology" of producing the crop and extending the frontier can be left unchanged but now the subsistence farmer simply becomes a full-time worker on the plantation, earning w, while the "rents" accrue to the plantation owner, as returns on his original investment in clearing the land on which the cash crop is cultivated.

The situation is perfectly analogous to the question of whether the typical "firm" in the primary producing sector in the United States, Canada, Australia, and Argentina is a family farm, the famous "forty acres and a mule", or a huge ranch or *estancia* with hired hands. Although the social consequences of these different arrangements are of course highly significant, they can be fitted into the same framework at the present level of generality.

5.4 CONCLUSION

The objective of this paper has been to provide a synthesis of the insights derivable from the "vent-for-surplus" and "staples" theories with the standard factor proportions formulation of comparative advantage, the key link being the concept of an endogenous land frontier. As we hope to have shown, the models of Section 5.3 conform in their implications to the main stylized facts of the patterns of resource-based export growth summarized in Section 5.2. In this concluding section we indicate the possibilities for further extensions and applications of the framework that we have attempted to construct.

While, as we have argued, there is an underlying similarity in the "opening up" phase in the development of all the staple export economies there has been an enormous diversity in the final "outcomes" of the process initiated by primary export growth. Within the regions of recent settlement the United States, Canada, and Australia have all followed growth paths that have led them to *per capita* incomes at the highest levels in the world. Argentina, however, has remained stagnant for decades since World War II. The plantation economies of Malaya (now Malaysia) and Costa Rica have attained the position of middle income countries, with Malaysia forging ahead rapidly in recent years on the basis of manufactured exports in addition to her traditional primary commodities. At the other end of the scale, the peasant export economies of Burma and Ghana, like Argentina, have been mired for decades in stagnation and even decline, after their highly promising beginnings around the turn of the present century.

Much of the explanation undoubtedly lies in "political economy" factors that, while partly exogenous, can also be linked to the ownership patterns and income distributions associated with their economic systems. Many important insights, still waiting to be explored, on these questions are contained in a splendid pair of early papers by Robert Baldwin (1956, 1963). More explicit discussion of the role of the state and political economy can be found in Hirschman (1977) and Findlay (1988).

The nature of the industrialization undertaken by the primary exporters is a problem of great interest and significance. Broadly speaking there have been two main avenues. One is resource-based industrialization (see Roemer, 1979, and Findlay, 1985, 1987) in which the primary export itself is processed further within the country. Another is import substitution for final consumer goods. Each has its own set of special problems that have been widely explored in the literature.

An important turning point in all the countries has been the "closing of the frontier," the challenge confronted by a society when it is no longer capable of "extensive" development. This sharpens the struggle over the rents generated by previous development, and is a key factor in the political economy of attempts by the state, as in Argentina, Burma and Ghana, to squeeze the primary producers by manipulating relative prices against them.

These and many other issues of comparable importance can be discussed within the framework developed here. In purely technical terms the models can be extended and enriched in many ways. Thus multiple primary exports, each with its own associated frontier, can readily be introduced, or more than one primary export can be produced on each type of "land." The manufacturing sector can be sub-divided into capital-intensive and labor-intensive components, and non-traded goods and services introduced. Moreover, the productive, as well as predatory, role of government can be accounted for along the lines of Clarida and Findlay (1992).

References

Adas, Michael (1974) *The Burma Delta: Economic Development and Social Change on an Asian Rice Frontier, 1852–1941* (Madison: University of Wisconsin Press).

Baldwin, Robert E. (1956) "Patterns of Development in Newly Settled Regions," *Manchester School*, May.

Baldwin, Robert E. (1963) "Export Technology and Development from a Subsistence Level," *Economic Journal*, March.

Bulmer-Thomas, Victor (1987) *The Political Economy of Central America Since 1920* (Cambridge: Cambridge University Press).

Bulmer-Thomas, Victor, *Studies in the Economies of Central America* (London: Macmillan, 1988).

Cardoso, Ciro F. S. (1977) "The Formation of the Coffee Estate in Nineteenth Century Costa Rica," in K. Duncan and I. Rutledge (eds.), *Land and Labor in Latin America* (Cambridge: Cambridge University Press).

Caves, Richard E. (1965) "Vent-for-surplus Models of Trade and Growth" in R. E. Baldwin *et al.* (eds.), *Trade, Growth and the Balance of Payments* (Chicago: Rand McNally).

Caves, Richard E. (1971) "Export-Led Growth and the New Economic History," in J. Bhagwati *et al.* (eds.), *Trade Balance of Payments and Growth* (Amsterdam: North-Holland).

Caves, Richard E. and R. H. Holton (1959) *The Canadian Economy: Prospect and Retrospect* (Cambridge: Harvard University Press).

Chambers, Edward J. and D. F. Gordon (1966) "Primary Products and Economic Growth: An Empirical Measurement," *Journal of Political Economy*, August.

Clarida, Richard H. and R. Findlay (1992) "Government, Trade and Comparative Advantage," *American Economic Review*, May.

Cortés Condé, Roberto (1985) "The Export Economy of Argentina 1880–1930" in R. Cortes Conde and S. Hunt (eds.), *The Latin American Economies: Growth and the Export Sector 1880–1930* (London and New York: Macmillan).

Diaz Alejandro, Carlos F. (1970) *Essays in the Economic History of the Argentine Republic* (New Haven: Yale University Press).

Diaz Alejandro, Carlos F. (1984) "No Less Than One Hundred Years of Argentine Economic History" in G. Ranis *et al.* (eds.), *Comparative Development Perspectives* (Boulder: Westview).

Di Tella, Guido (1982) "The Economics of the Frontier," in C. P. Kindleberger and G. Di Tella (eds.), *Economics in the Long View*, vol. 1 (London: Macmillan).

Easton, Stephen and C. Reed (1980) "The Staple Model," mimeo, Simon Fraser University.

Ferns, H. S. (1969) *Argentina* (New York: Praeger).

Findlay, Ronald (1970) *Trade and Specialization* (Harmondsworth: Penguin).

Findlay, Ronald (1985) "Primary Exports, Manufacturing and Development" in M. Lundahl (ed.), *The Primary Sector in Economic Development* (London: Croom Helm).

Findlay, Ronald (1987) "Intermediate Goods, Export Taxation and Resource-Based Industrialization" in H. Kierzkowski (ed.), *Protection and Competition in International Trade* (Oxford: Oxford University Press).

Findlay, Ronald (1988) "Trade, Development and the State" in G. Ranis and T. Schultz (eds.), *The State of Development Economics* (Oxford: Blackwell).

Findlay, Ronald (1990) "International Trade and Factor Mobility with an Endogenous Land Frontier," mimeo, Columbia University.

Furnivall, J. S. (1957) *An Introduction to the Political Economy of Burma* (New York: Institute of Pacific Relations).

Gunnarsson, C. (1979) "Malaysian Rubber Production: Patterns of Growth 1900–1975," *Meddelande fran Ekonomisk-historiska Institutionen*, No. 6, Lund University.

Hansen, Bent (1979) "Colonial Economic Development with an Unlimited Supply of Land," *Economic Development and Cultural Change*.

Hill, Polly (1963) *The Migrant Cocoa Farmers of Southern Ghana* (Cambridge: Cambridge University Press).

Hirschman, Albert O. (1977) "A Generalized Linkage Approach to Development, with Special Reference to Staples," *Economic Development and Cultural Change*, Special Supplement, vol. 25.

Hlaing, Aye (1964) *A Study of the Economic Development of Burma* (University of Rangoon).

Holmes, A. B. (1970) "The Gold Coast and Nigeria" in W. A. Lewis (ed.), *Tropical Development, 1880–1913* (London: Allen & Unwin).

Hopkins, A. G. (1973) *An Economic History of West Africa* (New York: Columbia University Press).

Innis, Harold A. (1930) *The Fur Trade in Canada* (Toronto: University of Toronto Press).

Innis, Harold A. (1940) *The Cod Fisheries* (Toronto: University of Toronto Press).

Jones, R. W. (1971) " A Three-Factor Model in Theory, Trade and History" in J. Bhagwati *et al.* (eds), *Trade, Balance of Payments and Growth* (Amsterdam: North-Holland).
Kravis, Irving B. (1956) "Availability and other Influences on the Commodity Composition of Trade," *Journal of Political Economy*, April.
Lewis, W. A. (1954) "Economic Development with Unlimited Supplies of Labour," *Manchester School*, May.
Lougheed, A. L. (1968) "International Trade Theory and Economic Growth," *Australian Economic History Review*, vol. 8, pp. 99–109.
Maddock, R. and I. W. McLean (1984) "Supply-Side Shocks: the Case of Australian Gold," *Journal of Economic History*, vol. 44, pp. 1047–67.
McLean, Ian W. (1989) "Growth in a Small Open Economy: A Historical View" in B. Chapman (ed.) *Australian Economic Growth* (Melbourne: Macmillan).
Meier, G. M. (1953) "Economic Development and the Transfer Mechanism: Canada 1895–1913," *Canadian Journal of Economics and Political Science*, February.
Myint, H. (1958) "The Classical Theory of International Trade and the Underdeveloped Countries," *Economic Journal*, June.
North, Douglass C. (1966) *The Economic Growth of the United States, 1790–1860* (New York: Norton).
Roemer, Michael (1979) "Resource-Based Industrialization in the Developing Countries: A Survey," *Journal of Development Economics*, vol. 6.
Samuelson, Paul A. (1971) "Ohlin was Right," *Swedish Journal of Economics*.
Solow, Robert M. (1956) "A Contribution to the Theory of Economic Growth," *Quarterly Journal of Economics*, February.
Szereszewski, Robert (1965) *Structural Change in the Economy of Ghana 1891–1911* (London: Weidenfeld & Nicolson).
Turner, Frederick J. (1921) *The Frontier in American History* (New York: Holt).
Viner, Jacob (1924) *Canada's Balance of International Indebtedness 1900–1913*, (Cambridge: Harvard University Press).
Watkins, M. H. (1963) "A Staple Theory of Economic Growth," *Canadian Journal of Economics and Political Science*, May.
Woodward, R. L. (1985) "Central America from Independence to 1870" in L. Bethel (ed.), *The Cambridge History of Latin America*, vol. 3 (Cambridge: Cambridge University Press).

6 Vent for Surplus, the Subsistence Fund, and the Evolution of Money

P. J. Drake

Hla Myint's 1970 paper contains in its conclusion the important point that the "implicit identification of capital with durable capital goods and complex machinery requires to be seriously qualified when applied to the underdeveloped countries. In the economic setting of these countries the older classical notion of capital as a 'subsistence fund' to support labor engaged in producing future output still retains great importance". Many years earlier, Myint had also observed that "... in Smith's time, fixed or durable capital played only a very small part in economic life and the bulk of investment was in the form of circulating capital or 'advances to labour'"[1].

This is the English classical view of capital, as distinct from the narrower concept of capital as the produced means of production. Schumpeter enunciated the distinction as follows "Since it was a requisite of production, capital consisted of goods... It is, however, one of the salient characteristics of the theoretical schema of the English 'classics' and their continental followers that they understood the term 'requisite of production' in a wider sense which included the consumers' goods that support labor during the process of production".[2] In this and other respects, Myint's analysis of the early stages of economic development in tropical — and predominantly colonial — territories is firmly rooted in the English classical tradition.

In a series of writings Myint has characterized the initial modern economic development of sparsely populated countries by the process known as "vent for surplus".[3] And vent for surplus has been much played upon by other writers in analyzing the early phases of economic development in countries of Southeast Asia and East and West Africa.[4] In these accounts, international trade confers value on any hitherto unused or untapped surplus output; and this is, according to Adam Smith, one of the main gains from trade.

One of the uses to which the output from hitherto untapped resources may be put is the creation of a subsistence fund. Although the importance of the subsistence fund is widely recognized, little direct attention has been given to the actual composition and mechanics of use of such a fund.

The purpose of this paper is to look more closely into the workings of the subsistence fund by addressing several questions. Of what items did the subsistence fund consist? By what mechanism did the components of the subsistence fund get into the hands of producer-investors? And how was the subsistence fund utilized? It becomes apparent that the subsistence fund featured in three roles: specialization and trade; capital formation and growth; and the development of money and credit. In particular, it transpires that the growth of monetized transactions and the supply of money forms to service them are closely connected to the nature, size and workings of the subsistence fund.

6.1 NATURE AND ORIGINS OF THE SUBSISTENCE FUND

6.1.1 Foodstuffs

Imagine a closed agricultural economy. Once any producer-consumer goes beyond complete subsistence and engages in specialized production in order to trade with others, he must obtain and set aside some foodstuffs to tide him over periods in which he is neither harvesting food crops nor receiving foodstuffs in exchange for other output. The more the farmer specializes in the production of non-food crops, the greater this subsistence fund has to be.

Commonly, the fund consists of food grains, in the tropical countries rice, which have a reasonable life-time in store. The provenance of rice may be from the home farm, from elsewhere within the domestic (national) economy, or from imports.

Risk-averse producers of non-food crops will try to maintain also their home production of rice; but those who become fully specialized in non-food production will rely on rice obtained from food growers elsewhere in the economy or importers. In the extreme case where the whole economy becomes specialized in the production of non-food crops, rice must be imported and exported goods given in exchange. The limiting cases, and the very wide range of intermediate, progressive arrangements are well illustrated by the experience of countries in Southeast Asia and the Pacific.

In Thailand, where the food crop (rice) served also as the export crop, the subsistence fund was largely provided by the farmers retaining a proportion of their production for their own use. In neighboring Malaya, which generally enjoyed self-sufficiency in rice on a national, aggregative basis, those producers who concentrated on such non-food exports as rubber and tin relied on rice to be supplied from other domestic producers. (Of course, many Malay peasants remained in the intermediate phase of part-time export production while also being self-sufficient in rice.)

The transfer of rice, by market forces, among the different producer-consumer units in the domestic economy could be effected via bilateral barter or (later) cash payments. Most commonly the transfer involved the activity of middlemen who procured rice from those who produced it for markets via barter of final consumer goods and distributed it to those producers of nonfood crops who looked to the barter market for a supply of the foodstuff. A very common further feature was that the middlemen also provided credit, in the form of advances of rice to the producers of rubber, tin, spices etc, which advances were requited at a later date by the delivery of the export products to the advancers.[5]

Much the same occurred in intra-regional trade in Southeast Asia, for which Singapore was the hub. In reflecting on what follows, one should always recognize the importance of the overseas Chinese community that was centered in Singapore but present in every port and trading hinterland in Southeast Asia. This extensive network of commercially astute people, bound by the trust that existed among them as a result of family and clan ties, gave Southeast Asia an unsurpassed commercial infrastructure for economic development.

In a path-breaking article from which I here draw extensively, W. G. Huff has shown that rice-based barter served as an effective alternative to cash in much of the entrepôt trade by which Singapore drew exports from, and funnelled imports into, the neighboring countries of Southeast Asia. "A major aspect of the credit given by Singapore traders as part of the barter trade was largely to finance late 19th century export expansion in Malaya and Netherlands India. The capital required for this expansion was chiefly circulating capital, or the 'subsistence fund' in the form of rice and simple manufactures".[6]

In respect of the areas that may be styled "rice-consuming", Singapore's trade with the West provided markets for tropical commodities against which the producers would accept rice in barter. The Singapore Chinese provided to export producers "circulating capital, principally in the form of rice to feed large work forces [the subsistence fund]".[7] "Moreover, the rice was made available on credit: Singapore Chinese characteristically took payment in tin and tropical produce at a later date. In this way barter not only obviated the need for cash except as a settling item; it also afforded a means to finance producers in the Malay states and Netherlands India".[8]

Furthermore, the fact that the rice was supplied on credit tied the exporters of other produce to their Singapore creditors thus ensuring the latter's lines of supply and pricing advantage for the future. For example, "In the Malayan gambier and pepper industry Singapore Chinese firms financed an initial waiting period of 18 months before the first crop, but finance then became a matter of short-term credit between harvests. Until the cultivator (if ever) could pay his original debt he was bound to a Singapore trader, who '... supplies him with rice, groceries and money for further planting, all at stipulated prices, and receives his produce in exchange, with deductions for weight according to a defined scale, and at prices...about 30 per cent below the actual market value'".[9]

To the infant, Chinese-owned tin industry in the Malay states, goods other than rice were also advanced. "The advancer naturally prefers giving kind, such as all foods and drink, clothing, etc., etc. His profit is larger on goods and his risk is less as he never knows exactly whether his cash advances may not be disposed of outside the mine and not brought to bear on the production of tin, the recipient gradually enriching himself."[10]

The credit element in the barter trade run by the Singapore Chinese kept the producers of commodities other than rice tied to Singapore suppliers of the grain; they could not turn directly to rice producing countries which could not match Singapore's credit facilities; "and for their part Singapore Chinese were anxious to ensure the supply of credit associated with barter trade, since 'advances to outport middlemen secure for the Singapore dealers a lien on the produce collected from the actual growers'".[11]

In dealing with the rice-producing countries, Singapore traders had need of cash because "Singapore imported a much higher value of rice than traders in the port could find goods to offer in return and the bulk of payment had to be in cash. But Singapore rice importers looked to barter to offset their purchases where possible.... In Siam, the acceptance of goods in barter from Singapore was not a hardship for the millers and exporters insofar as they could exchange these for paddy from the middlemen who themselves obtained paddy by bartering imported goods"[12]

Singapore's regional entrepôt role was underpinned by its conduct of barter, principally involving rice. Direct trade was long hampered by an inadequate stock of widely-acceptable money and indeed at times by a severe shortage of cash.[13] Although barter persisted in many uses, it was supplanted after the turn of the century by monetized transactions that grew rapidly for a variety of reasons: sound and internationally-convertible currencies evolved in the region; banks and other sources of credit developed and spread; producers increasingly sought payment in cash. Essentially, the growth in size and complexity of the Southeast Asian economies and their further integration into the web of international trade demanded ever-increasing monetisation. As this occurred, the nature of the subsistence fund changed.

6.1.2 Money

The points have often been made, but most recently and best by Barbara Ingham,[14] that indigenous monies existed long before the developing countries fell under the sway of international trade in the nineteenth century and that, in any primitive economy, money could take a variety of forms, reflecting the variety of specific economic and social purposes that different money forms emerged to serve.[15]

But international trade demanded general purpose money which could permeate the economy at all levels and serve all uses including the purchase of land and stocks, the payment of wage labor, the purchase of consumption and investment goods (whether from domestic or foreign sources) and the accumulation of liquid capital. In this context the subsistence fund began increasingly to take the form of cash, and hence gave a further stimulus to export in order to acquire money in return.

To the extent that the subsistence fund needed to take the form of internationally acceptable or convertible monies (coin, currency notes or money in the bank), a positive balance of international payments was generally needed (the exceptions being those territories in which gold or silver was mined). Coin and notes had to be provided to producers by traders, merchants, or banks and could be traced to prior international receipts of export revenue or capital investment inflow. Bank lending operations required the banks to maintain appropriate levels of cash reserves which, in turn, traced also to credit items in the balance of payments.

It is now time to look more closely into the mechanisms by which the cash subsistence fund was conveyed into the hands of producer-investors and subsequently spent on various purposes.

6.2 MECHANISMS OF OPERATION OF CASH SUBSISTENCE FUNDS

The sources of money to peasant producers were wages (in exchange for part-time labor) and sales of produce (whether for domestic use or export).

As Myint has described in several seminal works, the willingness of peasant producers to accept money in exchange for their produce or labor depended crucially on their acceptance of the utility of money.[16] This in turn came from the emergence of peasant demand for the enticing new manufactured goods that could be obtained only as imports and that ultimately could be bought only with internationally acceptable money.

Elsewhere I have recounted Myint's "vent-for-surplus" model of the process of economic growth in sparsely-populated under developed countries,[17] characterizing peasant production for export markets as Process I and wage employment as Process II. I then argued, adducing evidence from colonial Malaya, that Process II was paramount and that "… the entry of Malay peasants into the money economy was clearly dependent upon the prior establishment of foreign extractive industries on a large scale".[18]

The foreign-owned plantations, mines, and merchant firms promoted monetization of the indigenous economy not only through the payment of wages for local labor in primary industry and services but also through the introduction of incentive imported goods into the local society, cash payments for peasant produce and the provision of monetary credit into the peasant economy.

In the Malayan case, rubber plantation enterprises paid laborers in cash while peasant farmers could get cash from the sale of rubber (latex or smoked sheet) and other commodities to export merchants. Correspondingly, a smelting company in Singapore paid cash for tin ore, thus enabling mining enterprises to pay cash to their Chinese laborers who desired to spend it on — among other things — gambling and prostitutes. If a mine employer would not pay cash, the laborers would leave — in contrast to earlier times when labor was bound to a mine by payments in kind. Overall, the cash trail in mining ran from export proceeds or capital inflow to the banks to the smelter to the ore buyer to the mine owner to the laborers, and similarly via rubber agents and estates in the case of rubber.[19]

Barbara Ingham has noted similar developments in British West Africa "…co-incidental with the growth of cash crops for export during the nineteenth century was the introduction of British silver coin in payment for exports…Pressure for payment in silver came from the side of African producers and traders…."[20] Ingham goes on to argue that although the incoming silver coin had the appearance of a currency demanded for the sake of the imported goods that it could purchase, British silver was sought also to service the outlays involved in cash-crop production, particularly the purchase of land.[21] Moreover, the new money facilitated production not only for export but to supply goods and services for the home market. "Part at least of the income from exports [from Ghana]…appears to have been devoted to spending on domestically produced goods and services."[22]

The new money so introduced into peasant export economies was both of general-purpose form in local use and acceptable/convertible for external use in international payments. (It should be noted that the general-purpose and internationally acceptable features of money do not necessarily go together as they did in the colonial economies. The great closed economy of pre-Meiji Japan enjoyed general-purpose money that was not internationally acceptable; so too did island economies with their shell monies.) Thus modern forms of money facilitated and fostered both domestic and international trade, and constituted an ideal vessel for any individual's subsistence fund. Rather than stocks of foodstuffs that were perishable and subject to other risks of erosion or theft, the subsistence fund could now take the more lasting and less visible forms of coin, currency notes and bank deposits (this abstracts from price fluctuations that could affect the real value of both commodity stocks and money).

All told, the permeation of modern, general-purpose money through the developing economy was unstoppable once such money had taken root. Barter transactions and indigenous monies were displaced for spending on both domestic and imported consumption goods, and for domestic or overseas investment in the short term and the long.

Ingham notes too that the beginning of modern money was accompanied by far-reaching changes in economic and social structure. "Through [monetized] economic activity industrious young men gained the sort of status which had previously been restricted to those elders with knowledge of ritual and law."[23] In more recent times in the Pacific Island economies this is the phenomenon referred to as the rise of "the big men".[24]

There is a further development, beneficial to economic growth, arising from the change of nature of the subsistence fund from a store of goods to a store of money. This is that money permits the accumulation of savings to a far greater extent, and in more flexible form, than does any other store of value. Money constitutes not merely the most versatile store of the subsistence fund, working or circulating capital, but also the most efficient means of accumulation towards long-term capital investment. In the process, it may grow via compound interest (whereas physical stocks depreciate) and be a vehicle for speculation. Ingham has argued at length that the role of money and credit mechanisms associated with it in economic change and growth is more important in fostering long-term capital accumulation and a growing flow of production through time than in displacing the inefficiencies of barter and promoting exchange and specialization.[25]

6.3 THE SUPPLY OF MONEY

The money initially obtained by the developing export economies was either that of a metropolitan country, such as Britain, or consisted of coin or notes issued locally against the backing, usually in full, of foreign exchange assets.[26] In either case, the accretion of money in the developing colony was essentially a loan of real resources, free of interest, to foreign issuers of money by local moneyholders who preferred to hold money rather than consume or invest real resources. In other words, the progressive accumulation of a stock of modern money represented a cumulative balance-of-payments surplus in which the net increase in the money stock had its counterpart in a net real transfer of goods, services, or property rights to foreign interests.[27]

This general picture was modified but not displaced by the emergence of banks in the colonies. A rise in bank deposits represented a transfer of resources from depositors to banks. To some extent, the banks in the developing economies deployed the resources for local use via loans and advances, but until the late 1950s they also presided over a substantial transfer of capital funds from the colonies to the London capital market. In post-colonial times, there then occurred throughout the newly-independent territories of Asia and Africa a once-and-for-all surge of domestic credit expansion as the banking systems pursued local lending and ran down most of their reserves of foreign assets. Once excess reserves were expended, and the ability of banks to cover any foreign expenditure drain associated with local lending was depleted, further domestic credit expansion had to wait again on a positive balance of payments.

Thus in both early colonial and post colonial phases, monetary expansion in the developing export economies was dependent upon a surplus in the autonomous balance of international payments, and those economies were subject to deflationary pressures whenever the output of the economy expanded without any simultaneous improvement in the balance of payments.[28] Under systems where the nexus between foreign exchange reserves and domestic money expansion is tight, economic decline manifests itself not as a problem of international payments but as a fall in national income and employment.

6.4 CONCLUSION

Surplus-venting trade by the colonial economies was in significant part devoted to the acquisition of a stock of modern money. Modern money was sought within the colonial economy, first for domestic and international trade, secondly as the preferred means of holding circulating capital (the subsistence fund) and thirdly as the vessel for the accumulation of savings for purposes of long-term investment. Surplus venting, monetary acquisition and the establishment of short and long capital funds went hand-in-hand in colonial economic development.

Notes

1. Myint (1948), p. 5.
2. Schumpeter (1954), pp. 632–33.
3. Myint (1954) (1958) (1965).
4. For example, Caves (1965), Fisk (1962) (1964), Ingham (1979), Drake (1972) (1979).
5. Partadireja (1974).
6. Huff, (1989) p. 165.
7. *Ibid.*, p. 180.
8. *Ibid.*, p. 176.
9. *Ibid.*, p. 181, quoting Tan, 1902.
10. Martin Lister, 1889, quoted by Huff, p. 181.
11. Huff, pp. 182–3, quoting Report of Straits Settlements Trade Commission, 1934.
12. *Ibid.*, p. 176.
13. Drake (1981) pp. 4–7; Huff, p. 170.
14. Ingham (1981), Ch 4.
15. See also Drake (1980), Ch 4.
16. See also Fisk (1964).
17. Drake (1979), drawing especially on Myint (1965), Chs. 1–5.
18. *Ibid.*, p. 287.
19. *Ibid.*, pp. 278–9
20. Ingham (1981), p. 61.
21. *Ibid.*, p. 62.
22. *Ibid.*, p. 65.
23. *Ibid.*, p. 64.
24. Finney (1988).
25. Ingham (1981), Ch. 4, passim.
26. These issues are dealt with in the context of Singapore/Malaya in Drake (1981).
27. Ingham (1981), p. 106, n. 25, observes: "The proposition that money derives from foreign trade has a long history. It can be found in both Marx ('Grundrisse') and Weber ('General Economic History')."
28. Drake (1969), pp. 59–63 explains the deflationary bias in detail.

References

Caves, R. E. (1965) "'Vent for Surplus' Models of Trade and Growth" in R. E. Baldwin and others (eds), *Trade, Growth and the Balance of Payments* (Amsterdam: North-Holland Publishing).

Drake, P. J. (1969) *Financial Development in Malaya and Singapore* (Canberra: ANU Press).

Drake, P. J. (1972) "Natural Resources *Versus* Foreign Borrowing in Economic Development," *Economic Journal*, March.

Drake, P. J. (1979) "The Economic Development of British Malaya to 1914: An Essay in Historiography with Some Questions for Historians," *Journal of Southeast Asian Studies*, September.

Drake, P. J. (1980) *Money, Finance and Development* (Oxford: Martin Robertson).

Drake, P. J. (1981) "The Evolution of Money in Singapore since 1819" in *Monetary Authority of Singapore, Papers on Monetary Economics* (Singapore: Singapore University Press).

Finney, Ben (1988) "Culture and Entrepreneurship in the Highlands of Papua New Guinea" in Te's I. J. Fairbairn (ed.), *Island Entrepreneurs: Problems and Performances in the Pacific* (Honolulu: East-West Center).

Fisk, E. K. (1962) "Planning in a Primitive Economy: Special Problems of Papua-New Guinea," *Economic Record*, December.

Fisk, E. K. (1964) "Planning in a Primitive Economy: From Pure Subsistence to the Production of a Market Surplus," *Economic Record*, June.

Huff, W. G. (1989) "Bookkeeping Barter, Money Credit, and Singapore's International Rice Trade, 1870–1939," *Explorations in Economic History*, vol. 26.

Ingham, Barbara (1979) "Vent for Surplus Reconsidered with Ghanaian Evidence", *Journal of Development Studies*, April.

Ingham, Barbara (1981) *Tropical Exports and Economic Development* (London: Macmillan).

Myint, H. (1948) *Theories of Welfare Economics* (London: Longmans for the London School of Economics and Political Science).

Myint, H. (1954/55) "The Gains from International Trade and the Backward Countries," *Review of Economic Studies*, vol. XXII (2).

Myint, H. (1958) "The 'Classical Theory' of International Trade and the Underdeveloped Countries," *Economic Journal*, June. Reprinted in R. E. Caves and H. G. Johnson (eds.) (1968) *Readings in International Economics* (Irwin).

Myint, H. (1965) *The Economics of the Developing Countries* (2nd edn.) (London: Hutchinson).

Myint, H. (1970) "Dualism and the Internal Integration of the Underdeveloped Economies," *Banca Nazionale del Lavoro Quarterly Review*, June.

Partadireja, Ace. (1974) "Rural Credit: The Ajon System," *Bulletin of Indonesian Economic Studies*, November.

Schumpeter, J. (1954) *History of Economic Analysis* (New York: Oxford University Press).

7 Exports and Economic Growth

R. M. Sundrum

Economists have long been interested in the role of exports in promoting economic growth. Notwithstanding a large literature on the subject, there is still considerable confusion about both the statistical basis of the relationship and its analytical explanation. More data have recently become available. It is therefore worth reconsidering the subject once again in the light of these data.

7.1 STATISTICAL EVIDENCE

The historical experience of the western countries in the nineteenth and early twentieth centuries was marked by a close association between their modern economic growth and a considerable expansion of their exports. This experience led to the view of exports as an engine of growth. At the same time, there was also an acceleration of economic growth in many tropical countries which expanded their exports, especially of primary products. In their case, the export engine of growth seems to have been weaker (Lewis, 1969), so that they emerged at the end of World War II as typical less-developed countries.

Although some broad conclusions can be derived from the historical experience, sufficient data on exports and national income are not available for many countries on a comparable basis for a more detailed statistical analysis of the mechanism involved in the role of exports in economic growth. Such data have now become available for a larger number of countries for three or four decades of the post-war period. Further, the world economy has changed so drastically that the historical experience has become less and less relevant for the analysis of recent experience and its implications for future policies. Therefore, in this review of the statistical evidence, we shall concentrate on the period since World War II.

The influence of exports on economic growth may be studied through two types of statistical relationship. In many recent studies, the authors have investigated the relationship between the *growth* of exports and the

Table 7.1 GDP growth rates by export ratios

	Average GDP growth rates (GY) in					
		LDCs			*DCs*	
Export ratios (XR)	*1950s*	*1960s*	*1970s*	*1950s*	*1960s*	*1970s*
Below 5	5.7	3.4	4.2	3.2	–	–
5–10	4.0	4.9	5.6	6.0	5.6	2.9
10–15	3.6	4.0	4.8	6.7	7.4	4.5
15–20	4.1	4.4	4.5	4.9	5.3	4.2
20–25	4.0	5.2	5.0	4.2	5.0	3.5
25 & over	5.7–	5.7	3.7	2.8	4.5	2.8
Average GY	4.6	4.9	4.5	4.7	5.3	3.2
Average XR	24.1	23.6	27.4	21.3	22.5	28.8
Correlation between GY and XR	.363	.386	.216	–.429	–.394	–.123
Number of countries	49	78	82	22	23	23

Source: World Bank (1983).

growth of GDP. But we may also consider the relationship between the *level* (measured for example by the ratio of exports to GDP) and the growth of GDP. The cross-section data for developed and less-developed countries in the post-war decades are summarized in Table 7.1.

The relationship between the two variables is neither strong nor consistent, being positive for the LDCs and negative for the DCs in each decade of the post-war period. In both DCs and LDCs, the export ratio rose quite considerably from the 1960s to the 1970s, but the GDP growth rates declined, quite sharply in the case of the DCs.

Turning now to the relationship between the growth of exports and the growth of GDP, the data for the post-war decades are summarized in Table 7.2.

Now we find a consistently positive relationship between the two growth rates. Not only are the cross-section correlations very high, especially in the DCs, but the decline in the GDP growth rates in the 1970s is associated with a sharp fall in export growth rates. The high correlation between the two variables was noted by a number of economists writing in the 1960s and 1970s (for example, Balassa, 1978; Emery, 1967; Michaely, 1977). But, of course, we cannot draw any strong conclusions from these simple correlations. We must also allow for the influence of other variables commonly used to explain the growth of GDP, such as the growth of labor and the rate of investment. Using multiple regression methods, a number of

Table 7.2 GDP growth rates by growth of exports

Growth of exports (GX) (%)	LDCs 1950s	LDCs 1960s	LDCs 1970s	DCs 1950s	DCs 1960s	DCs 1970s
	Average GDP growth rates in					
Below 3	4.3	3.5	2.6	2.4	–	4.4
3 – 4	4.2	4.0	3.2	2.8	–	2.6
4 – 5	5.0	3.9	3.8	–	2.9	2.7
5 – 6	3.5	5.7	5.5	3.4	3.6	3.5
6 – 7	–	3.8	6.2	3.5	4.6	3.0
7 – 8	5.7	4.6	6.7	4.3	4.4	3.4
8 – 10	5.8	5.7	5.1	4.6	4.9	4.0
10 & over	5.9	7.2	6.6	7.1	7.0	4.5
Average *GY*	4.8	4.9	4.5	4.7	5.3	3.2
Average *GX*	5.2	6.4	4.6	8.3	8.8	5.7
Correlation between *GY* & *GX*	.311	.502	.583	.927	.917	.371
Number of countries	34	76	81	22	23	23

Source: World Bank (1983).

other writers have examined the influence of export growth together with other such variables; some of their results are reproduced in Table 7.3.

One important point about the Tyler and Kavoussi regressions (equations 1, 2 and 3) may be noted. They describe one of the explanatory variables as *GK* in their papers to stand for the growth of capital, but because data were not available, the variable actually represents the growth of investment (*GI*). This is a dubious step in their analysis, amounting in fact to using the second derivative of the time series of capital stock as a proxy for the first derivative.

In his study of 43 middle-income LDCs for the period 1960–77, Tyler (1981) included the growth rate of labour (*GL*) and of investment (*GI*) together with the growth rate of exports (*GX*) as explanatory variables of the growth rate of GDP (*GY*). In equation (1), GI is the most significant variable, while the export growth rate (*GX*) is barely significant. This is partly because of the multi-collinearity due to high correlation between *GI*

Table 7.3 Regression of *GY* on *GX* and other variables (*t* ratios in brackets)

Source/ sample	*GL*	*GI*	*IR*	*GY*	*Other variables* (GMX & GZ)*	*R2*
Tyler (1981)						
(1) 43 Middle	0.981	0.254		0.570		0.69
Income LDCs	(2.58)	(5.92)		(1.69)		
1960–77						
(2) Ditto	1.014	0.236			0.045	0.71
	(2.70)	(5.27)			(2.23)	
Kavoussi (1984)						
(3) 73 LDCs	0.400	0.241		0.105		0.57
1960–78	(1.69)	(5.84)		(3.72)		
Ram (1987)						
(4) 82 LDCs	0.304		0.079	0.186	0.217	0.49
1960–72	(1.39)		(3.05)	(4.70)	(4.19)	
(5) 79 LDCs	0.396		0.056	0.314	0.285	0.56
	(1.44)		(1.68)	(6.53)	(4.59)	

*Equation 2: GMX = Growth of manufactured exports.
Equations 4 and 5: GZ = Growth of government consumption expenditures.

and *GX*. His equation (2) shows that the growth rate of manufactured exports (GMX) has a more significant effect. Using the same method for a larger sample of LDCs, Kavoussi (1984) found that the influence of *GX* was more significant. In equations (4) and (5) in Table 7.3, Ram (1987) used *IR* (investment as a ratio of GDP) instead of GI, and also included the growth of government consumption expenditure (*GZ*). He also computed separate regressions for the 1960s and the 1970s. In both cases, he found the influence of *GX* to be even more significant. One reason is that his results are less affected by multi-collinearity, the correlation between *GX* and *IR* being smaller than that between *GX* and *GI*.

While these results show a strong connection between the growth of exports and the growth of GDP even after allowing for the influence of a number of other factors, some writers have been concerned that the observed correlations may be spurious to some extent because they are based on the accounting effect that the growth of exports is itself a part of the growth of GDP. For example, the 1968 OECD report on Development Cooperation argued that:

> This conclusion is not entirely unexpected considering that export earnings constitute for many developing countries a significant part of GDP. Expanding exports thus not only provides earnings with which to provide needed imports, but their production directly adds to GDP growth. (OECD, 1968, p. 107).

Similarly, Michaely (1977, p. 50) claimed that "Since exports are themselves part of the national product, a positive correlation between the two variables is almost inevitable, whatever their true relationship."

In order to eliminate such an accounting effect, Heller and Porter (1978) argued that the proper way to estimate the role of exports in economic growth was to correlate the growth of exports *GX* with the growth of non-export output *GD* (taking *D* as $Y - X$) rather than with *GY*. Using the same data as Michaely (1977), they found a rank correlation of 0.458 between *GX* and *GD*, higher than the rank correlation 0.380 between *GX* and *GY*, and concluded by asking "Could exports be that free lunch that economists have long sought?" However, a better measure of the quantitative relationship is given by the variate regression between the variables than by the rank correlations. Then, we get the following results:

$$\underset{(6.24)\ (6.90)}{GY = 1.61 + 0.27\,GX} \qquad R = .742 \qquad (6)$$

$$\underset{(5.56)\ (3.16)}{GD = 1.83 + 0.16\,GX} \qquad R = .452 \qquad (7)$$

The regression coefficient of *GD* on *GX* is positive suggesting that export growth is associated with some growth of non-export output as well, but is smaller and less significant than that of *GY* on *GX*.

But the problem is more complex. We must distinguish at least two ways in which export growth might accelerate the growth of GDP, namely by increasing a country's productive capacity either by increasing the resources of the economy or the efficiency of their use, and by fuller utilization of productive capacity. Some economists assume that resources are always fully utilized and hence take the entire rise in GDP growth associated with export growth as due to the increase in productive capacity. On the other hand, others concerned with the accounting effect assume that the growth of exports is achieved entirely by the fuller utilization of previously under utilized or surplus resources leading to an equivalent increase in GDP, and then measure the increase in productive capacity only by the increase in the output of goods for domestic use. In practice, the growth of exports may not be entirely due to fuller utilization of unemployed resources, and the real question from an analytical point of view is the extent to which a given increase of exports is additive, and the extent to which it substitutes for the growth of non-export output. Further, the growth of GDP brought about by increasing exports by fuller utilization of resources cannot be dismissed because it serves the useful function of providing a 'vent for surplus', one of the main arguments advanced by Adam Smith in his advocacy of free trade.

A convenient method of obtaining some indication of these two effects of export growth is by using the regression equation:

$$KD = a + b\,KX \qquad (8)$$

suggested by Kleiman (1980), where the *K*-ratios *KD* (= $\Delta D/Y$ and *KX* ($\Delta X/Y$) are, respectively, the non-export and the export components of growth. The constant term *a* represents the autonomous growth of GDP, that is, the growth of GDP that would have occurred in the absence of any export growth. If the growth of exports does not add to productive capacity and if productive capacity is always fully utilized, so that the growth of exports is achieved only by the shift of resources from non-export to export goods, then the regression coefficient *b* will be equal to –1. On the other hand, if the growth of exports does not lead to any increase in productive capacity but is achieved only by using hitherto unused resources, then *b* will be equal to 0. Any increase in productive capacity due to the growth of exports will then lead to higher values of *b* in both cases.

In order to compare his method with the other approaches, Kleiman estimated equation (8) with the same data used by Michaely and Heller and Porter. His results are shown in Table 7.4 under the combined sample.

Table 7.4 Regression of *KD* on *KX*: 1950–73

Parameters	*Combined sample*	*Sample A*	*Sample B*
a	1.58	1.70	5.69
b	0.53	–0.50	–1.02
R^2	0.093	0.001	0.480
Number of countries	41	34	7

Source: Kleiman (1980) for combined sample.

The correlation between *KD* and *KX* is lower than that between *GY* and *GX* and barely significant, but the regression coefficient is positive and quite large. Kleiman was surprised at the substantial spill-over effect of export growth indicated by the estimate of *b*. But this result is because his sample consists of two rather different types of economies, one set of 34 countries (sample *A*) being fairly typical LDCs, and another set (sample *B*) of seven countries (Greece, Israel, South Korea, Portugal, Spain, Taiwan, and Yugoslavia) at an intermediate or higher stage of development. When the exercise is carried out separately, we find that the regression coefficients are negative for each of the two samples. The regression coefficient is close to –1 in the more developed countries (sample *B*), indicating that the growth of exports was achieved mainly by diverting resources from domestic to export production. It was numerically smaller in the typical LDCs (sample *A*), indicating that a considerable part of export growth was achieved by fuller utilization of resources with a smaller diminution of non-export output.

More extensive data have since become available. The results of applying the method to these data are shown in Table 7.5.

The estimate of *b* is negative in all cases. Except for the 1950s, it was close to –1 in the DCs. It was numerically quite small in the LDCs. These results confirm that the role of export growth in bringing about fuller utilization of resources was quite strong in the LDCs and more limited in the DCs.

Finally, we may note a statistical analysis by Feder (1983) in which the role of exports in economic growth is separated into two parts, one due to a productivity differential between the export and domestic sectors and the

Table 7.5 Regression of *KD* on *KX*: 1950–81

Country/ period	*Estimate of b*	R^2
LDCs		
1950s	–0.385	0.06
1960s	–0.386	0.14
1970s	–0.276	0.04
DCs		
1950s	–0.107	0.02
1960s	–0.813	0.14
1970s	–0.797	0.29

Source: World Bank (1983).

Table 7.6 Regression of *GY* on *KX*, *GX*, and other variable: 1964–73 (*t*-ratios in brackets)

Explanatory variable	*31 Semi-industrialized LDCs*	*19 DCs*
Constant	.006 (0.60)	–.030 (2.61)
IR	.124 (3.01)	.141 (2.87)
GL	.696 (3.40)	.660 (1.48)
KX	.305 (4.57)	–.240 (1.31)
GX	.131 (4.24)	.494 (5.48)
R^2	.809	.815

Source: Feder (1983), Table 3, p.68.

other due to a spill-over effect of exports on the domestic sector. The former is measured by the parameter λ, the extent to which the marginal product of resources in the export sector exceeds that in the domestic sector as a ratio of that in the export sector; this differential is assumed to be the same for capital and for labor. The latter is measured by β, the elasticity of domestic output with respect to exports. Feder then derives the relationship

$$GY = a + b_1\, IR + b_2\, GL + (\lambda - \beta)\, KX + \beta GX \qquad (9)$$

where *IR* is investment as a ratio of GDP, *GL* is the growth rate of labor, and *KX* and *GX* have the definitions given above. His estimate of the parameters of this relationship are reproduced in Table 7.6.

The elasticity of domestic output with respect to exports is positive for both groups of countries, being greater in the DCs than in the semi-industrialized countries. In both groups of countries, there is a productivity differential in favour of the export sector, being greater in the semi-industrialized countries than in the DCs.

7.2 ANALYTICS

Having reviewed the statistical evidence, we turn now to the various theories that have been advanced in the literature to explain the role of exports in economic growth. Most of these theories have been so extensively discussed that only a brief summary is needed here.

7.2.1 Gains from Trade

In the conventional theories of international trade, the benefit that countries derive from participating in the international division of labor is analyzed mainly in terms of the gains from trade. Barring such exceptional cases as those where a country has some monopoly power, these gains are greater, the more closely countries trade according to their comparative advantage. Hence the main policy conclusion is in favor of free trade and the removal of trade distortions.

The analysis of these gains has been developed to a high level of sophistication in the modern theory of international trade. However, as Myint has pointed out in a number of papers, these effects of trade contribute little to the explanation of the role of exports in economic growth (for a recent summary, see Myint, 1987). The gains or losses associated with trade distortions as a percentage of GDP are generally of a small order of magnitude. These gains are essentially static and have only a once-over effect on growth. Further, according to the theory, there is an optimum amount of exports under conditions of free trade from which countries derive the maximum benefit in the form of gains from trade. But many countries, most notably South Korea and Taiwan, have achieved fast growth of GDP by giving special privileges to exporters and thus expanding their exports rapidly. Also while the rapid growth of GDP in the OECD countries in the quarter century after World War II was associated with a great expansion of their exports, it is difficult to interpret the trade of these countries in terms of their comparative advantage, as most of this trade was of an intra-industry type. By contrast, the trade between the tropical countries and the DCs in the nineteenth and early twentieth centuries was more in accord with their initial comparative advantages, but although the tropical countries enjoyed a rapid growth of GDP at the time, there was little effect on the domestic sector and they emerged at the end of the period with low incomes and slow growth.

To these arguments may be added another consideration of a statistical nature. To the extent that exports accelerate economic growth through the gains from trade, it is an effect that should be revealed by a relationship between the level of exports and the growth of GDP. But as we have seen, the statistical evidence does not show any strong positive relationship between these variables. Instead, it shows a much stronger relationship between the growth of exports and the growth of GDP. It is for this relationship that we need an analytical explanation that is not provided by the gains from trade argument.

7.2.2 Dynamic Advantage of Trade

The main reason why the gains from trade contribute little to the explanation of the effect of exports on economic growth is that they are based on the assumption of a given comparative advantage of trading countries. Therefore, a number of authors have tried to explain the relationship by invoking some dynamic effects of trade in changing the comparative advantage of countries. Thus, Lockwood (1954, esp. p. 320) explained the economic growth of Japan after the Meiji Restoration by the effect of trade in introducing knowledge of new products and new techniques, and spoke of trade as a 'highway of learning'. The educative effects of foreign trade in introducing new wants, new techniques, and new forms of economic organization were also stressed by Myint (1958). Haberler (1959, p. 705) considered trade as "the most important vehicle for the transmission of technological know-how", and Johnson (1977, p. 427) also referred to "the educational effects of exposure to foreign competition and foreign ways of doing things".

The improvement of technology is certainly a major source of economic growth in all countries. But, as Myint (1987, p. 118) himself remarked on a later occasion, "The real question is how these technological improvements are introduced into the process of export expansion," that is, the question why they depend peculiarly on export growth rather than in other ways such as import substitution growth or investment in human capital.

7.2.3 Relaxation of the Foreign Exchange Constraint

The growth of less-developed countries depends not only on savings to finance investment in a non-inflationary way but also on sufficient foreign exchange to import capital goods that cannot be produced domestically. One argument that has been extensively discussed in the literature, most notably in the two-gap theory, is that the economic growth of these countries may be constrained by a scarcity of foreign exchange in the sense that the rate of growth permitted by the available supply of foreign exchange is lower than that corresponding to the rate of saving. Then, an expansion of exports will lead to faster growth of GDP by relaxing this foreign exchange constraint.

The theory was very popular in the 1960s and was used mainly to advocate more foreign aid to the developing countries. The experience of these countries, however, does not show any significant relationship between their rates of growth and the amounts of foreign aid received. The main reason is that the theory is based on some rather special assumptions of rigid structural relationships between growth and its import requirements, which have not always been valid. In practice, many countries have used increases in their foreign exchange receipts, whether provided by aid or earned from higher prices for their exports, as in the case of some OPEC countries, to raise their consumption of imports with little effect on their growth. Therefore, Myint (1969) has argued that the growth of LDCs depends more on the efficiency with which they use their available resources, and has criticized the tendency of some economists to harp constantly on the foreign exchange constraints on growth.

7.2.4 Vent for Surplus

One feature of the above theories is that they all seek to explain the role of exports in economic growth mainly in terms of the supply factors of expanding resources and their optimal use. These supply factors are certainly important for economic growth but it is doubtful whether their magnitude is sufficient to explain the significant effect that export growth seems to have had on growth of GDP. Thus Krueger (1981, p. 4) says:

> On the one hand, the classical free-trade arguments while indicating the superiority of free trade do not provide any hint as to why that superiority should be demonstrated in a more rapid rate of growth (as contrasted with a higher level of income after sustaining once-and-for-all losses associated with protection). On the other hand, even if the losses from first-best optimality were several times as great as traditional theory would suggest, the differences in growth rates seem to be greater than can conceivably be accounted for by the exporting sector of the economy.

Similarly, Myint (1987, pp. 116–17) has suggested that "the gains from the removal of the static distortions seem to be too small to explain the rapid growth of the (export-oriented) countries". It is therefore useful to consider also the demand factors, especially the role of exports as a source of demand. One way in which exports play this role was already emphasized by Adam Smith in his vent-for-surplus theory. After suffering much neglect by modern neoclassical economists because of their characteristic assumption of continual full employment, the theory was revived by Myint (1958) especially in explaining the economic growth of LDCs associated with their export orientation in the nineteenth and early twentieth centuries. He has summarized his argument as follows (Myint, 1987, p. 121):

The vent for surplus theory was particularly suited to explain the rapid expansion of agricultural exports from the relatively sparsely populated countries of Southeast Asia and West Africa. After the initial opening up of these countries in the late nineteenth and early twentieth centuries, agricultural exports grew typically about five percent a year for many decades. This happened without any important change in agricultural techniques, simply by bringing more land under cultivation. The additional labour was drawn from the subsistence sector. Unlike the situation in the densely populated countries, the underemployment was caused not by a shortage of land but by the limited local demand for the agricultural output that the existing underemployed labour could have produced with the existing uncultivated land. Hence the role of international trade as a vent for surplus. I believe that the vent for surplus theory provides a more powerful argument for free trade than the conventional comparative advantage theory. The direct gains from using the previously underutilized resources will be many times greater than the conventional gains from a more efficient reallocation of the given resources.

Further, as we have seen in the statistical analyses reviewed in the first part of the paper, part of the economic growth especially of LDCs associated with export growth in the post-war period may also be explained by the fuller utilization of under-employed resources.

Nowadays the standard way of studying the demand effects is, of course, the Keynesian analysis. It is therefore interesting to examine the vent for surplus theory from the Keynesian point of view. In that analysis, some sources of demand, such as consumption and imports, are endogenous in the sense that they depend on the level of income, and cannot therefore be used to explain the level of income. But other sources of demand, such as exports, investment, and government expenditures are exogenous in the sense that they do not depend on the income of the countries concerned, though of course they will be affected by their policies. When there are under-utilized resources in an economy, an increase in these exogenous sources of demand will not only increase output by the same amount but will also have multiplier effects as explained in the standard textbooks on macro-economics. On this argument, the important point is that exports play a significant role in economic growth because they are an exogenous source of demand.

The vent-for-surplus theory of the role of exports is primarily concerned with the increased output in the export sector in response to external demand, but the increase in demand also has multiplier effects. In the case of the LDCs, however, these multiplier effects have generally been small. One reason was that simultaneously with the expansion of exports, there was also a rise in the propensity to import which dampened the multiplier effects. Another reason was that much of the increase in income associated with export expansion accrued to foreigners who transferred their incomes to their own countries instead of spending them in the domestic economy (see, for example, Singer, 1950).

While the vent-for-surplus theory is a powerful explanation of the historical experience of LDCs, it is less applicable to other cases of export-led growth. For example, as we have seen, the growth of exports in LDCs in the post-war period was achieved by using under-employed resources to a smaller extent and was accompanied by some diminution in the growth of non-export output. This was even more so in the case of the DCs which enjoyed full employment conditions at least until the early 1970s. Therefore, we must consider some further explanation of the role of exports in these cases.

7.2.5 Interaction of Supply and Demand Factors

If the observed relationship between growth of exports and growth of GDP, especially in the post-war decades, cannot be fully explained by the greater utilization of under-employed resources, as envisaged in the vent-for-surplus theory, it must be due to some increase in productive capacity associated with the growth of exports. In other words, a growth of exports increases the demand not only for existing surplus productive capacity but also for expansion of productive capacity. Such a relationship has been traditionally ignored in the literature because of the widespread tendency among economists to treat supply and demand factors as independent of each other. But in fact, as Cornwall (1972, Ch. 4) has particularly stressed, there is a considerable interaction between these factors.

Take for example the case of investment. It is an important source of economic growth, and most fast growing countries have had high rates of investment. Investment contributes to economic growth not only by increasing the stock of capital but also as a vehicle for technological progress. But we must also explain why investment rates vary so much between countries. The subject is so little understood that Keynes even suggested that it was determined by the animal spirits of entrepreneurs. In neoclassical economics, the standard explanation is that investment is determined by savings behavior through equilibrium adjustments of the rate of interest. But voluntary savings are not the only way to finance investment; it may be financed by the banking system or by foreign capital.

Table 7.7 Correlation between growth of exports (*GX*) and growth of investment (GI)

Period	Correlation coefficient between GX and GI in LDCs	DCs
1950s	–.079	–377
1960s	.236	.641
1970s	.368	.187

Source: World Bank (1983).

A more plausible explanation is that investment is determined by profitable opportunities to invest rather than by *ex ante* savings. Where these opportunities exist, resources can usually be found to finance the induced investment. Where they do not exist, the result will be a weak inducement to invest, as Nurkse and Lewis argued was the case in LDCs, and their savings efforts will be frustrated. According to this theory, the growth of exports will provide the demand for high rates of investment by creating profitable opportunities to invest. The strength of this relationship is indicated by the correlation between the growth of exports (*GX*) and the growth of investment (*GI*) shown in Table 7.7.

Except for the 1950s, there is a positive correlation between these variables, which is particularly high in the DCs in the 1960s. The rapid growth of GDP in these countries was due to high and growing levels of investment, but these rates of investment were in turn induced by the rapid growth of exports brought about by a great liberalization of world trade.

Similarly, for a long time, technological progress was viewed as an exogenous process like manna falling from heaven. But recent studies have shown that it is much more an endogenous process, in particular that it is highly responsive to demand factors, as shown particularly by the work of Schmookler (1966). Rapid technological progress depends also on high rates of investment, as stressed in the learning by doing theories. Hence a rapid growth of exports leads to faster technological progress, both by increasing the demand for innovations and by inducing a high rate of investment. The high rate of investment and the faster technological progress will in turn expand exports further by improving the country's competitive position in international markets. The resulting cumulative process has been described by Cornwall (1977, pp. 165ff) as the virtuous circle of export-led growth.

The classic example of such growth is Taiwan. It experienced an average GDP growth rate of nine per cent in the period 1952–86. One reason was, of course, a high rate of investment. It was rather low to begin with, averaging 13 per cent of GDP in 1952–65, financed to a considerable extent by foreign capital. It rose to 22 per cent in 1966–70 and 30 per cent in 1971–80, financed entirely by domestic savings. The result was a rise in capital per worker at about five per cent per annum in the 1970s. Taking the post-war period as a whole, output per worker also increased at over five per cent per annum. Such a rapid growth of productivity cannot be explained only by the accumulation of capital, on any reasonable estimate of the elasticity of output with respect to capital. Much of it must therefore be attributed to a high rate of technological progress.

These high rates of capital accumulation and technological progress, however, are only the proximate causes of rapid economic growth. We must also explain how these high rates of capital accumulation and technological progress came about in Taiwan. The most likely explanation is that they were induced by the spectacular growth of exports that occurred at the same time. Starting from only nine per cent in the 1950s, it rose to 22 per cent in the 1960s and 14 per cent in the 1970s. These high rates of export growth sustained over such a long period could not have been achieved by only the fuller utilization of under-employed resources. Any under-utilized resources that may have existed to begin with must have long since been exhausted, especially as exports consisted of non-traditional goods, particularly manufactures. In the early stages, it was because of a considerable diversion of labor from domestic-use products to exports; but in the later stages, it was due to a greater extent to the increase in productive capacity.

The important point, however, is that the increase in productive capacity itself was induced to some extent by the growth of exports. This can be seen quite clearly in the case of investment. Table 7.8 shows the correlation between *GX* and *GI* with various lags between the variables.

Table 7.8 Correlation between growth of exports and growth of investment

Lag of investment growth behind export growth	*Correlation between growth of export and growth of investment*
–2	.077
–1	.317
0	.156
1	.153
2	.706
3	.397

It shows that while there is some correlation between *GX* and *GI* when *GX* is lagged behind *GI*, the correlation is higher when *GI* is lagged behind *GX*. We may therefore conclude that the growth of exports in Taiwan was not only facilitated by rapid capital accumulation; it was also an important cause leading to the growth of investment, an illustration of the interaction between supply and demand factors. (For more details on the data and the analysis of the Taiwan experience, see Sundrum, 1990, section 10.4.)

In general, the strength of the interaction varies with the commodity composition of exports. The interaction is particularly strong in the case of manufactures, which depend heavily on investment and use of modern techniques. Hence export growth was a major source of economic growth of DCs in the post-war period, and also of those LDCs like Taiwan which expanded their exports of manufactures rapidly. By contrast, the interaction is much weaker in the case of primary products which were the main exports of the tropical countries in the historical period. The growth of their exports was achieved mainly by using surplus land and labor with very little change in techniques or the use of capital. What was missing in this case was the growth of productive capacity. The growth of GDP in these countries was almost entirely based on the vent-for-surplus role of exports, though it was a long drawn out process. Eventually, with the exhaustion of surplus resources and the decline of external demand, these countries emerged as typical less-developed countries.

References

Balassa, B. (1978) "Exports and Economic Growth," *Journal of Development Economics*, vol. 5, pp. 181–9.

Cornwall, John (1972) *Growth and Stability in a Mature Economy* (London: Martin Robertson).

Cornwall, John (1977) *Modern Capitalism* (London: Martin Robertson).

Emery, R. F. (1967) "The Relationship of Exports and Economic Growth," *Kyklos*, vol. 20, pp. 470–84.

Feder. G. (1983) "On Exports and Economic Growth," *Journal of Development Economics*, vol. 12, pp. 59–73.

Haberler, G. (1959) *International Trade and Economic Development* (Cairo: National Bank of Egypt).

Heller, P. S. and R. C. Porter (1978) "Exports and Growth," *Journal of Development Economics*, vol. 5, pp. 191–3.

Johnson, H. G. (1977) "Trade, Growth and Economic Stability" in *Trade and Employment in Asia and the Pacific* (Manila: Council for Asian Manpower Studies).

Kavoussi, R.M. (1984) "Export Expansion and Economic Growth," *Journal of Development Economics*, vol. 14, pp. 241–50.

Kleiman, E. (1980) "Exports and Growth: Evidence and Interpretation", mimeo (Canberra: Australian National University).

Krueger, A. O. (1981) "Export-led Industrial Growth Reconsidered" in W. Hong and L. B. Krause (eds), *Trade and Growth of the Advanced Developing Countries in the Pacific Basin* (Seoul: Korean Development Institute) pp. 3–27.

Lewis, W. A. (1954) "Economic Development With Unlimited Supplies of Labour", *Manchester School*, vol. 22, pp. 139–201.

Lewis, W. A. (1969) *Aspects of Tropical Trade* (Stockholm: Almqvist & Wiksell).

Lockwood, W. W. (1954) *The Economic Development of Japan* (Princeton: Princeton University Press).

Michaely, M.(1977) "Exports and Growth," *Journal of Development Economics*, vol. 4, pp. 49–53.

Myint, Hla (1948) *Theories of Welfare Economics* (London: Longmans).

Myint, Hla (1958) "The Classical Theory of International Trade and the Underdeveloped Countries," *Economic Journal*, vol. 68, pp. 317–37.

Myint, Hla (1969) "International Trade and the Developing Countries" in P. A. Samuelson (ed.), *International Economic Relations* (London: Macmillan).

Myint, Hla (1987) "Neoclassical Development Analysis: Its Strengths and Limits" in Gerald M. Meier (ed.) *Pioneers in Development* (London: Oxford University Press).

Nurkse, R. (1953) *Problems of Capital Formation in Underdeveloped Countries* (London: Oxford University Press).

OECD (1968) *Development Cooperation*, Paris: OECD.

Ram, R. (1987) "Exports and Economic Growth in Developing Countries," *Economic Development and Cultural Change*, vol. 36, pp. 51–72.

Schmookler, J. (1966) *Invention and Economic Growth* (Cambridge: Harvard University Press).

Singer, H. W. (1950) "The Distribution of Gains between Investing and Borrowing Countries," *American Economic Review*, Papers and Proceedings (May).

Sundrum, R. M. (1990) *Economic Growth in Theory and Practice* (London: Macmillan).

Tyler, W. G. (1981) "Growth and Export Expansion in Developing Countries," *Journal of Development Economics*, vol. 9, pp. 121–30.

World Bank (1983) *World Tables* (Third Edition) (Washington: World Bank).

8 Peasant and Plantation in Asia

Yujiro Hayami

Peasant and plantation are two contrasting modes of agricultural production in less developed countries (LDCs). The term "plantation" refers here to a large farm estate producing a crop (or crops) for commercial purposes and employing a relatively large number of hired wage laborers organized under a central management hierarchy.[1] It is a new institution brought by Western colonialism in order to extract tropical agricultural products for export to home countries. In tropical Asia it became common especially after the 1870s with major innovations in transportation such as opening of the Suez Canal and use of steamships and railways.

Such a system is in sharp contrast with the age-old peasant mode of production, in which crops are produced in small-sized farm units based mainly on family labor. Their production is geared principally for subsistence purposes, and any small surpluses above home consumption requirements are exchanged in the market.

One of the major contributions by Hla Myint was to set these two institutions in a proper perspective in the "vent-for-surplus" development process that is characteristic of land-surplus economies newly opened for international trade. A traditional paradigm developed under colonialism had been to identify plantation as a modern enclave geared for the international market and peasant as dominated by subsistence orientation and irresponsive to profit incentives created by changes in market demands and technological opportunities.[2] The iconoclasm of this old belief was accomplished almost concurrently by three great development economists, Theodore W. Schultz (1964), Hla Myint (1965), and W. Arthur Lewis (1969, 1970).

Schultz convincingly argued that peasants in traditional agriculture are rational and efficient in resource allocation and that they remain poor not because they are irresponsive to economic incentives but because only limited technical and market opportunities are available to which they can respond. Myint, drawing mainly on the experience of Southeast Asia, demonstrated how peasants responded vigorously to market incentives in opening new lands for cultivation of export cash crops while maintaining subsistence food crop production. This observation for the Southeast Asian case was found by Lewis to be no exception in tropical development from the late nineteenth to the early twentieth century.

Both Myint and Lewis recognized that, while plantations played an important role in opening up new areas for export production, they were usually unable to compete with peasants where the peasants had established fairly permanent agricultural structures and were allowed to have access to new lands. Yet, the plantation system has subsisted long since the demise of colonialism and the closing of land frontiers under rapid population growth.

This essay aims to develop a proper perspective on the roles of peasant and plantation in the development of tropical economies. The task done by Myint and Lewis two decades ago shall be reexamined in the light of new theoretical developments as well as emerging policy problems such as the role of multinational corporations in agriculture and privatization of collective and state farms in socialist economies.

8.1 PEASANT CROPS VERSUS PLANTATION CROPS

For the explanation of why the two contrasting production organizations have emerged in tropical agriculture, the difference in demand structures is clearly not sufficient. It is true that subsistence food crops, such as rice, wheat, and maize, are grown almost exclusively by peasants, whereas plantations grow cash crops for export demand. However, some export crops such as cotton and tobacco are also produced by peasants. Further, rice production for export in some newly opened deltaic areas, such as the lower delta of Chao Praya River in Thailand, has been carried out under the peasant system.

An apparently more convincing explanation has resorted to the difference in production technology or production function between the "plantation crops", such as sugar and rubber, grown exclusively in tropical environments and the "peasant crops", such as wheat, more suitable to temperate environments. This theory was popularized among economists by an influential paper of Robert Baldwin (1956). Baldwin assumed that the production function of the plantation crops as compared with the peasant crops is characterized by (i) significant scale economies, (ii) much higher intensity of labor relative to capital, and (iii) much lower elasticity of factor substitution. These characteristics are considered to underlie the emergence and continuation of the plantation system using a large number of unskilled laborers under the command of central management. Further, he generalized to a more sweeping hypothesis that it is difficult for the plantation economies to achieve sustained growth with decent equity because the route is closed for plantation laborers to advance to owner operators since the optimum point on such a production function is too far to reach with their limited financial capacity.

The direct evidence on the shapes of production functions by crop is very scanty. Limited statistical evidence and experts' assessments, however, indicate that the crops subject to scale economies sufficiently strong to make large-scale plantation operations necessary are rather few, being only tea and banana among major tropical export crops (Binswanger and Rosenweig, 1986; Lim, 1968; Pim, 1946; and Wickizer, 1951, 1960).[3] Even for these crops, scale economies are not quite so decisive at the farm-level production, although the private profitability of some operations that have externalities, such as pest management, tends to be greater for larger operations.

Significant increasing returns emerge only at the levels of the processing and marketing activities. The vertical integration of a large farm unit with a large-scale central processing and/or marketing system is called for because of the need to supply farm-produced raw materials in a timely schedule. A typical example is fermented "black tea". The black tea manufacturing requires a modern machine plant into which fresh leaves must be fed within a few hours after plucking (Wickizer, 1951, 1960). The need for close coordination between farm production and processing underlies the pervasive use of the plantation system for black tea manufacture. Unfermented "green tea", in contrast, remains predominantly the product of peasants in China and Japan.

In the case of bananas for export, harvested fruits must be packed, sent to the wharf, and loaded to a refrigerated boat within a day. A boatful of bananas that can meet the quality standards of foreign buyers must be collected within a few days (Hayami, Quisumbing, and Adriano, 1990). Therefore, the whole production process from planting to harvesting must be precisely controlled so as to meet the shipment schedule. Although the plantation system has a decisive advantage for this export banana production, bananas for domestic consumption are usually produced by peasants.

On the other hand, for the crops for which centralized processing and marketing are not necessary, plantations have no significant advantage over peasants. Typical examples are cocoa and coconuts. The fermentation of cocoa and the drying and smoking of coconuts to make copra can be handled in small lots with no large capital requirement beyond small indigenous tools and facilities. These crops are grown predominantly by peasants. In Ceylon, where more than 80 per cent of tea acreage was held by plantations, about 70 per cent of coconut acreage was in small peasant holdings, as recorded for the 1940s to the 1950s (Wickizer, 1960). In the Philippines where large landownership holdings for coconuts are common, large-scale plantation operations based on hired wage labor is less common than small-scale tenant operations on subdivided plots (Hayami, Quisumbing and Adriano, 1990).

For other tree crops such as coffee and rubber the advantage of the plantation system is also not so significant. The quality of these products tends to be higher when processed in modern facilities in plantations. Yet, the lower product prices that peasants receive can be effectively compensated for by the lower costs of using family labor with low opportunity costs. Indeed, in major rubber exporters, such as Indonesia and Malaysia, peasant operations have not only coexisted with plantations but increased their share over time (Bauer, 1948; Thoburn, 1977; and Wickizer, 1960).

Sugar is frequently cited as a classic case of scale economies stemming from the need of coordination between farm production and large-scale central processing (Binswanger and Rosenweig, 1986). Efficient operation of a centrifugal sugar mill requires the steady supply of a large amount of canes over time. Coordination of production from planting to harvesting with processing is required. This coordination, however, need not be as stringent as for tea and bananas. The rate of sugar extraction decreases as the processing of cane is delayed, but this loss is in no way comparable with the devastating damage that delayed processing has on the quality of tea and bananas. Sugar cane can be hauled from relatively long distances and stored for several days. Therefore, the need for vertical integration is not so large, and the necessary coordination can be achieved through contracts of a sugar mill with cane growers on the time and quota of cane delivery. In fact, an efficient sugar industry with small holders has developed in Australia and Taiwan. In tropical Asia, too, sugar production has been carried out in the peasant system in India and Thailand, whereas it has traditionally been based on the plantation system in Indonesia (recently shifted to the small-holder operation). Within the Philippines, the peasant operation has been common in old-settled areas on the island of Luzon, whereas the plantation mode has predominated in newly-opened areas such as the islands of Negros and Mindanao.

From those observations, it should be clear that the "plantation crops" of the Baldwin sense are rather exceptional among tropical export crops. His production function determinism on the patterns of agrarian organization and economic development seems to have but limited applicability. It is important to recognize that "no definite or permanent line can be drawn between agricultural products as regards suitability for plantation or peasant methods of production" (Pim, 1946, p.177). The classification between "peasant crops" and "plantation crops" can be useful only when it is understood that they range in a continuous spectrum.

8.2 ADVANTAGES OF THE PEASANT SYSTEM

Although the plantation system is an important component in tropical agriculture, it has never been the major sector relative to the peasant sector, at least, in Asia. Not only have staple food crops been produced exclusively by peasants, but they have also held significant shares in the production of tropical export crops. According to FAO's *1970 World Census of Agriculture*, even in countries like Indonesia, Malaysia, and the Philippines characterized by comparative advantage in the production of tropical export crops within Asia, less than 20 per cent of farmland area was operated by estates above 50 hectares and more than 50 per cent was cultivated by small holders below 5 hectares (UN-FAO, 1981). Moreover, peasants' share in the total output of export crops has increased over time as shown for the history of Indonesia (Booth, 1988).

Thus, the peasant system has demonstrated remarkable resilience and viability in the process of commercialization under colonialism as well as after independence in tropical Asia. This experience adds to counter evidence against the Marxian prediction. A theory advanced by Karl Marx (1867) and later elaborated by Karl Kautsky (1899) and Vladimir Lenin (1899) asserts that modern technology and the institutions of capitalism polarize the peasantry into large commercial farmers and wage laborers. Institutions of precapitalist village society such as communal land ownership, mutual-aid associations, and patron-client ties are thought to provide for an egalitarian distribution of assets and income that assures at least a minimum subsistence. As those traditional institutions are replaced by modern market institutions, village elites begin to accumulate land for commercial production by encroaching on commons, evicting tenants, and purchasing small peasant holdings. This process is augmented by modern agricultural technology based on large machinery, which raises the efficiency of large-scale operations relative to small-scale operations. The higher efficiency of large commercial farms drives off small peasants and converts them into landless laborers, many of whom are not able to find employment in the rural sector and are forced to migrate to the cities.

As conceived by Marx, large-scale commercial farming based on landlords, capitalist tenants, and wage laborers, established in England after the second enclosure movement, is the ideal type of the polarization process.

Marx realized, however, that patterns in other countries would likely deviate from the ideal. In fact, Germany and other European countries in the late nineteenth century showed the opposite trend. Even in the United States, despite dramatic increases in mechanization, family farms continued to exist. Large-scale farms characterized by hired labor and management hierarchy did not become a dominant mode of production in agriculture, and this led to a major controversy between Marxian orthodoxy and revisionists (de Janvry, 1981; Mitrany, 1951).

A major reason for the failure of Marx's prediction seems to be the inherent difficulty of labor enforcement in agricultural production. In urban industries, work is highly standardized and easy to monitor. The biological process of agricultural production, however, is subject to infinite ecological variations. Different ways of handling crops or animals are often necessary because of slight differences in temperature and soil moisture. The dispersal of agricultural operations over wide space adds to the difficulty of monitoring. This difficulty multiplies as the farming system becomes more complex, involving more intensive crop care, crop rotations, and crop-livestock combinations: "In areas more suitable for multiple enterprise farms, family operations have the advantage. Increasing the enterprises so multiplies the number of on-the-spot supervisory management decisions per acre that the total acreage which a unit of management can oversee quickly approaches the acreage which an ordinary family can operate" (Brewster, 1950, p. 71). In fact, large plantations are limited largely to monoculture.

This constraint of managerial ability and family labor on operational farm size is exacerbated by the danger of reckless use of draft animals and machines by non-family operators that results in capital loss. Therefore, "a landless person with a family who owns animals and/or machines and possesses some managerial skill will find it more profitable to rent in land than to hire out his endowments separately. Similarly, a large landowner will find it more profitable to rent out land than to manage a large operation because of scale diseconomies arising from the use of hired workers" (Binswanger and Rosenweig, 1986, p. 524). In other words, technological scale economies arising from the use of indivisible inputs such as managerial ability and animals/machines are countervailed by scale diseconomies from the use of hired labor so that the nuclear family farm becomes optimum except for some plantation crops that need close coordination with large-scale processing and marketing.

Another advantage of peasant operations is the ability to utilize the low-opportunity cost labor of women, children, and aged family members who have little employment opportunity outside their own farm. Although the wage cost is thus lower for peasants, their capital cost may be higher than for plantations because of more difficult access to the credit market. On this ground, the argument has been developed that plantations have advantage in the tree crops that are characterized by long gestation periods from planting to maturity (Binswanger and Rosenweig, 1986). However, the opportunity costs of labor and capital applied to formation of the tree capital are not necessarily high for peasants. Typically they plant the trees in hitherto unused lands. If such lands are located nearby their residence, they open the new lands for planting by means of low opportunity cost family labor mainly in idle seasons for the production of food crops in the farm lands already in use. When they migrate to frontier areas, a typical process is to slash and burn jungles, and plant subsistence crops such as maize, potatoes, and upland rice, together with seedlings of the trees. Such complex intercropping is difficult to manage with hired labor in the plantation system.

In this way, the cost required for the formation of tree capital by peasants could be much lower than those of plantations that must employ hired wage labor for opening new lands, planting, and caring for the trees until maturity. The economic development strategy based on capital formation by the use of low opportunity cost resources, envisaged by Ragner Nurkse (1953) for densely populated economies characterized by "disguised" unemployment, seems to be more applicable to the vent-for-surplus stage in which land frontiers are open for peasants to push forward.

8.3 CONDITIONS FOR THE PLANTATION SYSTEM

With their organizational advantage in both current production and capital formation as described above, peasants proved to be highly responsive to market incentives in increasing the supply of cash crops for export in the vent-for-surplus situation that emerged since the 1870s in many areas of tropical Asia. In regions where peasant communities had already been established, the plantation system usually failed to make inroads. Western traders found it more profitable to purchase tropical agricultural commodities from peasant producers in exchange for imported manufactured commodities than to produce these commodities themselves in the plantation system. This was particularly convenient during the mid-nineteenth century when the industrial revolutions in the Western nations made it possible for these countries to produce and supply manufactured products at much lower cost than if these products were produced by the manufacturing sector in the tropical economies.

The establishment of plantations in less developed economies became a necessity when the demand for tropical products by the industrialized nations continued to rise, although the regions in the less-developed economies physically suited for the production of these products had no significant peasant population that could produce and trade in these commodities.

Opening frontier lands for the production of new crops entailed high capital outlays. Virgin lands had to be cleared and developed; and physical infrastructure such as roads, irrigation systems, bridges, and docking facilities had to be constructed. Capital, in the form of machinery and other equipment, had to be imported and redesigned to adapt to local situations. Laborers were not only imported from the more populous regions but also had to be trained in the production of these crops.

The establishment of plantations requires huge initial capital investments. For the investors to internalize the gains from investments in these "public goods" or infrastructure, the farm size must inevitably be large. Furthermore, to shorten the transition period before a systematic production process can be firmly established so as to obtain decent return from large initial investments, planters often had no choice but to let the laborers work by command under a management-foreman hierarchy. The relative efficiency of the command system increased when new sophisticated technologies were imported from abroad, which native people often found difficult to master in a short period of time.

Given these historical conditions, that is, the continuing rise in the demand for tropical commodities by industrialized nations and the urgency of opening new lands to reap the gains from the production and marketing of high-valued crops, the establishment and the development of plantations in areas where labor and social capital were deficient (or nonexistent) were therefore inevitable. Viewed from this perspective, it follows that the plantation system evolved not because it was generally a more efficient mode of productive organization than the peasant mode but because it was the most effective type of agricultural organization for extracting the economic benefits accruing from the exploitation of sparsely populated virgin areas.

In this perspective it is easy to understand why the same crop is grown mainly by peasants in one place and by plantations in another, for example, for sugar cane production the peasant mode is more common in old settled areas of Luzon and the plantation system predominates in the newly opened Negros, both in the Philippines.

Of course, technologies associated with production, processing, and marketing have made certain crops more suitable for peasants and others more suitable in plantations. For example, tea plantations were established not only in such places as Assam, India, which had been endowed with abundant unused lands and thin indigenous population of permanent agricultural settlement, but also were established in West Java, Indonesia, characterized by relatively dense peasant population.

On the other hand, rice which is characterized by absence of scale economies in terms of both farm-level production and coordination with processing and marketing has been produced exclusively under the peasant system irrespective of initial conditions and development process (Barker and Herdt, 1985). Lower deltas of major rivers in continental Southeast Asia, such as Irrawaddy in Burma, Chao Praya in Thailand and Mekon in Vietnam, had very few indigenous settlements until they were opened for the production of rice from the late nineteenth to the early twentieth century for export, first to Europe as a cheap food for industrial labor population and, later, to the insular and peninsular parts of Southeast Asia for their plantation workers. Landlords invested in building infrastructure, such as canals and dikes, needed for both human settlement and rice production. Despite this large capital outlay, the plantation system did not emerge in these rice bowls. Instead, landlords preferred to rent out lands in small parcels for cultivation by peasants who were invited from old-settled areas (Feeny, 1982; Wickizer and Bennet, 1941).

In addition to the technical characteristics of crops, colonial policies especially with respect to land policies were an important determinant of the production organization. A major factor underlying the development of large plantations in the central highlands in Ceylon, initially for coffee and later for tea, was the British colonial government's policy of selling a large tract of unclaimed land to European planters on very favorable terms (Craig, 1970). In Indonesia, the development of the plantation system was facilitated by a Dutch policy to give village headmen the authority to sign contracts on the rotational lease of village lands to sugar companies (Geertz, 1970; Van Leeuwen, 1970). In the Philippines, the emergence of huge banana and pineapple plantations in Mindanao frontiers under the management of multinational corporations was not possible without the National Development Company, a public corporation established for the purpose of leasing public lands to agribusiness (Hayami, Quisumbing and Adriano, 1990).

8.4 CHANGING ROLE OF PLANTATIONS

Although actual development of the plantation system has been subject to several factors such as crop nature and government policy, it should hold true that its efficiency relative to the peasant system tends to be higher in the initial opening-up process of land-abundant and labor scarce economies characterized by absence of public infrastructure. It should be recognized, therefore, that the plantation system made a very important contribution to rural and national development particularly during the initial stages, when it virtually opened up virgin lands for the production and marketing of new crops. Without it, infrastructure in remote areas would have remained much less developed and the introduction of advanced technologies associated with the production and marketing of new crops destined for the export market would have been slower. The result would have been lower rural employment, incomes, and foreign exchange earnings. Plantations absorbed labor from densely populated areas, thus relieving population pressure in the old settlements.

After considering the contributions of the plantation system to less developed economies, let us examine its disadvantages. First, the plantation system tends to substitute capital for labor. This is because of the inherent difficulty in supervising wage laborers in spatially dispersed and ecologically diverse farm operations. Second, agricultural lands tend to be cultivated less intensively in the plantation system that employed mainly wage labor and produced essentially a monoculture crop. Complicated crop rotation and crop-livestock combinations are more difficult to manage in the command system. This implies that both labor input and income per hectare were lower in the plantations. In contrast, small-sized family farms, tend to cultivate land more intensively.

Third, plantations usually specialize in a single crop. This bias for the production of a monocrop reduces the flexibility of these productive organizations to respond to changing demand by shifting to the production of other crops. Moreover, continual cropping of a single crop tends to result in soil degradation and an increase in pest incidence. Counter application of fertilizer and chemicals causes serious stress on environment and human health.

Fourth, the specialization of plantation workers in specific tasks inhibits the development of their managerial and entrepreneurial capacity (Baldwin, 1956; Myint, 1965; Beckford, 1972).

Fifth, the plantation system is the source of class conflicts between laborers and managers/capitalists. The presence of a plantation enclave in rural economies where the peasant mode of production predominates has often strained relationships in rural communities. In terms of the criterion of social stability, therefore, the plantation system is no match to the system of relatively homogeneous small producers owning small assets, however small they might be.

Overall, whether the net contribution of the plantation system is positive or negative depends on the man–land ratio of the region, the development of public infrastructure, the nature of the crop produced, and the quality of management employed in plantations. It is, however, inevitable that the negative impact of the plantation system tends to outweigh its positive contributions as population increases in once-sparsely populated regions and as unused lands become scarce.

8.5 TOWARD A STRUCTURAL REORGANIZATION

In view of the increasing negative aspects of plantations as tropical economies shift from the land-abundant to the land-scarce stage, what structural reorganization may be desirable for sustaining growth with equity? Through the painful experiments of the former Soviet Union and other socialist countries, cooperative and state farm operations have proved incapable of achieving this goal.

The design of a new structure must be based on a clear understanding of the pros and cons of the plantation versus the peasant system. The advantage of the peasant system is the high work incentive and the low cost of enforcing family labor, so that peasants are capable of managing complicated crop rotation and crop–livestock combination by making productive use of low-opportunity-cost labor on scarce land. The advantages of the plantation system are (i) the low transaction costs associated with the supply of farm-produced materials to central processing and/or marketing characterized by scale economies, (ii) internalization of external effects such as provision of public infrastructure and prevention of contagious pest and disease, and (iii) low credit costs.

These advantages of the two systems can be combined in the so- called "contract farming" system in which an agribusiness enterprise manages the processing/marketing process and contracts with small growers on the assured supply of farm-produced raw materials. The contract may include stipulations not only on the time and quantity of material supply but also on prices, credit and technical extension services.[4]

A gradual reorganization of the existing plantation system into an efficient contract-farming system appears quite feasible, provided that the multinationals apply their high management capability to this endeavor. Under present conditions, however, since the prevailing mode of plantation management is both efficient and profitable, the multinationals do not see the need for such a reorganization.

Thus, a policy design is necessary to create an incentive mechanism to induce efforts for organizational change toward that direction. The design might include (i) gradual phasing-out of special treatments, such as public land leases at favorable terms and special allocation of import licenses and foreign exchange, and (ii) more strict application of labor and environment codes to corporate farms. At the same time, government must invest in education, research, and extension for developing the capability of small growers to operate effectively the contract farming scheme.

Another approach might be to encourage the organization of cooperatives for processing and marketing. Inefficiency in organizing farm production by cooperatives has been amply illustrated by the experiments of centrally planned as well as some market economies. On the other hand, examples of successful cooperatives in organizing agricultural product marketing and processing are not rare, for example, horticultural marketing cooperatives in Netherlands and cooperative creameries in Denmark. The best services of marketing and processing will be provided to both consumers and farm producers in an environment in which cooperatives and private marketing agents compete with each other and among themselves. Their services are bound to degenerate if monopoly is granted to the cooperatives, as demonstrated by the Japanese experience (Hayami, 1988).

Plantations have been and will continue to be an important sector in tropical Asia. While negative aspects of plantations have been looming larger over time, government direct controls on their operations will likely prove damaging to both national development and the well-being of rural people. The entrepreneurship and management capability of agribusiness enterprises, including multinational corporations, in the area of agricultural marketing and processing are very valuable inputs that developing economies can not afford to lose. The rational approach, therefore, should be to design an inducement mechanism toward an agrarian organization that may be able to combine the merits of both the plantation and peasant systems.

Notes

1. In a broader definition, for example, Jones (1968), farm estates based on forced labor, such as slavery, corvee, and serf, instead of free wage labor may also be called plantations. These estates based on forced labor were established typically before the onset of the industrial revolution in Europe and North America. They had a major impact on United States South and Latin America (*hacienda*), as well as Eastern Europe (such as the Junker estates in Prussia) but had little effect in Asia. The plantations dealt with in this chapter are those established in tropical Asia in the late nineteenth to the early twentieth century. From the beginning their operations were based on wage laborers, even though many laborers were imported from densely populated

economies such as China and India under long-term contracts, often tied by credit, akin to debt peonage.

2. A typical expression is found in Boeke (1953). For a sociological perspective on peasants' motivation and behavior, see Rogers (1969).
3. Among less important crops, sisal and pineapple are also characterized by strong scale economies for the same reason as for tea and banana that shall be explained below.
4. This is the system under consideration in the privatization of state-owned plantations in Indonesia.

   As evidence for viability of this option in tropical Asia, see my comprehensive report on field visits to sugar plantations in the Philippines: Hayami, Quisumbing and Adriano (1990, Chs. 5 and 6).

References

Baldwin, Robert E. (1956) "Patterns of Development in Newly Settled Regions," *Manchester School of Economics and Social Studies*, 24 (May): 161–79.

Barker, Randolph, and Herdt, Robert W. (1985) *The Rice Economy of Asia* (Washington, D.C.: Resources for the Future: distributed by The Johns Hopkins University Press).

Bauer, P. T. (1948) *The Rubber Industry* (London: Longman & Green).

Beckford, George L. (1972) *Persistent Poverty: Underdevelopment in Plantation Economies of the Third World* (New York: Oxford University Press).

Binswanger, Hans P. and Rosenweig, Mark R. (1986). "Behavioural and Material Determinants of Production Relations in Agriculture," *Journal of Development Studies*, 22–3 (April): 503–39.

Boeke, Julius S. (1953) *Economics and Economic Policy of Dual Societies as Exemplified by Indonesia* (New York: Institute of Pacific Relations).

Booth, Anne (1988) *Agricultural Development in Indonesia* (Sydney: Allen & Unwin).

Brewster, John M. (1950) "The Machine Process in Agriculture and Industry," *Journal of Farm Economics*, 32–1 (February): 69–81.

Craig, J. Edwin (1970) "Ceylon," in W. Arthur Lewis, ed., *Tropical Development 1880–1913* (London: Allen & Unwin) pp. 221–49.

de Janvry, Alain (1981) *The Agrarian Question and Reformism in Latin America* (Baltimore: Johns Hopkins University Press).

Feeny, David (1982). *The Political Economy of Productivity: Thai Agricultural Development 1880–1975* (Vancouver: University of British Columbia Press).

Geertz, Clifford (1970) *Agricultural Involution: The Process of Ecological Change in Indonesia* (Berkeley and Los Angeles: University of California Press).

Hayami, Yujiro (1988) *Japanese Agriculture under Siege: The Political Economy of Agricultural Policies* (London: Macmillan).

Hayami, Yujiro, Quisumbing, Ma. Agnes and Adriano, Lourdes S. (1990) *Toward an Alternative Land Reform Paradigm: A Philippine Perspective* (Quezon City, Philippines: Ateneo de Manila University Press).

Kautsky, Karl (1899) *Die Agrarfrage* (Stuttgart: Dietz).

Jones, William O. (1968) "Plantations," in *International Encyclopedia of the Social Sciences*, vol. 12 (New York: Macmillan and Free Press) pp. 154–59.

Lenin, Vladimir I. (1960; original publication, 1899) *The Development of Capitalism in Russia: The Process of Formation of a Home Market for Large-scale Industry*, vol. 3, pp. 23–607 in Lenin, *Collected Works*, 4th ed. (Moscow: Foreign Languages House).

Lewis, W. Arthur (1969) *Aspects of Tropical Trade, 1883–1965* (Stockholm: Almqvist & Wiksell).

Lewis, W. Arthur (1970), "The Export Stimulus," in W. Arthur Lewis, ed., *Tropical Development, 1880–1913* (London: Allen & Unwin) pp. 13–45.

Lim, Youngil (1968) "Input of the Tea Industry on the Growth of the Ceylonese Economy," *Social and Economic Studies* 17–4 (December): 453–67.

Marx, Karl (1909; original publication, 1867) *Capital: A Critique of Political Economy, Vol. I: The Process of Capital Production* (Chicago: Kerr).

Mitrany, David (1951) *Marx Against the Peasant* (Durham, NC: University of North Carolina Press).

Myint, Hla (1965) *The Economics of Developing Countries* (New York: Praeger).

Nurkse, Ragner (1953) *Problems of Capital Formation in Underdeveloped Countries* (Oxford: Basil Blackwell).

Pim, Alan (1946) *Colonial Agricultural Production* (London: Royal Institute of International Affairs and New York: Oxford University Press).

Rogers, Everett M. (1969) "Motivations, Values, and Attitudes of Subsistence Farmers: Toward a Subculture of Peasantry," in Clifton R. Wharton, Jr., ed., *Subsistence Agriculture and Economic Development* (Chicago: Aldine) pp. 111–35.

Schultz, Theodore W. (1964) *Transforming Traditional Agriculture* (New Haven, CT: Yale University Press).

Thoburn, John T. (1977) *Primary Commodity Exports and Economic Development* (London: John Wiley & Sons).

UN-FAO (1981) *1970 World Census of Agriculture, Analysis, and International Comparison of Results* (Rome: United Nations Food and Agriculture Organization).

Van Leeuwen, Robert J. (1970) "Indonesia," in W. Arthur Lewis, ed., *Tropical Development, 1880–1913* (London: Allen & Unwin) pp. 250–82.

Wickizer, V. D. (1951) *Coffee, Tea, and Cocoa: An Economic and Political Analysis* (Stanford: Stanford University Press).

Wickizer, V. D. (1960) "The Smallholder in Tropical Export Crop Production," *Food Research Institute Studies*, 1-1 (February): 49–99.

Wickizer, V. D. and Bennet, M. K. (1941) *The Rice Economy of Monsoon Asia* (Stanford, CA: Food Research Institute).

9 Traders and Development*

Peter Bauer and
Gerald M. Meier

This essay emphasizes the positive contributions of traders to the development process, especially in its early phases.

When economists discuss wholesaling and retailing in advanced Western economies they focus on such subjects as the organization of these activities, the nature and extent of competition, concentration, economies of scale, vertical integration, and restrictive practices. The emphasis is on the efficiency in the provision of distributive services — in broad terms, the link between production and consumption. It is unusual to examine the possibility of any relationship between the activities of traders and the growth of the economy, except to the extent that efficiency in the provision of their services releases resources for other purposes. In short, the emphasis is on the allocation of given resources. In this respect, trading activity is treated very much like any other branch of economic activity.

This orientation is justified. It focuses on the main issues of interest to both economists and policy-makers. But this orientation, though appropriate now, would be misleading if it were applied to the same economies as they were two or more centuries ago. Yet in that earlier period those economies were in many ways far more advanced than most of the less developed countries (LDCs) today. In particular, they were already very largely exchange economies in which subsistence or near subsistence production was relatively unimportant. It has been recognized by some historians that the economic repercussions of trading activities in, say, seventeenth- and eighteenth-century England went well beyond those of efficiency in the use of resources in the trading activities themselves. For example, the authors of a book on shopkeeping in eighteenth century England conclude:

> If the major purpose of all these activities by shopkeepers was to drum up business, by so doing they eased the flow of goods and at the same time helped to stimulate as well as satisfy an increasingly widespread

*This is a revised and extended version of "Traders and the Development Frontier," in Peter Bauer, *The Development Frontier: Essays in Applied Economics* (Cambridge, Massachusetts: Harvard University Press, 1991), pp. 1–5.

> demand, a demand that encouraged expansion in industry and overseas trade. It was not an unimportant contributor to the overall economic development of the country — industry, overseas trading and inland distribution moved in tandem, each fructifying the other.[1]

Professor Jacob Price has observed that in seventeenth- and eighteenth-century Britain the activities of merchants "left behind" much more than "specific markets for specific products." Their activities helped to create commercial institutions and practices and to raise the level of human capital, which proved to be "of great utility to the entire economy in the ensuing era of rapid industrialization and attendant export growth".[2] Richard Grassby wrote that it was "merchant capital which created markets, financed manufacturers, floated the American colonial economies and launched banking and insurance".[3]

And in the words of Adam Smith, a contemporary observer, "the habits besides of order, economy and attention to which mercantile business naturally forms a merchant render him much fitter to execute, with profit and success in any project of improvement".[4]

These observations about trading activity in seventeenth- and eighteenth century on the eve of what is still known as the industrial revolution apply at least as cogently to development in many LDCs. Indeed, the historian Sir Keith Hancock has rightly called West Africa "the traders' frontier".[5]

Nevertheless, the pertinent considerations are still ignored in the formulation of official policies in many LDCs, and for that matter are also neglected in many influential academic publications.

As another analyst of markets in developing economies has observed: "marketing has been almost totally neglected in the literature on economic development. Instead, most theoretical and empirical studies in this area stress the importance to development of such things as capital formation, land reform, educational reform, and improved productive techniques."[6] It is suggested that this neglect may be attributed to a number of factors, including the intangibility of marketing, the association of marketing with high-level, not low-level economies, the inattention to marketing problems in economists' competitive models, and allied with this point, the feeling that marketing is a passive, accommodating activity that will be performed somehow once production is increased.[7]

Occupational statistics, especially for the colonial period, have not given due consideration to the number of traders. Other information such as the proportion of the population living in towns and the very large number of dispersed producers of cash crops indicate a large volume of trading activity. A large number of market stall owners and hawkers' licenses reflect a multitude of selling points. But such information provides only an imperfect idea of the multitude of people engaged either part-time or whole-time in selling small quantities of goods or conveying them to dispersed points of sale. In the aggregate, there is an enormous amount of activity the quantitative significance of which is obvious to the observer. The misleading impression created by official statistics derives from the inappropriateness of classification by distinct occupational categories in a less-developed economy in which occupational specialization is imperfect. The economic activity of a large proportion of the population of West Africa, for instance, is better described as the performance of a number of different activities rather than as the pursuit of a definite occupation. In many of the so-called agricultural households the head of the household actually trades part-time even during the normally short farming season, and more actively outside the season, while members of the family trade intermittently throughout the year.[8] Many others outside the agricultural community are also engaged in trade.

Entry into small scale trade is easy, as at this level no technical or administrative skills are required and only very little capital. Trade is attractive even for very low rewards in view of the absence of more profitable alternatives. Women and children are also available for trade, partly for social reasons.[9]

In emerging economies the indispensable task of commodity distribution is expensive relatively to available resources: of the available resources, capital is scarce and unskilled labor is abundant. The multiplicity of traders is the result of the mass use of unskilled labor instead of capital in the performance of the task of distribution. The labor intensity of trading activity reflects in part the low opportunity costs of the time and effort and large numbers of people. The rewards of trading, meager though they may be, are relatively attractive to many because of the absence of more satisfactory alternative sources of employment. There is an extensive demand for the services of intermediaries, and there is a large section of the population available to perform these services at a low supply price in terms of daily earnings.[10]

The report of the East African Royal Commission also called attention to the "Marketing and Distributive System" (Ch. 7, p. 64) and stated:

> Division of labor in Adam Smith's phrase, is the necessary, though very slow and gradual consequence of a certain propensity in human nature … to truck, barter, and exchange one thing for another. This propensity has long been in evidence in East African tribes. More than half a century ago Sir Harry Johnston wrote, "All Africans are fond of trade …

commerce has a great attraction for them. The men and women both make long journeys to sell their goods." It would be a serious mistake to underestimate the importance of commerce among the indigenous populations even today. Dr Chalmers Wright in a valuable report says that the traditional system of commerce which prevails among the indigenous peoples involves every man and woman, and that "in countless daily transactions, commodities produced by Africans are exchanged, whether simultaneously or in separate operations, whether with or without the use of money, for other commodities produced by Africans" ... "This indigenous commerce," he adds, "must not be confused with the distributive system in occidental and oriental peasant societies. The rural shopkeeper who devotes himself more or less exclusively appears to be generally unknown to African societies." This does not mean that African shops do not exist. There are, indeed, thousands of Africans shops in East Africa.

Economic development begins with the replacement of subsistence activities by production for sale. There is a need for some economic agents to activate the "vent for surplus". Production for sale is not possible without an outlet. Moreover, producers will move out of subsistence only if they see an advantage in doing so. All production of cash crops usually also requires the purchase of some inputs. Traders provide outlets and they supply consumption goods and inputs. Consumption goods serve as incentive goods (a term that has largely dropped out of the contemporary development literature), thereby widening the horizons of producers by showing the possibilities of a more varied and richer pattern of consumption. It helps to overcome what has sometimes been called the wantlessness of backward peoples.

Some have claimed that the international operation of the "demonstration effect" has been a handicap for a poor country. It is argued that the demonstration of advanced consumption in rich countries has excessively raised the propensity to consume in the poorer countries and has thereby limited capital accumulation.[11] To the extent that the demonstration effect operates in favor of raising the consumption of imported commodities, it operates *pari passu* on the incentives to work and produce more. Classical economists stressed the incentive side of the demonstration effect, and from the standpoint of accelerating development, this may well outweigh the effect on the consumption side. When the transition to an exchange economy has not been completed, the demonstration effect stimulates more effort to create a marketable surplus of agricultural products since the ability to purchase new types of consumer goods depends on money income. Extension of the exchange economy entails greater specialization and increased production, and eventually, additional saving. The general point is that the demonstration effect tends to stimulate the "aspiration to consume" as well as the "propensity to consume"; as long as it affects the aspiration to consume, it may actually lead to greater effort and more production.

Traders both large and small create new opportunities. With their knowledge of the requirements of local, regional, and export markets, traders provide outlets for farm products. They buy the traditional products and at the same time acquaint farmers with new products and the methods of growing them. Further, they make available to them the necessary inputs such as seeds, fertilizers, and implements. Thus the traders encourage new wants, convey new opportunities, and help farmers to take advantage of them. The activities of traders set in motion and maintain the process by which participation in the exchange economy replaces subsistence production.

Considering a peasant export economy, Myint also connected the activities of trade with the introduction of money.[12] In a peasant export economy, at the beginning of each trading year, the foreign export import firms brought in a certain amount of circulating capital in the form of trade goods and "cash". The "cash" may be British shillings as in the earlier phase in the African countries or sterling converted into local currency at a fixed exchange rate. In either case there was a sufficient inflow of the medium of exchange to transact the foreign trade. After the annual harvest was exported, the entire amount of circulating capital — i.e., the value of trade goods and cash — was turned over with a large profit margin and repatriated, the whole process taking place all within the same trading year covered by the trade statistics. Hence the export surplus in peasant export economies right from the beginning of the "opening up" process. In contrast, in a mining economy, long-term capital investment had to be sunk for many years before the profits could be repatriated in the form of an export surplus.

One implication of the "vent-for-surplus" theory is that anything which contributes to the increase in output, including export production, may be regarded as "capital". Thus "capital" in this sense would emphasize circulating capital in the form of cheap consumer goods that provided the incentive to peasants to expand exports and also the local knowledge and skills of traders and money lenders who contributed to the export expansion. Moreover, the colonial monetary arrangements were an economical way of financing exports, because different peasant export economies had different harvest periods. Thus the circulating capital that flowed into one country during its harvest season, after being repatriated with profits, promptly flowed into another peasant economy with a different harvest season. This continual "rolling over" of capital funds among different countries contributed to a lowering of transaction costs and interest charges.

In view of the various contributions of traders, it is misleading to look upon the network of traders in an LDC as serving as only a pipeline for conveying from producer to consumer a given volume and composition of output. Although the traders are not trying to transform the economy, their perception and pursuit of opportunities for profit encourage that process.

In many LDCs, large numbers of people in rural areas respond to the incentives and opportunities conveyed to them through traders. That response often involves capital formation. The investment includes the establishment, extension, and improvement of agricultural holdings, taking such forms as the clearing of bush or jungle, the terracing of soil, fencing, drainage, and the planting of crops, often tree crops, which begin to yield returns only after several years. Related categories of investment include consideration of storage facilities and the acquisition of simple farming and transport equipment.

These types of capital formation are often undertaken by farmers with very low incomes. In order to secure improved living standards in the future, they work harder and give up some of their leisure. A large volume of effective capital investment has been undertaken in LDCs by people who are very poor by Western standards.

There is a very large volume of direct investment in agriculture by small-scale producers in LDCs, investment encouraged and made possible by the activities of traders. This category of capital formation is generally ignored in the development literature.[13] This neglect results in a misleading picture of economic activity in LDCs in that it suggests that small farmers there are unable or unwilling to save. Moreover, this disregard of their capital formation has had practical consequences. It means that the repercussions of official policies are not fully recognized. For example, a government wishing to encourage capital formation is likely to frame its taxation rather differently if it recognizes the importance of direct investment in agriculture than if it believes that farmers do not save and invest.

Traders, including small-scale traders, also build up capital in the form of buildings, transport equipment, and stocks of goods. They also often provide credit to their farmer customers, which facilitates both production for the market and capital formation on the farms.

In LDCs traders both use and provide credit. This applies from small-scale traders, even petty traders, to large European and Levantine merchant firms. These firms lend to their trustworthy local customers, mostly substantial traders, who in turn lend on to smaller traders, who then in turn lend to farmers. Thus, at several removes, external finance, including bank finance, provides credit to local traders and farmers.

Many traders in LDCs also own and farm land. Thus they can be classified as farmers as well as traders. The pioneers of manufacturing and processing activities have often come from their ranks. In LDCs traders have been among the first to operate repair shops and transport enterprises, to establish plants for the processing of farm produce (cotton ginneries, for example, and nut-crushing plants), and to set up manufacturing establishments. When such businesses prosper, they can develop into substantial enterprises. Such developments are not surprising. Trading activity, as Adam Smith observed in the passage already quoted, serves as preparation for other economic activities that call for the same attitudes and attributes as does trading itself. All this applies to farmer traders as well — that is, to farmers, often small farmers, who also undertake some trading.

Such movement from trading to other economic activities, including manufacturing, is familiar in the economic history of the advanced economies as well as in the recent history of the contemporary LDCs. In the early history of textile manufacture in Europe, the merchant entrepreneurs occupied a key position as organizers of production, supplying materials to outworkers, providing finance, and marketing the products. In eighteenth-century Britain merchants involved themselves in many financial and industrial enterprises, either directly or as major investors. Such giant enterprises as Royal Dutch Shell and Unilever had their origins in very small trading enterprises established a century or so ago.

In British West Africa in the 1950s, every single successful local industrialist had started his business life as a trader. Much the same is true of Southeast Asia. Indeed, the history of these two regions provides examples of the transformation of large economies in which the role of traders has been critical along the lines analyzed here.

Studies of the role of merchants and marketing in India are particularly instructive. One study of rural merchants, for example, focuses on a "lively and enterprising" group rarely mentioned in the development literature, but one that, by selling hundreds of millions of dollars worth of vital fertilizers and irrigation equipment helped make agricultural gains in India possible.[14] The study suggests that ready made and inexpensive merchant networks could adapt quickly and effectively to other tasks if strong political resistance to a private merchant role can be overcome. It shows that the economic and political rationales that have been put forward for limiting the merchant role are manifestly unsubstantiated. This study contends they are largely a cover for political positions that could not be openly justified. It also proposes that there be a greatly increased use of local merchant networks as promoters and commercializers of development-linked goods and activities. This study shows that such networks are ubiquitous in India, and that they can spread rapidly and flexibly into new geographic and product areas with a minimum of incentive and encouragement.[15]

Another study of marketing in the North Indian sugar industry demonstrates the effectiveness of Indian distribution from the viewpoint of both the Indian economy and of the individual businessman.[16] Of special interest is the positive assessment of the roles of the selling agents, brokers, wholesalers, and retailers.

The process of transformation can also operate, however, in reverse, and this can be observed on the contemporary scene. The maltreatment of traders and the suppression of trading activity in many LDCs, especially in Africa and to some extent in South Asia, have been contributory factors to economic stagnation, retrogression, and even collapse, including reversion to subsistence production with all its hazards. The Sahel, Ethiopia, Tanzania, Uganda, and Zaire have provided examples of such negative, even destructive effects.

The central theme of this essay has been the role of trade in helping to propel and maintain the development of an exchange economy from a subsistence base. Although trading activity in LDCs is highly important in securing the effective deployment of available resources, often in uncongenial conditions, the emphasis here has been on the expansion and advance of an economy, and on the dynamic effects of trade. Trade contributes to material progress in various ways, including among others by the husbanding of scarce resources, notably capital; by the extension of markets, with the resulting promotion of specialization and of production for sale, and thus the creation of an agricultural surplus; by stimulating the accumulation of capital; by bringing to prominence and influence trader-entrepreneurs accustomed to an exchange economy; and by acquainting people with the processes of the exchange economy and promoting the habits and attitudes appropriate to it. Moreover, by linking local communities to the outside world and acquainting people with the habits of a money economy, trade promotes the disintegration of the traditional local attitudes, customs, and institutions.[17]

This emphasis on the dynamic effects of trade has been deliberate because these beneficial effects have been so largely ignored, both in the development literature and development policy.

Notes

1. Hoh-cheung and Lorna H. Mui, *Shops and Shopkeeping in Eighteenth Century England* (London, 1989) pp. 291–92.
2. Jacob M. Price, "What Did Merchants Do? Reflections on British Overseas Trade, 1660–1790," *Journal of Economic History,* 49 (June 1989) pp. 267–284.
3. Richard Grassby, "English Merchant Capitalism in the Late Seventeenth Century," *Past & Present*, no. 46 (February 1970) p. 106.
4. Adam Smith, *The Wealth of Nations* (London, 1776) bk III, Ch. 4.
5. W. K. Hancock, *Survey of British Commonwealth Affairs* (London: Oxford University Press, 1940) vol. II, pt 2, Ch. II.
6. Reed Moyer, *Marketing in Economic Development* (Institute for International Business Management Studies, Michigan State University, 1965) p. 1.
7. Reed Moyer and Stanley C. Hollander, eds., *Markets and Marketing in Developing Economies* (Homewood, Illinois: Richard D. Irwin, Inc., 1968) p. 1.
8. P. T. Bauer and B. S. Yamey, *Markets, Market Control and Marketing Reform* (London: Weidenfeld and Nicolson, 1968) pp. 4–5.
9. *Ibid.*, pp. 6–7.
10. *Ibid.*, pp. 9, 27. The labor-intensity of trading operations in less developed countries has also been noted by others: Sydney W. Mintz, "The Jamaican Internal Marketing Pattern," *Social and Economic Studies*, March 1955; Alice G. Dewey, *Peasant Marketing in Java* (New York, Free Press, 1962); Leon V. Hirsch, *Marketing in an Underdeveloped Economy: The North Indian Sugar Industry* (Englewood Cliffs, N.J.: Prentice-Hall, Inc., 1961).
11. The "international demonstration effect" was first applied to relations between the United States and western European countries in connection with the post-war dollar shortage problem — a situation quite different from development. See W. F. Stolper, "A Note on the Multiplier, Flexible Exchanges and the Dollar Shortage," *Economia Internazionale*, August 1950, pp. 772–73.
12. The following is derived from the summary of a lecture by Myint at the University of Oxford, 1955.
13. Two early examples are *The Indian Second Five Year Plan* (Delhi, 1956) and the World Bank Report on *The Economic Development of Nigeria* (Baltimore, 1955). These influential documents served as models for other countries.
14. Paul A. London, *Merchants as Promoters of Rural Development: An Indian Case Study* (New York: Praeger Publishers, 1975) pp. v–vi.
15. *Ibid.*, p. vi.
16. Leon V. Hirsch, *Marketing in an Underdeveloped Economy: The North Indian Sugar Industry* (Englewood Cliffs, N.J.: Prentice-Hall, Inc., 1961).
17. For elaboration, see P. T. Bauer, "Some Aspects and Problems of Trade in Africa," in Reed Moyer and Stanley C. Hollander, eds., *Markets and Marketing in Developing Economies, op. cit.*, p. 49.

10 Development as a Societal Problem in a Colonial Setting

W. W. Rostow

10.1 INTRODUCTION

This essay focuses on the writings of three pre-1945 analysts of development — Vera Anstey, R. H. Tawney, and Joyce Cary. In so doing, it presents variations on the theme of colonialism and development plus further reflections on two observations made rather tersely in my *Theorists of Economic Growth Since David Hume*.[1]

The first observation was the lack in modern economic development theory of concepts which linked in a systematic way the economics of development to the other dimensions of society — to the process of modernization as a whole, its politics in particular. Reviewing nine of the World Bank's Pioneers in Development, I noted the recurrence in their final reflections, in moods ranging from anguish to outrage to gentle philosophic acceptance, of a sense that bad politics had often frustrated good economics.[2] But there was little serious analysis of the politics or sociology of modernization. I concluded:[3]

> In short, politics was generally more important than economics in the developing world; and the critical political issues were substantially different from those of the advanced industrial countries. Here, I believe, is the reason for the inadequacy of, say, Bauer's plea that aid only be granted to those governments that relied on the market and thus moved toward democracy or, say, Myrdal's and Singer's easy transfer of the canons of the post-1945 social-democratic welfare state in Northwestern Europe to the developing world — a view that Myrdal finally recanted. It will be recalled that others among our pioneers ended up in puzzlement and disappointment at the extent to which politics frustrated the economic development outcomes they envisaged or hoped for.

The second observation was that the central technical debate among development economists between "neoclassicists" and "structuralists" does not make a great deal of sense if it is abstracted from the stage of modernization at which a particular society has arrived and from its current politics.[4]

As for the three analysts discussed here, all took it for granted that the critical problem of the societies examined — that is, massive poverty of the most persistent and degrading kind — could not be permanently alleviated without profound political and social as well as economic change, including escape from colonialism or quasi-colonialism — a process that, as we shall see at the end, took longer than generally reckoned.

Unlike most post-1945 development economists, our central figures related the policy changes they commended to the historical past. Anstey and Tawney were rooted in the vital setting of the inter-war London School of Economics and Political Science, which included two remarkable medieval economic historians, Eileen Power and M. M. Postan. Tawney was himself a towering figure in the analysis of the transition from medieval to modern Europe and a great stylist. A sense of history pervades the work of Anstey and Tawney including sensitivity to — but not rigid analogy with — the complex transformation of early modern Europe from its medieval mold to the industrial revolutions of the late eighteenth and early nineteenth centuries. And when Joyce Cary, colonial civil servant and novelist, came to formulate his views on policy towards Africa, in *The Case for African Freedom* and in later essays, he also included a good deal of historical material, some out-dated by subsequent scholarship, but nevertheless broadly relevant to the Africa he vividly evoked.

The uniqueness of Cary's work on African development, however, lies elsewhere. As the Introduction of the enlarged (1962) edition[5] observed, Cary's study is "a rare example of a creative artist working in a political and economic field".[6] Analytically, this has a special meaning. As an artist, Cary's obsessive concern is the unique human being caught up in the human condition, in his special time and place. Working out from this micro-perspective, Cary arrived in his African novels at precisely the macro-policy conclusions he makes explicit in his later expositions of economic, social, and political policy towards Africa. Much in *Mr Johnson*, for example, clearly foreshadows his policy essays. There is no significant discontinuity between Cary as a novelist and Cary as a politico-economic pamphleteer; although a conventional social scientist, doomed to read the jargon of his profession, is likely to find the freshness of Cary's prose, where every word counts and communicates, a source of delight and, perhaps, despair. As Christopher Fyfe concludes:[7] "What shines through these pages (as through everything he wrote) is Cary's own humanity, his hatred of the theorist who sees people as statistics or concepts, his compassionate concern with people as individuals, not as abstractions."

Against this background, we shall pose three questions of Anstey on India, Tawney on China, Cary on Africa: How did they introduce a dynamic historical perspective into their analyses; how did they link economic analysis to broader societal variables, politics in particular; and how did they relate colonial or neo-colonial relationships to economic development.

10.2 ANSTEY ON INDIA (1929)

When first published, Vera Anstey's *The Economic Development of India* (1929, 1931, 1936) was the product of some 16 years immersion in the facts and problems of Indian life: first, in Bombay (1914–20) with her husband who was for those years Principal of the Sydenham College of Commerce; then, after his death, as a lecturer on Indian economic topics at the London School of Economics and Political Science. Her 600 page study of Indian economic development is the first major synthesis of, even then, a considerable body of literature contained in monographs and official reports; for, however one assesses the virtues and demerits of British rule of India in the first quarter of the twentieth century, it generated a massive volume of data and analyses covering every significant sector of the Indian economy including education, public health, economic and social policy.

To frame her majestic survey and prescription for the future Anstey places India in two settings, one broad, the other narrow.

The first evokes medieval Europe to assist the Western reader grasp the forces that gripped Indian society and impeded its development:[8]

> First and foremost, medievalism is manifested in the striking predominance of religion and its influence on, and control over, every other aspect of life... [it] controls the social activities of all classes, with the numerically very minor exception of a certain proportion of those who have received a Western education.
>
> Next we come to the absence of the idea of progress. It has been said [Eileen Power] that "a great deal of the strangeness between East and West is due to the fact that we of the West habitually measure civilization by an essentially modern criterion, the idea of Progress; and progress in the mind of the average man is apt to be narrowed down to material progress". In the West "material progress" is almost a spiritual thing to the philosophical mind. It entails the possibility of a higher

level of life for the mass of the population, and "opportunity for all, instead of a parasite bloom of civilization, drawing its life from a slave class without hope". But in India earthly existence is still looked upon as but a passing phase, preparatory to the life or lives to come. Hence the ideal of the religious leaders is to subdue the appetites rather than to satisfy them, whether such appetites be their own or those of their fellow-men....

Another feature of Indian society that is strongly reminiscent of medievalism is the nature of the social divisions. As under the feudal system in Europe in the Middle Ages, the social ideal, under the caste system in India to-day, is static, and social divisions are horizontal....

Owing to the prevailing type of social organization, we find that custom, tradition, and superstition continue to predominate, and that the scientific spirit is lacking. It is sometimes assumed that the absence of the scientific attitude is an inherent characteristic of the Indian mind. When, however, we consider the entirely unscientific spirit of the Middle Ages in Europe, the persecution of those who refused to accept authority but insisted on thinking for themselves and testing prevailing assumptions, and when we follow out the history of development and triumph of scientific thought, need we despair of India?...

In many cases the outstanding economic institutions and methods characteristic of mediaeval life, such as the self-sufficing agricultural unit, primitive methods of agricultural and industrial production, and the organization and control of industry and commerce by means of local gilds, still prevail in India. These features are not anything like as strongly marked as they were some fifty, or even some twenty-five, years ago, but they have not yet by any means entirely disappeared.

Thus, as in the modern study of medieval Europe, Anstey viewed India in dynamic terms: in a transition to modernity, but still heavily weighed down by its own, historically determined, medieval past.

She then turns to a highly professional survey of India's resources, physical and human; the economy's institutional structure; a survey of sectors, traditional, transitional, and modern; foreign trade, commerce and finance; the upshot for the people's standard of living; and a remarkably solid and prescient summary and conclusions. Seven appendixes, 35 pages of statistical tables, as well as a thorough bibliography follow.[9]

Although, as indicated earlier, Anstey had the advantage of a large body of compulsively detailed government reports, *The Economic Development of India* is unique in the pre-1945 development literature and remains a worthy beginning for the study of India's modern economic history.

From the perspective of this essay two features of the study warrant further comment: the dynamic and wide-ranging character of the technical chapters; and Mrs Anstey's conclusions.

Together with the discussion of the functional dimensions of the economy, Indian history, social structure, and the evolution of British policy are flexibly interwoven with detailed conventional economic analysis. There is no pedantic, disciplinary self-consciousness as she moves from productivity measurements, to the influence of the caste system, to pre- and post-1900 British policy. This is as true of her casting up the pluses and minuses of the British building and management of the Indian railway system (Chapter VI) as it is for the treatment of public health (Chapter IV) or the Indian land system (Chapter V). She is also quite willing to pause and lay out a basic framework of technical analysis, as she does in capturing in general terms the interaction between public health and the level and pace of economic development (pp. 66–72).

But the unforced societal view Vera Anstey brought to her work is revealed most clearly when, having concluded that India as of 1929 was a case of "arrested economic development", she identifies the obstacles to be overcome if India's development is to proceed with continuity and vigor. Her conclusion, with its primacy for social and political factors — India's independence above all — is worth quotation.[10]

> from the purely material, technical point of view there is no reason why rapid advance should not be made... But I am convinced that no such rapid advance can take place in the absence of fundamental social reorganization....
>
> [I]t can be said that India's economic future depends, in the main, not upon the inauguration of particular schemes of development, or the adoption of particular lines of policy, but upon more fundamental social reforms and reorganization, directed towards controlling the size of the population, breaking up the existing over-rigid social stratification, stimulating enterprise and energy, promoting education, and replacing the forms by the spirit of religion. India is crying out for the persistent and unstinted efforts of her people — male and female — inspired by a clear vision of the potentialities of the future, unshackled by bitter and unavailing reflection upon the past, to help her loosen the bonds of tradition, caste, and superstition. Thus and thus only will she at last attain her rightful position as a free — and free internally, not only externally — and prosperous member of the Commonwealth, not merely of the Empire but of the Nations of the World.

Behind this conclusion was more than rhetoric. Mrs Anstey examines in some detail the intensely debated question of whether India received more from Britain than it transferred to London: the famous question of the "drain".[11] Like a good many others who have dealt with this issue as an analytic problem rather than an item for political debate, she concludes that there were some "financial extravagances and injustices", but, on balance, the Indian economy gained, on a narrow calculus.

In broader terms, however, she concluded that British administration of India was a fundamental obstacle to India's coming to grips with its most basic problems. The following passage typifies her final judgment:[12] "It is a curious paradox that nothing would end British rule in India more quickly than any attempt to introduce just those reforms which would do most to improve the well-being of the masses." Mrs Anstey had in mind, above all, measures to reduce the Indian birth rate.

I shall return later to this paradoxical theme in a broader context.

10.3 TAWNEY ON CHINA (1931–32)[13]

As the title and table of contents of Tawney's study indicate,[14] his focus, in the first instance, is on agriculture and rural life where something like three quarters of a population of about 450 million lived in the 1920s. (The World Bank estimate for 1988 is 50 per cent of a population of 1.1 billion).

In setting a historical framework for his study, Tawney presents a more complex analogy to pre-modern Europe than Anstey's, with both unshared and shared elements of historical experience:[15]

> The hackneyed reference to the Middle Ages is sadly over-worked, and leaves a good deal unsaid. It is misleading, indeed, both in principle and in detail. On the one hand, it implies a comparison of stages of development, as though the Chinese version of civilisation, instead of differing in kind from the European, were merely less mature. On the other hand, it ignores the sharp contrasts between them, not only — the most important point — in spirit and quality, but in circumstance and environment. The most obvious of the economic characteristics of medieval Europe — to mention no other — was that its population was small, its uncultivated area available for colonisation large, and its sea communications of exceptional excellence....
>
> In certain of the arts of production, and, still more, of life, she [China] had been a pioneer. But the era of invention, which in the West followed that of natural science, in China preceded it. Having made her discover-

ies, she left it to peoples of coarser fibre to reap their fruits, as though conscious that her genius required for its expression more sensitive media....

Such contrasts between the static civilisation of China — as it was formerly called — and the more mobile economy of the West are easily drawn and easily misinterpreted. They are misinterpreted when the differences which they emphasise are assumed to be the expression of permanent characteristics. History, with its record of the movement of leadership from region to region, lends little support to the theory that certain peoples are naturally qualified for success in the economic arts, and others unfitted for it, even were the criteria of such success less ambiguous than they are.

The traditionalism which has sometimes been described as a special mark of Chinese economic life is the characteristic, not of China, but of one phase of civilisation which Europe has shared with her. Rapid economic change as a fact, and continuous economic progress as an ideal, are the notes, not of the history of the West, but of little more than its last four centuries; and the European who is baffled by what appears to him the conservatism of China would be equally bewildered could he meet his own ancestors.

Turning to agriculture and rural life, Tawney describes with an expertise acquired in his work on medieval and early modern Europe the quality of the soil, rainfall, land tenure, the regional distribution of crops, agricultural technology, and institutions of credit marketing.

Along the way he underlines several striking features of the still basically traditional character of Chinese agriculture. First, it was not feudal:[16] "Agriculture, in China is a peasant industry. It is the business of some seventy million farmers and their families. Small-scale cultivation may co-exist with a regime of great landed estates ... But there is no landed aristocracy in China; When great estates are formed, they normally disappear in a few generations by division among heirs...." Second, Tawney notes the sharp demographic distinction between China and Medieval Europe: rural population pressed, in a painful Malthusian cycle, against arable land in the former case, generating extraordinary skills in irrigation and the control of the water supply. There was still a good deal of available frontier land in the latter. Relative to most European farmers, the Chinese was a gardener working a small plot with great intensity, using sophisticated but traditional methods. Third, pressed close to the margin of subsistence the Chinese farmer was extremely vulnerable to flood and drought, war and famine.

Thus, although China's geography and soil as well as land tenure, social system, and politics differed from India's, the consequences for the peasant family were much the same in the sense that the margin of subsistence was an almost visible presence and there was no long term expectation that the lives of grandchildren would differ much from that of their grandparents.

Tawney draws his portrait of Chinese rural life to a close in a chapter of synthesis and prescription: "The Possibilities of Rural Progress." He first distinguishes two types of problems: those indigenous to the physical circumstances of Chinese agriculture; and those stemming from "defects of economic organization or in social habits".[17] Both, he argues, must be recognized in a development program where "[It] is necessary to eschew both the facile sentimentalism which makes light of the burdens imposed by nature, and the fatalism which ignores the possibilities of social art. In so far as the disorders of Chinese agriculture belong to the second category, they are acute in degree but not unique in kind. They are one species of a genus which has been widely diffused, and which is characteristic, not of this nation or that, but of a particular phase of economic civilization."[18] Thus, gracefully, Tawney moves over from the analysis of a unique society to the biology of growth and, then, to public policy.

Drawing on elements of experience in the individual countries of Europe, India, and China itself, as well as the quite different circumstances of machine farming in land-rich Russia and the United States, he distills an agenda for agricultural progress:[19]

> Communications, science and education, co-operation in credit and marketing, and the formation, where possible, of compact farms out of dispersed fragments of land, appear everywhere, in short, to be the fundamental conditions of agricultural progress.

Tawney then proceeds to explore the possibilities and problems of moving forward on each agenda item in China. He concludes by arguing that although an agricultural program along those lines is fundamental to ameliorating the pathology of Chinese rural life, it can not, in itself assure a substantial advance in the standard of life of the rural population:[20]

> The larger problems are of a kind with which these and similar well-intentioned reforms do not begin to cope. The fundamental fact, it is urged, is of a terrible simplicity. It is that the population of China is too large to be supported by existing resources. While, in China as a whole, its mean density is low compared with that of most western countries, in certain areas it is appalling. Whole provinces, as large as European

> states, may properly be described as congested districts. The struggle of a swarm of human beings for a bare physical existence is an ever present reality. All the phenomena of rural distress — minute holdings, tiny incomes, female infanticide, starvation — are the unavoidable result of it ... Famine is the economic, civil war the political, expression of the pressure of population on the means of subsistence.

At this point Tawney examines the real but limited possibilities and turns to the potential creative role of industrialization. "The deliberate limitation of the size of families" he leaves for later.

With great compression Tawney draws a striking portrait of the organization of traditional industry in China that still dominated when he wrote:[21] "The industrial system characteristic of China is that which predominated in most regions of the west till the nineteenth century."

Turning to the enclaves of modern industry, he notes that they are "preponderant" in the ports; limited but growing along the lines of rivers and railways; with limited impact and virtually no local roots in the hinterland. Regions containing 10 per cent of the area of China (36 per cent of the population) accounted at that time for 92 per cent of foreign trade, 53 per cent of railways, 42 per cent of motor roads, 64 per cent of coal and iron-ore production, 93 per cent of cotton yarn, 92 per cent of silk reeled, 87 per cent of electric power capacity.

Would modern industrialization spread across the face of China? With this question Tawney launches a subtle, multi-dimensional analysis that occupies roughly the last third of his book. Here, in summary, is the sequence of his argument.

— The catching up of other countries with Britain's initial industrial leadership came, in some cases, swiftly; for example, Germany and Japan:[22] "Once the ice is broken, the current is apt to run, given the necessary conditions, with surprising rapidity."

— The necessary conditions did not exist in China over the past century — neither peace, nor adequate communications, nor a strong national government, nor an adequate agricultural base, nor an indigenous entrepreneurial class:[23] "What is surprising in such circumstances ... is not that the modernization of industry has taken place gradually, and in isolated areas, but that it has taken place at all."

— As for the future, Tawney arrives at his most profound insight:[24]

> If China desires to modernise her industry, it is improbable that she will continue for long to be baulked merely by the existence of psychological obstacles.

Does she genuinely desire it? Or is her real aim a more subtle one — to use western technique as an instrument, while resisting domination by the mentality behind it? Only a Chinese can say, and, perhaps, not even he.

Chinese who applaud the triumphs of the machine rarely mean what the West means when it uses the same phrases. The latter hails it as a master, the former accept it as a servant. When they reflect on the weakness of their own country in the face of foreign Powers, they feel like a giant outwitted by a dwarf. They admire the devices which give success to the barbarian, as a European may admire the skill of a native tracker who follows game through the bush, or kindles a camp fire by rubbing sticks. To neutralise his capacity for mischief, so prodigious and incalculable, and gain what is good he has to offer, they must master his tricks. But tricks, after all, are but tricks; means are means, and nothing more. Apart from a handful of ex-students educated in America, most Chinese would as little dream of succumbing to the philosophy of the West, and endorsing its ends, as the European of exchanging his life for that of the bushman.

Their reactions to industrialism are, consequently, not simple and decided, but complex and hesitating. They would take the thing, for it is useful, but they would take it on their own terms; wise men, who know good and evil, do not surrender their souls. It is a question, in short, not of acceptance or imitation, but of adaptation and adjustment. Adjustment demands time, and one reason for the slow advance of economic change in China, compared with its swift progress in Japan, is psychological. It is that an interval is required in which the alien elements can be digested and assimilated. In the process of assimilation those elements themselves undergo a subtle sublimation. Fused with their Chinese environment, they change their chemistry; they take up new properties, which blend with and transform them. Whether, thus qualified and subdued, capitalist industry will retain the economic qualities which constitute its attraction, only time can show; but one prophecy may be hazarded. It is that, like all other movements which have been imported from abroad and acclimatised in China, it will be propagated in a Chinese version or not at all.

... The long view is one thing, the short another. Whether the space between them is to be measured by decades or by centuries, a stranger cannot say. The conditions of economic progress — peace; cheap and easy communications; a uniform and stable currency; the ruthless curtailment of military expenditure; the widest possible diffusion of education among all sections of the population; the formation of a body of competent technicians; reasonable sense and honesty in the management of affairs of state and of corporate undertakings; the improvement of agriculture and, thereby, of the home market; measures to prevent the exploitation of the cheap labour which is the curse of Chinese industry and a perpetual clog upon the improvement of its technique — such commonplaces are as familiar in China as in the West. The difference between them appears to be that, while part of the latter are relapsing into poverty by destroying some of these prerequisites of prosperity, China remain in poverty through the slow growth of all of them.

An observer may suspect that the political and social impediments to her industrial development will not be permanent, but he has no means of gauging the rate of their disappearance.

After concluding that the physical endowments of China are adequate for widespread industrialization, Tawney identifies three economic imperatives for success:[25] improved communications; tariffs for "manufacturing industries ... struggling to their feet in the teeth of the competition of well-established rivals..."; and a "Scheme of Priorities" implemented effectively by an administrative unit of a strong national government. (Tawney drew cautious comfort from the creation in November 1931 of a National Economic Council.)

But he finds critically important obstacles in the social, psychological and political circumstances of China in an early stage of the transition from a traditional to an industrial society. First, the excessive birth rate. Tawney is quite explicit about the demographic transition but notes correctly that the birth rate does not move decisively downward until "some two generations" of industrialization have passed. China can not, therefore expect early demographic relief from industrialization. On the contrary, measures of public health may raise the rate of population increase in the short run. On economic grounds he advocates "substituting the deliberate restriction of births for the removal of part of the surplus by death" — the reigning form of population control in traditional China.[26]

Second, as the good Fabian he was, Tawney concerns himself with the social conditions and real wage of industrial labor in a society experiencing the pressure of excessive population increase. In China's industrial enclaves he clearly feels himself back in Great Britain of the 1840s. He advocates trade unionism and industrial legislation;[27] and he elaborates a program along lines that would impose standards "...not on any plan of impracticable excellence, but at the highest level which undertakings conducted with reasonable efficiency can at any given moment attain, and shall periodically be raised".[28]

In a final chapter Tawney turns to what he regards as the basic and overriding task for the Chinese to create "a stable and unified political system, in the absence of which it is idle to talk either of national independence or of economic reconstruction".[29]

Earlier Tawney, in an economic context, had quoted Sun Yat Sen's description of China as a colony.[30] The Opium Wars, the Japanese invasion of 1895, and the extra-territorial rights extracted from the Chinese created a semi-colonial situation in China heightened by the pressure of Russia and Japan on the North after the turn of the century and the role of Germans and other foreigners in the railways and mines. But 1931 was the year of the Japanese take-over of Manchuria. The issue of national independence was inescapable. Tawney argued:[31] "Unequal treaties, extra-territoriality, concessions, the Manchurian question — these matters, if China succeeds in setting her own house in order, will settle themselves. Unless she does so, they will not be settled at all."

Tawney then pulls back and explains why China, a unified civilization rather than a modern state of the West, had been able to survive without strong central government. But that was no longer the case. Anticipating the conclusion painfully arrived at by most of the World Bank's Development Pioneers forty year later, Tawney concludes:[32] "... in the present circumstances of China, the *Maxim économique prime la politique* is less true than its converse". He proceeds in some detail with a practical vision of how the Nationalist government, with the help of the League of Nations, might develop a system of efficient administration over a limited area and then gradually extend it over the country. This process would require rapid expansion and improvement in the quality of education on which Tawney comments shrewdly:[33]

> Questions of organisation, though important, are not the central problem. The root of the matter was expressed, perhaps, by the Chinese president of a university, when he complained that the universities were on the way to be commercialised.... As a result, it is hardly an exaggeration to say that in some of them everyone graduates and no one is educated. What a country requires, however, is men with education, not graduates without it.

Tawney, a man of university life, then proposes six essential administrative measures for the Chinese university system.

Tawney's essay on development, clearly one of the best such pieces ever written, closes with a peroration that still has meaning for mainland China more than sixty years later:[34]

> Much talk of the Westernisation of China is remote from realities. It is a kind of incantation, which proceeds, not only from foreigners, but, occa-

sionally, also from Chinese themselves. ...Conscious of the feebleness of their country, and eager for its progress, they would lift its burden by transplanting to it the apparatus of material prosperity whose vast power has dazzled them. China requires, it is true, the scientific and technological equipment of the West; poverty and weakness such as she endures to-day are dreadful evils. If western nations could bring themselves, instead of regarding her as a field of enterprise, to realise that, on a long view, her major interests are also theirs, and to help her to attain them, they would reap a harvest of gratitude which would more than repay them. But the problem is more complicated....

[T]he imitation of America or Europe, which has profoundly influenced Chinese education, offers no solution of the deeper problems of China. It was a necessary stage in her evolution; till she knew the West, she could not fully know herself.... But, though a nation may borrow its tools from abroad, for the energy to handle them it must look within.

Erquickung hast du nicht gewonnen,
Wenn sie dire nicht aus eigner Seele quillt.
(One does not achieve rejuvenation
unless it arises from one's own soul.)

It is in herself alone in her own historical culture, rediscovered and reinterpreted in the light of her modern requirements, that China will find the dynamic which she needs. The most fundamental achievements of her revolution are still to come. The problem is to translate political rejuvenation into the practical terms of social institutions, and to build with a modern technique, but on Chinese foundations. It is to her schools and universities that she must look for the builders.

10.4 CARY ON AFRICA

Before turning to Cary's more conventional work, *The Case For African Freedom*, we should consider briefly the best of his African novels, *Mr Johnson*, characterized by Christopher Fyfe as "...one of the most moving and perceptive pictures of the British colonial situation ever made".[35] As intended, however, it is a novel not a political tract. Mr. Johnson is a boy called up from a mission school to be temporary clerk to the local British administrator, Judge Rudbeck. But he belongs, in fact, with Cary's gallery of incandescent personalities, touched with grace, believing in their own magic. Mr Johnson ends up executed with reluctance and compassion by his British master, as a thief and murderer, by a shot in the back of his head rather than the hanging that should legally have taken place. Perhaps only Cary could have reconciled that tragic denouement with this, his own picture of the character he created:[36] "Mr Johnson is a young clerk who turns his life into a romance, he is a poet who creates for himself a glorious destiny." And then, responding to critics of his narration of the novel in the present tense, Cary goes on:[37] "And as Johnson swims gaily on the surface of life, so I wanted the reader to swim, as all of us swim, with more or less courage and skill, for our lives."

Mr Johnson's romance is with the modern world as he perceives it through the prism of British administration. At one point he says to an old native trader: "Come then, Mr Benjamin — we are going to be rich soon. We go home to England, we see the King and Pallament."

> He begins to sing "England is my home, de King of England is my King," and dances with the peculiar, loose, boneless step which expresses his patriotic sentiment.

Closer to home is the story of Judge Rudbeck's motor road — a symbol of modernization. Its native advocates argued it would bring "Traders to the village wanting shelter from the men and food from the women. Along this road motors will come to take them and their produce to market."[38] It is Mr Johnson who galvanizes the work force and, in a paroxysm of effort, as pipers and drummers set the pace,

> work becomes a kind of festivity, something between a spree and a battle … Johnson in a torn pair of trousers and a carrier's straw hat, is chopping, swearing or singing, improvising and exhorting from before dawn till long after dark. He is always dirty, streaked with layers of sweat and dirt in which the new sweat trickles crookedly like water on a varnished boat, leaving bright black trails.… He doesn't feel anything except music, noise, the movement of the work, the approbation and nearness of Rudbeck and Rudbeck's triumph which is his own. He lives in this glory, which is expressed by every yell, in every obscene joke, kick, jump or swing of the matchet. He does not need to think, "Rudbeck's road, the great, the glorious, the wonder of the world, is about to be finished and I have helped to finish it. He knows it in every muscle."[39]

But when it is all over, Rudbeck has second thoughts:[40]

The road itself seems to speak to him. "I'm smashing up the old Fada — I shall change everything and everybody in it. I am abolishing the old ways, the old ideas, the old law; I am bringing wealth and opportunity for good as well as vice, new powers to men and therefore new conflicts. I am the revolution. I am giving you plenty of trouble already, you governors, and I am going to give you plenty more. I destroy and I make new. What are you going to do about it? I am your idea. You made me, so I suppose you know."

Rudbeck, staring at the road, feels rather than understands this question and he feels again a sense of confusion and frustration.

Mr Johnson's romance with his British connection and the modern world he glimpses is only part of the story. In the background is the round of life of an impoverished traditional society. At its best, it is captured by the beautiful ferryman's daughter whom Mr Johnson marries, a child of her family and tribe, untouched by the fevered dreams of her husband.

Here is Cary's stark portrait of the physical setting of life:[41]

Fada is the ordinary native town of the Western Sudan. It has no beauty, convenience or health. It is a dwelling-place at one stage from the rabbit warren or the badger burrow; and not so cleanly kept as the latter. It is a pioneer settlement five or six hundred years old, built on its own rubbish heaps, without charm even of antiquity. Its squalor and its stinks are all new. Its oldest compounds, except the Emir's mud box, is not twenty years old. The sun and the rain destroy all its antiquity, even of smell. But neither has it the freshness of the new. All its mud walls are eaten as if by smallpox; half of the mats in any compound are always rotten. Poverty and ignorance, the absolute government of jealous savages, conservative as only the savage can be, have kept it at the first frontier of civilization. Its people would not know the change if time jumped back fifty thousand years. They live like mice or rats in a palace floor; all the magnificence and variety of the arts, the ideas, the learning and the battles of civilization go on over their heads and they do not even imagine them.

Fada has not been able to achieve its own native arts or the characteristic beauty of its country. There are no flowering trees or irrigated gardens; no painted or moled courtyard walls.

The young boys, full of curiosity and enterprise, grow quickly into old, anxious men, content with mere existence. Peace has been brought to them, but no glory of living; some elementary court-justice, but no liberty of mind. An English child in Fada with eyes that still see what is in front of them, would be terrified by the dirt, the stinks, the great sores on naked bodies, the twisted limbs, the babies with their enormous swollen stomachs and the hernias; the whole place, flattened upon the earth like the scab on a wound, would strike it as something between a prison and hospital.

Nevertheless, it is to his native life, and ties to nature that Mr Johnson turns as he chants his farewell, with the Sergeant guarding him and a few friends joining in:.

> "We'll be sorry to say good-by."
> "So will I, friends. Have some more whisky? I don't mind hanging, but I dont want to say good-by."
> "Oom-oom-aah," Button-stick sings:
> "I said good-by to my little house.
> "Good-by, my little house, my little dog".
> Stink-fish, Johnson and Button-stick sway together, to the rhythm of Button-stick's oboe and the sergeant's soft hand-clapping. Then Pepper and Stink-fish join in:
> "Good-by, my little father, my little mother.
> "I'm going for the white man's war."
> Good-by, my little river, my little village.
> "Good-by, my sun," Johnson sings in English.
> "Good-by, my wind."
> Good-by, my rivers, wash me with your soft hand.
> Good-by, my worl', good-by, my father worl'.
> Good-by my mother sky, stretch your arms all round.

Thus, Cary captured Africa, starting thousands of years back, caught between two worlds, attracted, baffled, and demeaned by its colonial masters and the civilization from which they came — masters profoundly uncertain of the right course to follow as they perceived the acuteness of the dilemma into which they had stumbled.

The Case for African Freedom explores the dilemma that Cary defines quite lucidly. It turns out to be a double dilemma.

First, is the ultimate case for granting independence by the colonial power:[42]

> In many parts of Africa racial feeling enforces a strong moral case. The natives feel not only the bitterness of race discrimination but a sense of moral outrage. They say to whites: "You call yourselves Christian people and you treat us like animals. When you first came to our country, you hunted us like vermin. Now you have taken us captive, you keep us as beasts of burden, pack horses, plough mules."

African governments have sometimes tried to ignore the moral charge; none of them has been able to forget the danger of a race war.

Second, if the convergence of morality and the need to avoid a race war argue for early independence, the nature of development argues that the colonial power, having for whatever reasons, assumed the responsibility of rule, must act to prepare the society for modernity and civilized self-rule with whatever time history may grant:[43]

> You cannot give liberty to people by a wave of the hand, as you throw open a cage. If you attempted it you would find that your victims, like cage birds turned loose, would only injure or poison themselves. They would be lucky if, more or less damaged, they found at last another cage, however small, to creep into.
>
> The whole conception of producing freedom by a sudden political act belongs to a school of thought which never did face the root problem of liberty; which did actually believe, or try to believe, that Robinson Crusoe had more liberty than an ordinary British or American citizen. To make a man free you have to create a whole social order of a special kind: the democratic.
>
> The growth of freedom in Europe, of education, of wealth, of social and political organization, has been a long and slow process, with frequent interruptions by political dictators. These interruptions have become shorter, as real freedom increased....
>
> But in Africa, there has been no growth. African peoples know no other government but dictatorship, direct or indirect, and it is quite easy for the African dictators to think and even to speak in public of the natives as helpless serfs or slaves.
>
> This, as I have said, does not make the position in Africa any less dangerous; it makes it only more difficult.

In this race against time Cary was blunt in articulating the danger that if the African states were granted independence before a democratic social order was created, they might fall into the hands of African despots. Thus, Cary's original tract, without its later essays, ends with this assertion of the primacy of democratic freedom:[44]

> To have freedom on your side is the only security of all government. And since freedom is never satisfied while it is held back by any bounds not strictly accountable to reason and justice, only one policy is open to government, the quickening of all powers, in mind and body, to the

man, that as a responsible citizen he may become his own judge of what is necessary and just; and the devolution of all authority that to the sudden and terrible challenge of freedom cannot answer, 'I am your servant.'

In his earlier chapters, Cary expounds a highly pragmatic economic, social and political program.[45]

He starts with the nature of African poverty, evoked in *Mr Johnson* with his portrait of Fada (see p. 158), a poverty that leaves the natives mortally vulnerable to the depredations of nature, their own understandably short-sighted acts of deforestation, and the fluctuations of a world economy to which their real income is sensitive. Cary's theme is:[46] "Political liberty, and even education, is no good to a starving man ... the first steps therefore towards African freedom are economic. Those are the more urgent because African economy is not merely primitive; it is ruinous."

After underlining the extraordinary diversity of the continent he concludes:[47] "Diversity of governments and races in Africa is not the basic problem, which is economic and social. Make all its peoples richer and more secure, give them better health and education, and the political aspect will change in accord with social reality."

Short chapters follow on specific aspects of the African scene:

— A brief, subtle analysis of the virtues and deficiencies of indirect colonial rule and remedies for the latter in a post-1945 era when economic development rose in priority in British Colonial policy.

— A comment on tasks of development amidst the forbidding race problems of the Union of South Africa and Kenya.

— An unconventional answer to the question: "Where to Begin?"[48]

"But the one-step method, the slow approach, has already failed. The best answer to the question where to begin, seems to be 'everywhere at once.'" Cary drives home his dictum by citing the extraordinarily rapid transformation of African army recruits from "dull, drop-jawed loafers" into "brisk youngsters who pick up English and signalling and even simple arithmetic in a few weeks. ...the reason for this transformation, of course, is that African recruits get not only clothes, good food and quarters, and instruction, but doctoring. They are freed from the inevitable worms; often of fever, too. At the same time, they are removed at one blow from tribal influence."[49]

After paying his respects to individual doctors and engineers who apply the highest professional standards in Africa, Cary offers a prescription from hard-won experience:

> The doctor is right, like the engineer, to give the best opinion, regardless of any financial or human consideration. But engineers and scientists are notoriously bad political advisers....
>
> The African problem of health cannot be separated from the economic, educational, racial complex in which it is a factor. Bad nutrition, for instance, is agreed to be the cause of the low stamina of the African, but malnutrition arises partly from poverty, partly from ignorance.
>
> Therefore I cannot help feeling that the political officer, taking into account all these aspects of the situation, and especially the character of a primitive people, should rather urge a wide attack, however, amateurish, than a limited service of high quality. I think a native dispenser in each district or group of villages, a native forestry assistant, even if he can't write his own name, and a score of native elementary teachers, though they never heard of algebra, are of much more value to progress than a first-class hospital two hundred miles away, a European doctor of science attached to the Governor-General, and a model school, equipped with desks and European notebooks, in each capital town.

A chapter on administration follows that ought to be read in every school of public policy or administration. It captures in a series of aptly manufactured quotations the typical perspective of a full hierarchy of British administrators, from London to the bush. Cary notes that they fall into two categories: those asking for more centralization of authority; or more devolution. He proposes a scheme of reconciliation including a new development department at the center plus a bit more scope for local administration; but he concludes with an over-riding judgment:[50] "If the idea, still a new idea, of creating [in Africa] as soon as possible a modern civilization, is firmly grasped and locally pursued, then bureaucratic forms matter little...."

Cary then devotes four chapters to facets of education, including especially education for adults and women. As elsewhere his argument is freshly stated and rooted in the linkage between education and freedom; and, still deeper is his transcendent view of the latter:[51] "When we say that we believe in freedom we are finally asserting a moral, or, if you like, a religious belief. First that freedom is good for the personal soul; and then, that what is good for one cannot be denied to others."

We only get to economic development in the narrow sense with essays on "Small Industry and Co-operation" and "Large Industry and Finance." In the first he argues, with vivid illustrations (one echoing Judge Rudbeck's and Mr Johnson's great road) that small enterprises can not only be beautiful but play a critical role in the transit from tribal stagnation to African modernity. He notes along the way

> [T]hat those who support co-operation as a natural alternative to the tribe, will be disappointed. Supporters of this kind are usually the idealists, spoken of above, who have been accustomed to think of the tribesman as a noble savage and the tribal life as a golden age of simplicity and social happiness. They argue that co-operation is the ideal simplicity and social happiness. They argue that co-operation is the ideal substitute for the tribal life of communal interests and fraternal equality. But just as the equality of tribesmen is not that of brothers, but of slaves, so the community of co-operators is not that of equals, but of ambitious individuals. The members co-operate not to produce a communal wealth but a better return for themselves. A flourishing co-operative society does not produce equality, but inequality. The more energetic and intelligent members, taking full advantage of the society, soon grow richer. The slack and stupid stay where they are.[52]

Cary then turns sharply on those who would withhold large-scale industrial development from Africa on either Gandhian grounds of nostalgia for a golden age of eternal peace or to appease those at home who fear competition from industry using cheap African labor. And, two centuries on, he argues against this latter day mercantilism with a fervor worthy of David Hume and Adam Smith:[53]

> If any European government did begin to develop competing industries in its African dependency, it would certainly be fiercely attacked by representatives of those industries at home.
>
> But such a development is absolutely necessary to African economy. Africa is a poor country, and a poor country especially must have the best possible industrial organization to support itself at a reasonable standard. The fact that Africa is so far from such an organization now must not prevent understanding of its need; as a final aim, it should be in the mind of all responsible governments. Fear of competition has prompted obstruction to every development of industry, in the East, in India, Russia, Southern Europe; but the actual results of that advance have been an enormous increase in the world's wealth and in immense expansion of markets.... Competition has been the result everywhere of progress, and it cannot be avoided unless progress is stopped. Its evil result in causing unemployment may and should be avoided; but any attempt to prevent the use of new process, better machinery, in order to

> avoid competition between factories or unions, and the dislocation of trade routine, is reactionary and stupid. It would prove a certain method for bringing any country that practised it to decay and ruin.
>
> ...European governments must be prepared therefore to encourage the development of competing industry in Africa, and when the setting up of such an industry would be of advantage to local economy they should not be frightened from it by clamour at home.

Cary's tract closes by affirming the inevitability of African nationalism; the terrible urgency of modernization in this "vast slum among nations;" and the ultimate rationale for this course as a pre-condition for human freedom. Later, hopeful in the wake of the Colonial Development Act of 1945, he set down memorably his faith in the staying power of African culture in the face of modernization and the contribution such a modernized Africa will bring to world society:[54]

> As for those who fear that Africa, in gaining a modern equipment, will lose by that its own quality, colour, humour, its exuberance and native dignity, and above all, that positive affirmation of life, which in extremest misery and oppression has been the strength of the Negro and the Bantu, one can only ask if any great and rich culture ever weakened a race. Did Greek scholarship ruin Italian art in the fifteenth century? Did the Renaissance destroy the French architecture or English poetry of the sixteenth? Did English philosophy and science bring decadence upon the French of the eighteenth century, or the painting of Turner and Constable discourage the native genius of contemporary Paris schools?
>
> "The secret of a rich local and national culture throughout the world is not the shutting out of foreign ideas and arts, but the assimilation.
>
> "...There is no fear that tropical Africa will lose its local qualities when it is permitted to take its place in the world; rather it will bring to the world a new African civilization, new arts, new religion."

10.5 REFLECTIONS ON THE TRANSITION FROM COLONIAL TO DEVELOPMENT ECONOMICS

What can we distill from these three portraits that bears on the central theme of this volume?

The first and most important conclusion about colonial economic policy is that it was not constant. Colonialism begins with an act of aggression motivated, in Sir Josiah Child's old mercantilist phrase, by a desire for "profit and power", in combinations often difficult to disentangle. In further pursuit of those goals, the imperial authority usually undertook some actions which introduced elements of modernization, for example, ports, roads, railroads, the mobilization of raw material exports, elementary education, measures of public health. And, with the passage of time, in India and Africa, there was a gradual trend towards assuming some responsibility for encouraging less explicitly self-interested measures of development. Both Anstey and Cary note this trend in the twentieth century, which is also illustrated by the 1931 Shanghai conference for which Tawney's monograph was commissioned. A positive concern for development evidently took a quantum jump in the wake of World War II. With the accelerated drive for independence induced by the war, the emergence of the United Nations, and, only a bit later, the Cold War, definitions of self interest shifted among the advanced industrial countries. Decolonization became inevitable, and policy addressed itself to relations with the foreseeably independent governments. By the early 1950s development economics was roaring along. But this essay dramatizes, via the three figures treated, that a wholly recognizable development mentality antedates World War II among important intellectual figures; and they articulated their case from an historical, moral, and human perspective rarely matched in the post-1945 literature.

I would guess, however, that more powerful as a stimulus to modernization than positive development measures undertaken by the colonial power, in narrow self-interest or for larger purposes, was the demonstration effect of Western behavior and gadgetry. Of all the demonstrations, the most influential in the long run was the Western capacity to seize and hold power, to occupy and impose humiliating conditions in places far from home. Out of this daily demonstration arose an ambivalence: a tendency to emulate; and a zenophobic nationalism determined to drive the rascals out.

This strand in the story must, of course, be put in a larger context. The nature of Indian society — the values of its elites, its social structure and land tenure system — certainly contributed to the delay in the India take-off. On the other hand, British rule was sufficiently flexible to permit enterprising Indians, usually from lesser castes, to make of Gujarat something of an Indian São Paulo and to set in motion an iron and steel as well as a modern textile industry. But the scale of the problem of modernizing the Indian economy was such that Indian leaders would have had to address themselves to the task in a unified and concentrated way to move India into take-off while under British rule. That never happened.

It has also been argued that British political policy within India, notably after the Mutiny (for example, the elevation of the native princes), made it difficult or impossible to focus Indian leaders around the goal of modernization. But, in my view, the fact of alien rule was decisive in leading the literate Indian middle class to concentrate a great deal of its creative energy, starting in the last quarter of the nineteenth century, on politics and what became the struggle for independence.[55] Significant elements in economic modernization went forward; but, as in China during the same period, the leadership of a succession of generations addressed its talents to problems of politics and power rather than economics and welfare.

Thus, the greatest delaying consequence of British rule arose from its becoming the primary target for the energies of literate and competent Indians. Creation of the preconditions for take-off, from a base in a traditional society, requires great energy and purposefulness in both public policy and among the inevitably thin ranks of well-trained private leaders. British policy and Indian reaction to it combined to make that stage peculiarly protracted.

On this view it is wholly logical that the Indian take-off can be dated from 1952 and the first-five year plan. Indian progress thereafter was not brilliant. But, clearly, the long period of income *per capita* oscillating around an essentially static low level was over.

In China there was also a mixture of emulation and zenophobic nationalism, as Tawney vividly captures; but the political problem differed from India. There Britain had built a central authority that united the subcontinent in relative peace. Indians merely had to persuade the British, in one way or another, to turn it over to them; although once turned over, British India painfully fractured. In China, as Tawney perceived, the creation of an effective central authority was the key task; and, in the end, the Communists won a civil war to decide who would control that authority and undo the sequence of external humiliations that had begun with the Opium wars. Again, a new phase in Chinese economic history began with Mao's first Five Year Plan in 1952, launching a period of erratic, distorted but real economic progress.

In both cases the story of colonialism and escape from colonialism left unfortunate marks on post-1952 development theory and practice. The Indian political leadership of the first generation, at least, influenced by a mixture of anti-imperialist and anti-capitalist doctrine, sentimentality about Soviet planning, and an inherited massive bureaucracy with a lively interest in its self-perpetuation generated an excessively protectionist system, with an overblown state sector, reluctant to import private capital or to confront the rigors of international competition. Moreover, a full generation had to pass, and the back-to-back monsoon failures of 1965–67, before an agricultural policy with adequate peasant incentives was introduced, and the notion that agricultural production had a colonial taint was more or less put to rest. All this caused a considerably lower rate of growth than India might have attained over its first forty years of independence.

The Chinese Communists began with Stalin's First Five Year Plan as the explicit model and have only partially and painfully escaped over, roughly, the same time period. In both cases, the passage of time has moved policy in the right directions; but the point here is, simply, that the experience of colonialism (or quasi-colonialism) has, through rather complex routes, cast long shadows on development policy in the first four decades of post-independence development policy.

With India and China we are considering the birth pangs of vast modern nations, likely to remain unified despite some fragmenting tendencies, well on their way to full industrialization in the next half century.

But Africa remains still fragmented as of the 1990s. The heritage of colonialism can still be discerned in all the African states; but the cases vary greatly and generalizations are not easy.

In some colonies, independence was achieved under the leadership of classic romantic revolutionaries of the kind prefigured in Cary's chapter on "African Nationalism";[56] for example, Nkrumah, Ben Bella, Secou Toure. In other cases, the transition — like India's in relation to Great Britain — was, despite an internal convulsion, relatively tranquil, as with Bourguiba's Tunisia and Nyerere's Tanzania.

Their economic performances have also varied, not only with the character of their escape from colonialism but also with resource endowments, the vicissitudes of domestic politics, and export prices. In general they were held back by an unhelpful package of policies not unlike those which retarded India's post-independence development but (except Nigeria) they were mainly small countries, in some cases too small to be economically viable in the long run; and virtually all suffered from arbitrary national boundaries which cut across tribal lines making it difficult to generate an authentic sense of nationhood. The small African countries also began, of course, much further back in the preconditions for take-off than India. The simple fact is that, as of 1991, no sub-Saharan African country has yet moved into take-off. Despite severe distortions, take-off began in India and China in the 1950s and both countries have moved beyond in the progressive absorption of modern technology.

There are, nevertheless, some typical signs in Africa of progress in movement though the pre-conditions for take-off; for example, increases in the proportions of the relevant age groups attending primary and secondary school. Increases in tertiary education are modest and leave most countries in the 1–2 per cent range of enrolment for the 1980s as opposed to India's remarkable 9 per cent. Similarly, the proportion of urban population has risen as well as (more unevenly) the proportion of GDP generated in manufacturing; but the figures are generally typical of the World Bank's low-income economies — a categorization confirmed by small if any declines in birth rates, overwhelmed by still greater decline in death rates, although the latter still remain high and perhaps worsening with the diffusion of AIDS. But the tragic truth is that sub-Saharan Africa has not yet entered the hopeful side of the demographic transition.

Data for the 1980s also reflect the setback caused by the severe debt crisis of that period; but it is clear that independence came to an Africa much further back in the process of modernization than post-1945 India and China or, even feudal Japan of the mid-ninteenth century. Emperor Meiji and his samurai supporters took over in 1868 a large capital city, an experienced central administration, a people suffused with a sense of national identity, a Confucian aspiration for literacy and learning, a sophisticated national domestic trading system, and virtuousity in pre-modern manufactures. It was not surprising that the Japanese could move into take-off less than twenty years later. Nevertheless, as Cary perceived, there is ample evidence that there is an underlying determination in Africa to modernize and for the African states to become part of the modern world in terms of their own cultures and tradition. It's just taking a long time.

Perhaps the greatest shadow cast by the colonial experience on the struggle for modernization in the post-independence world as a whole was more subtle. As already suggested, colonization of its nature forced the occupied peoples to focus their attention unnaturally on the imperial power in a mixture of often admiring emulation and determination to throw off a humiliating yoke. E. M. Forster's *A Passage to India* captures this duality well in the painful discussion early in the book between Hamidullah and Aziz. The former evokes the authentic friendship that he experienced when in England with a British family and how it became impossible on both sides to perpetuate in colonial India.[57] In different ways both Tawney and Cary also capture this inescapable, distorting ambivalence. The best educated among the colonial peoples who, inevitably, moved later to positions of authority, felt most acutely this complexity.

Thus, when independence was formally achieved, the colonial mentality of ambivalent obsession with the old masters did not promptly dissipate. It had its impact on development policy through a tendency to indentify free competive enterprise with imperialism and through excessive emphasis on the impact of what the advanced industrial nations did or failed to do, as opposed to the problems that could only be overcome at home if development was to proceed well.

This distortion was accentuated by the emergence of the Cold War at precisely the time that the old colonial empires were being rapidly liquidated. Although the reaction among a good many formerly colonial states was to assert their independence of the Cold War contestants via collective proclamations of neutrality, in fact their policies tended, again, to place excessive emphasis on the external world as a cause of their difficulties, while they played if possible, one Cold War contestant off against another.

Certainly an American whose country achieved independence by playing the French off against the British and subsequently expanded its territory to the Pacific substantially by continuing this divide and rule policy should have no difficulty understanding with some sympathy this phase of policy in the developing regions. My point here is positive not critical. The Cold War is being dismantled. The reduction of leverage on Washington and Moscow, the return of Cuban soldiers to their stricken island has forced Africans and others to look more closely at their own problems. At just this time the "charismatic populists" are passing from the scene — often forcefully removed.[58] The coming to authority of a new generation, freed of memories of colonialism and, even, of identification with the authentic glories of the struggle for independence, should yield in the decades ahead, no doubt after many vicissitudes, the emergence of formerly colonial states with governments prepared to assume full responsibility for the modernization of their societies in harmony with their own cultures and traditions as, each in a unique way, Anstey, Tawney, and Cary envisaged. As this happens they will become confident partners in the affairs of the world community; and, at last, the costs of the colonial experience will have withered away.

Notes

1. W. W. Rostow, *Theorists of Economic Growth Since David Hume with a Perspective on the Next Century* (New York: Oxford University Press, 1990). For comments on the "lack of a solid analytic political base" in post-1945 economic development theory, see, especially, pp. 426–27. For references to Vera Anstey, see pp. 4, 206–7, 315; R. H. Tawney, pp. 4, 207–8, and 315–17; Joyce Cary, p. 318.
2. Gerald M. Meier and Dudley Seers, *Pioneers in Development* (New York: Oxford University Press for the World Bank, 1984).
3. *Theorists of Economic Growth*, p. 426.
4. *Ibid.*, pp. 419–426.
5. Christopher Fyfe of Edinburgh University provided the Introduction to the 1962 edition of *The Case for African Freedom* (Austin: University of Texas

Press, 1962). It includes Cary's 1944 edition of *The Case for African Freedom*, originally published as a pamphlet in 1941; a 1946 pamphlet, *Britain and West Africa* (reprinted with an added appendix in 1947); plus three magazine pieces on Africa published in the period 1951–54.

6. *Ibid.*, p. ix.
7. *Ibid.*, p. xiii.
8. *The Economic Development of India*, pp. 2–4.
9. The scope and thoroughness of Anstey's survey is suggested by its table of contents (1936 edition) which includes the following chapters: The Resources of India; Population, Social Organization, and Economic Development; Public Health and Economic Development; Economic Organization; Transport and Communications; Agricultural and Allied Problems and Policy; The Co-operative Movement; The Trend of Industry and Industrial Policy; India's Large-Scale Industries; The Protection of Industrial Labour by the State and by Voluntary Organization; The Trend of Foreign Trade and of Commercial Policy; The Financial System and Financial Developments; Banking and Currency; The Prosperity of the People.
10. Extracted from *ibid.*, pp. 474–87.
11. *Ibid.*, pp. 509–11.
12. *Ibid.*, p. 474.
13. R. H. Tawney, *Land and Labour in China* (London: Allen & Unwin, 1932). Tawney's study originally took the form of a long memorandum commissioned for a conference held in Shanghai in November, 1931, by the Institute of Pacific Relations. The final chapter, a subtle and prescient essay on "Politics and Education," was added after the Shanghai conference.
14. The contents are: The Rural Framework; The Problems of the Peasant, (Methods of Cultivation, Marketing, Credit, Land Tenure, Poverty, War and Famine); The Possibilities of Rural Progress (Analogous Problems Elsewhere, Agrarian Policy, Communications, Science and Education, Co-operation, Land Tenure, Drought and Flood, Population, Migration and the Development of Industry); The Old Industrial Order and the New (The Legacy of the Past, The Growth of Capitalist Industry, Problems of Social Policy); Politics and Education.
15. Extracted from *ibid.*, pp. 18–22.
16. *Ibid.*, p. 31.
17. *Ibid.*, p. 78.
18. *Ibid.* Here is Tawney's vivid description of the genus (that is, the general characteristics of a basically stagnant traditional agriculture), *ibid.*, p. 79: "The persistence of an empirical technique based on venerable usage and impervious to science; the meagre output of foodstuffs which that technique produced; the waste of time and labour through the fragmentation of holdings; the profits wrung from the cultivator by middleman, usurer and landlord; the absence of means of communication and the intolerable condition of such as existed; the narrow margin separating the mass of the population from actul starvation and the periodical recurrence of local famines — such phenomena, if exception be made of a few favoured regions, were until recently the commonplaces of western economic life since men first reflected on it. Scientists analysed them; philanthropists deplored them; governments legislated for them; common men confronted their results, sometimes with

patient acquiescence, sometimes with violent revolt; in England and France a whole literature arose to expose and correct them. From the Middle Ages to the nineteenth century the social problem of most parts of Europe, in spite of natural advantages of soil and climate, was what in China and India it is to-day. It was the condition, not of the industrial wage-earner, but of the peasant. Its solution, in so far as it has been solved, is a thing of yesterday."

19. *Ibid.*, p. 82.
20. *Ibid.*, p. 103.
21. *Ibid.*, p. 121.
22. *Ibid.*, p. 128.
23. *Ibid.*, p. 129.
24. *Ibid.*, extracted from pp. 130–32, and 137.
25. *Ibid.*, pp. 138–40.
26. *Ibid.*, p. 142.
27. *Ibid.*, p. 150.
28. *Ibid.*, p. 160.
29. *Ibid.*, pp. 162–63.
30. *Ibid.*, p. 129.
31. *Ibid.*, p. 162.
32. *Ibid.*, p. 169.
33. See, especially, *ibid.*, pp. 190–93.
34. *Ibid.*, pp. 193–95.
35. *The Case for African Freedom*, p. ix.
36. *Mr Johnson* (New York: Harper, 1951). p. 257, "Author's Note," from the English Carfax edition.
37. *Ibid.*, p. 261.
38. *Ibid.*, p. 172.
39. *Ibid.*, pp. 177–78.
40. *Ibid.*, pp. 186–87.
41. *Ibid.*, pp. 105–6.
42. *The Case for African Freedom*; p. 23.
43. *Ibid.*, pp. 26–27.
44. *Ibid.*, p. 136.
45. The table of contents includes these chapters: Conquest of Africa; The Case for Freedom; African Poverty; Problems of Reconstruction: Political; Political: Direct and Indirect Rule; The Union of South Africa and Kenya; Where to begin?; Administration; Information Officers and Public Relations; Adult Education: General; Importance of Women's Education; English and the British Institutes; Small Industry and Co-operation; Large Industry and Finance; African Nationalism; Political Reality; The Future.
46. *Ibid.*, p. 27.
47. *Ibid.*, p. 49.
48. *Ibid.*, p. 73.
49. *Ibid.*, p. 73.
50. *Ibid.*, p. 92.
51. *Ibid.*, p. 112.
52. *Ibid.*, p. 119.
53. *Ibid.*, pp. 122–23.
54. *Ibid.*, pp. 194–95.

55. Although not relevant here, it is worth noting a remarkable passage in Joyce Cary's *African Freedom* (pp. 125–30) on the interplay between middle class leaders and the impoverished people in anti-colonial revolts. Cary draws on analogies from the French, Russian, and other revolutions.
56. *Ibid.*, Ch. 16.
57. E. M. Forster, *Passage to India* (New York: Harcourt, Brace, 1924), especially, pp. 10–13.
58. I owe this excellent phrase to *World Press Review*, August 1991, p. 141, heading an article by Victoria Brittain reprinted from *New Statesman and Society.*

11 From Colonial Economics to Development Economics

Gerald M. Meier

More than two centuries after Smith's *Wealth of Nations*, economists still inquire why the whole world is not developed. As earlier chapters have indicated, their analyses have evolved through various phases. The early period of development economics from approximately 1945–60 provides an especially significant phase. This chapter concentrates on those early days of transition from "colonial economics" to "development economics" when economists began to analyze more rigorously the problems of the latecomers to development.

11.1 EARLY ANALYSIS

As decolonization spread in the postwar period, the emerging nations sought more rapid economic development. If classical economists had focused on the "progressive state" and the determinants of economic growth, only to have the neoclassicists subsequently neglect the subject in favor of marginalism and the formal analysis of the market price system,[1] the post-war rebirth of interest in growth or development called for a "new development economics".[2] As latecomers to development, the countries of Africa, Asia, and Latin America encountered some special problems that differed from those faced by the now advanced countries when they were the early-comers to development. The leaders of the new nations insisted that international attention be given to their development problems. Areas that had been considered in the eighteenth century as "rude and barbarous", in the nineteenth century as "backward", and in the pre-war period as "underdeveloped" now became the "less developed countries" or "the poor countries" — and also the "emerging countries" and "developing economies".

But how was development to be achieved? Although political independence could be legislated, economic independence could not. Nationalism could intensify the demand for accelerated transformation of the economy, but the process could not be simply willed. An understanding of the forces of development was necessary.[3] And the design of appropriate policies to support these forces was essential. To accomplish this, the creative participation of economists was needed.[4]

The earlier study of colonial economics would no longer suffice. Previous courses in colonial economics had catered mostly to those working in, or hoping to enter, the colonial services. Trade fluctuation had been a basic problem of the inter-war years, and the main objective, implicitly at least, had been stabilization. This reflected both the needs of the colonial powers and the Keynesian fashion then current. In so far as social and political changes were considered, they were depicted as elements of gradual progress requiring economic stability. The economic role of the state remained very limited.

The war not only disrupted the colonial system; it upset this narrow way of perceiving the problems of poor countries. The newly independent governments were now under pressure to achieve development, not merely the stability of colonial regimes. Immediately before and after World War II the main concerns of economists were (1) the ways in which the economy deviated from competitive behavior and competitive efficiency, and (2) unemployment.[5] These concerns shaped development analysis in the post-war decade. From the viewpoint of development economics, Keynesian unemployment theory gave encouragement to models in which labor played no constraining role. Although the dynamic Keynesian growth models were relevant for the unemployment problem of only the developed countries, these theories nonetheless provided support for development planning. The second area of attention — market imperfections and market failure — had been elaborated by Marshall, Pigou, and by the newer concerns of welfare economics. For some development economists, underdevelopment was now attributed to pervasive market imperfections. Again, the remedy was to be sought through governmental interventions.

Early attention was given to a major manifestation of market failure — the market's failure to achieve equality of wage rates in different sectors of the economy. This provided a basis for the dual economy hypothesis. Having been associated during the war with a study group at the Royal Institute for International Affairs on problems of "underdeveloped countries", Paul N. Rosenstein-Rodan published his "Problems of Industrialization of Eastern and Southeastern Europe" in 1943.[6] Rosenstein-Rodan introduced four concepts that contributed to the emerging theory of economic development.[7] First was a concern with "excess agrarian population" (disguised unemployment), which, although a weakness, may also represent a source of development. The second was the concept of "pecuniary" external economies which yielded economies of scale — that is, increasing returns that were treated in Marshall's footnotes but considered to be only a "second order of smalls". To take advantage of them, however, Rosenstein-Rodan argued that planned industrialization comprising simultaneous planning of several complementary industries is needed. The third new idea was that before building consumer goods factories, a major indivisible block of social overhead capital or infrastructure must be built and sponsored because private market initiatives were not created in time. The fourth concept was the emphasis on "technological external economies", which are not due to indivisibilities but are very largely due to "inappropriability". The training and education of workers under competitive market conditions would be below optimum while the process of industrialization of underdeveloped countries was believed to depend on the advantages of training, learning on the job, and the formation of human capital (without using this terminology in the article).

Rosenstein-Rodan also maintained that the market mechanism does not realize the "optimum" either in one nation or between nations because it relies on such unrealistic assumptions as linear homogeneous production functions, and hence no increasing returns or economies of scale or of agglomeration, and no phenomenon of minimum quantum or threshold. He maintained that this obscures the nature of the development process and the risks involved.

In 1947, Kurt Mandelbaum attempted to present a quantitative model of industrialization for the overpopulated and "backward areas" of eastern and southeastern Europe.[8] Mandelbaum believed that the "depressed areas" of this region suffered from lack of industrial development, which was driving the growing population into rural and urban occupations of very low productivity. He argued that the economic case for the industrialization of "densely populated backward countries" rests upon the "mass phenomenon of disguised rural unemployment". The principal barriers to higher employment were lack of demand and scarcity of capital. To overcome these, he asserted that state intervention was necessary so that redistributive measures might raise "necessary consumption" and thus counteract the potential deficiency of demand and directly relieve poverty. Such governmental measures might also institute a regime of state-enforced savings in support of a higher rate of capital formation. The increase in the rate of output and some needed adjustments of technology were derived from the aim of attaining full employment within about one generation.

From Rosenstein-Rodan on, a number of dual-economy models have been formulated. Dualism was long recognized as a characteristic of an underdeveloped country. The term came into prominence in association with the colonial status of many underdeveloped countries. A history of nineteenth century Jamaica, for instance, is entitled, *Two Jamaicas*: two cultures — two ways of life — were represented by the African Jamaica and European Jamaica. The Dutch economist, J. H. Boeke, also emphasized in his study of Indonesian development the differing social organizations and cultural contrasts that result in "social dualism" — "the clashing of an imported social system with an indigenous social system of another style".[9] The early development economists did not follow these views on dualism. Instead, they emphasized a dualism in economic organization and concentrated on economic forces.

Among the several economic models of dualism, that formulated by W. Arthur Lewis (1954) is the simplest in construction but still among the richest in perceptive insights.[10] Lewis presents his model as an aid to "interpreting development with unlimited supplies of labor" when there is organizational dualism between a "traditional" and "capitalistic" sector. In emphasizing the differences in the conditions of employment in the two sectors, Lewis returns to Adam Smith's distinction between "productive" and "unproductive" labor. His interpretation of Smith on this point also corresponds to that of Myint (1948, Ch. 5) who argues that Smith's preference for productive labor arose not from any "materialistic fallacy but from a desire to promote growth over stagnation". Myint recalls that "the classics from Smith to Marx all assume, or argue, that an unlimited supply of labor was available at subsistence wages. They then inquired how production grows through time. They found the answer in capital accumulation ... " Similarly, in presenting his dual sector model, Lewis (1954, p. 139) states that

> the central problem in the theory of economic development is to understand the process by which a community which was previously saving and investing four or five percent of its national income or less, converts itself into an economy where voluntary saving is running at about 12–15 percent of national income or more. This is the central problem because the central fact of economic development is rapid capital accumulation (including knowledge and skills with capital).

The fundamental relationship between the two sectors in Lewis's model is that when the capitalist sector expands, it draws labor from the reservoir in the non-capitalist sector. Labor is "unlimited" in the sense that when the capitalist sector offers additional employment opportunities at the existing wage rate, the numbers willing to work at the existing wage will be greater than the demand: the supply curve of labor is infinitely elastic at the ruling wage. Employment in the capitalist sector is constrained only by demand, not labor supply.

Lewis's recollection of how he postulated the fundamental relationship in his model is illuminating. He states that he was concerned with the sources of capital formation in a developing economy. It was clear to him that in the nineteenth century the bulk of finance for Europe came from a rising share of profits in the national income. But what caused this rise in the share of profits? Lewis could not find an answer in either neoclassical economics or Keynes's model. Instead, he stated:

> What we were getting from the neo-classicists … were demonstrations of how to combine long run savings constancy with short run savings volatility. This was of no use to us, since what we were trying to understand was long term rise in the savings propensity.
>
> As I was walking down a road in Bangkok one morning in August 1952, it suddenly occurred to me that all one needed to do was to drop the assumption — then usually (but not necessarily) made by neoclassical macroeconomists — that the supply of labor was fixed. Assume instead that it was infinitely elastic, and that productivity was increasing in the capitalist sector, and one got a rising profits share. It also occurred to me that this model would solve another problem that had bothered me since undergraduate days: What determined the relative prices of steel and coffee? I had been taught that marginal utility was the answer to this question. But this answer made no sense to me. If, however, one assumed an infinite elasticity of labor in terms of food to the coffee industry, and an infinite elasticity also in terms of food to the steel industry, then the factoral terms of trade between steel and coffee were fixed, and marginal utility was out the window. So in three minutes I had solved two of my problems with one change of assumptions (Lewis 1984, pp. 132–33).

In Lewis's dual sector model, the traditional sector withers away as investment in the capitalist sector absorbs the surplus labor from the traditional sector. As did the classicists, Lewis assumes that all wages are consumed and that profits in the capitalist sector constitute the only source of savings. The rate of growth is therefore equal to the product of the rate of profit and the propensity to save out of profits. The major conclusion is that the rate at which surplus labor will be absorbed in the capitalist sector depends on the size of the capitalist sector and the ratio of profits in national income: the larger the capitalist sector, and the greater the share of profits in national income, the more rapidly will surplus labor be absorbed. Again in his *Theory of Economic Growth* (1955, p. 236) Lewis emphasized that "if the process of converting an economy from a five to twelve percent saver is essentially dependent upon the rise of profits relatively to national income, it follows that the correct explanation of why poor countries save so little is not because they are poor, but because their capitalist sectors are so small".[11]

The fact that the capitalist sector would have to pay a wage higher than the social opportunity cost of drawing labor from the reservoir in the non-capitalist sector led many to advocate policies that would subsidize and protect the modern industrial sector. The advocacy of import substitution industrialization became prominent. Such an inward-looking strategy was advocated not only because of market failure but also because of export pessimism with respect to exportation of primary products. Many came to believe that primary producing countries suffered a secular deterioration in their terms of trade. The Prebisch–Myrdal–Singer hypothesis received much attention.[12]

An early critic of import substitution and protectionist policy was Jacob Viner (1953), who rejected the Prebisch–Singer doctrine of secular deterioration of the terms of trade and argued against import substituting industrialization.[13]

In his 1954 article, Lewis also argued that in the long run it is the factoral terms of trade that determine the commodity terms, and not the other way around. Although he recognized that the factoral terms have moved continually against the developing countries since the beginning of the nineteenth century, he suggested that the basic way to stop this is to raise continually the productivity of farmers producing for the domestic market, thereby increasing the supply price of export crops.

Contrary to the neoclassical view of international trade, Gunnar Myrdal went on to argue that international trade may actually operate as a mechanism of international inequality. He was particularly concerned with backwash effects on the latecomers to development. "If left to take its own course, economic development is a process of circular and cumulative causation which tends to award its favors to those who are already well endowed and even to thwart the efforts of those who happen to live in regions that are lagging behind. The backsetting effects of economic expansion in other regions dominate the more powerfully, the poorer a country is" (Myrdal, 1956, p. 10).

In the 1950s, another argument against the agricultural export strategy came from the school of Dependencia. Believing in the domination of the "periphery" by "the center" and "an interminable metropolis–satelite chain, in which the surplus generated at each stage is successively drawn off toward the center", dependistas in Latin America advocated independent growth for the latecomers to development. It was argued that a form of dependency is manifested in neocolonialism and in the domination of the manufacturing sector in the periphery by multinationals, and through dependence on the center for technology and factors of production.[14]

As corollaries of their emphasis on capital accumulation, the early development economists also promulgated the policies of a "big push" and "balanced growth". Rosenstein-Rodan (1943, p. 205) maintained that "Complementarity of different industries provides the most important set of arguments in favor of a large-scale planned industrialization.... The planned creation of such a complementary system reduces the risk of not being able to sell, and since risk can be considered as cost, it reduces costs. It is in this sense a special case of 'external economies'."

Rosenstein-Rodan also argued that "existing institutions of international investment are inappropriate to the task of industrialization of a whole area. They deal with too small units, and do not take advantage of external economies." (1943, p. 204). "There is a minimum level of resources that must be devoted to ... a development program if it is to have any chance for success. Launching a country into self-sustaining growth is a little like getting an airplane off the ground. There is a critical ground speed which must be passed before the craft can become airborne... Proceeding bit by bit will not add up in its effects to the sum total of the single bits. A minimum quantum of investment is a necessary, though not sufficient, condition of success. This, in a nut shell, is the contention of the theory of the big push. This theory seems to contradict the conclusions of traditional static equilibrium theory and to reverse its famous motto, '*natura non facit saltum*'" (Rosenstein-Rodan, 1957, p. 70).

Recognizing Allyn Young's earlier article on increasing returns (1928), Rosenstein-Rodan maintained that "increasing returns accrue to a firm not only with the growth of its size but also with the growth of the industry and with the growth of the industrial system as a whole. Greater specialization and better use of resources become possible when growth helps to overcome indivisibilities generating pecuniary external economies" (1943, p. 207). Accordingly, Rosenstein-Rodan believed that more emphasis should be given to increasing returns through attention to the indivisibility of demand and indivisibility in the production function.

Reviewing his 1943 article, Rosenstein-Rodan has said that "In terms of contemporary theory, the essence of the 1943 article may seem to rest on the basic question whether perfect future markets can exist for all the commodities in the context of a future which is both open-ended and uncertain. Although I recognized that future markets and future prices could provide necessary additional signalling devices, I stated that 'It is a moot point whether perfect future markets for all goods can exist. [My] suspicion (without proof) is that they cannot exist for the same reasons for which perfect foresight is impossible. In reality they certainly do not exist' " (1984, p. 210).[15]

Reinforcing Rosenstein-Rodan's "big push" argument was Nurkse's emphasis on "balanced growth." The two concepts are connected insofar as balanced growth plus economies of scale equal the big push.[16] The idea of balanced growth emphasized the simultaneous creation of demand on a broad front. As Nurkse said:

> ... the solution seems to be a balanced pattern of investment in a number of different industries, so that people working more productively, with more capital and improved techniques, become each other's customers.... In this way a pattern of mutually supporting investments in different lines of production can enlarge the size of the market and help to fill the vacuum in the domestic economy of low income areas. This, in brief, is the notion of balanced growth. (Nurkse, 1958, p. 171).

> A frontal attack — a wave of capital investments in a number of different industries — can economically succeed while any substantial application of capital by an individual entrepreneur in any particular industry may be blocked or discouraged by the limitations of the pre-existing market. Through the application of capital over a wide range of activities, the general level of economic activity is raised and the size of the market enlarged. (Nurkse, 1953, pp. 13–15)

Responding to the question of whether balance might not be achieved by keeping the economy open to foreign trade, Nurkse also expressed export pessimism in believing that a world excess supply of primary products would worsen the terms of trade for the primary producing developing countries. "[E]xternal demand conditions do not favor the traditional pattern of 'growth through trade'" (Nurkse, 1958, p. 173). Instead, balanced growth domestically was "a means of getting out of the rut, a means of stepping up the rate of growth when the external forces of advance through trade expansion and foreign capital are sluggish or inoperative" (Nurkse, 1958, pp. 171–72).

Viewing the latecomer as a stationary economy that needed a stimulus to get off dead center, other economists joined Rosenstein-Rodan and Nurkse in emphasizing the need for capital accumulation. Nelson (1956) formalized the situation with an analysis of the "low-level equilibrium trap". And Leibenstein (1957) propounded the "critical minimum effort" thesis: if the latecomer resembles a stationary state or is in a low-level equilibrium trap, then to become a more developed state the economy must receive a stimulus to growth that is greater then a certain critical minimum size. This is because growth itself sets up not only income-raising forces but also income-depressing forces such as population growth, declining saving rate, and dis-economies of scale. A critical minimum effort must therefore be exceeded so that the income-raising forces surpass the income-depressing forces; again, a considerable amount of investment became identified with the critical minimum effort.

Rostow's "stages of growth" analysis was also to have considerable appeal (Rostow, 1952, 1960). Again, this analysis comprised some elements of the big push, balanced growth, and critical minimum effort principles. Rostow viewed the historical course of development as a linear path along which all countries pass. The path runs through a series of stages: the traditional society, the emergence of the preconditions for take-off, the take-off, self-sustaining growth, the age of high mass consumption. Rostow indicated three essential conditions for the take-off: a rise in the rate of productive investment from, say, five per cent or less to over ten per cent of national income; the development of one or more substantial manufacturing sectors; and the existence or quick emergence of a political, social, and institutional framework that exploits the impulses for expansion in the modern sector.

Although there were several political and ideological arguments for government playing a central role in promoting development,[17] the policy implications of much of the early development thought also supported development programming and development planning. The focus on imperfect competition, other conditions of market failure, and elements of increasing returns supported a case for central coordination in the allocation of resources. Moreover, the newly-expanding subject of welfare economics that paralleled the early development economics provided considerable rationale for government policies. Unlike the tenets of neoclassical theory, the structuralist school also believed that prices need not clear markets.

A prominent role was given to the state in the process of capital accumulation in order to break the vicious circle of poverty with a "big push" and "balanced growth" that would establish complementarity in demand, achieve a "critical minimum effort", and fulfill the conditions of the "take-off". It was believed that a planning agency should correct the market prices and allocate resources in accordance with the corrected "shadow" prices. Above all, it was thought that the price system must be superseded when the determination of the amount and composition of investment is too important to be left to a multitude of uncoordinated individual investment decisions, and when the challenge to a latecomer was to achieve large structural changes over a long period instead of simply marginal adjustments in the present period. If there is to be an industrialization program, secondary industries had to be created on a large scale and supported by sufficient overhead capital. Government was to have an increasing role in the accumulation through taxation, the formation of financial institutions, control of consumption imports, and policies to improve the country's terms of trade. Savings had to be mobilized and resources allocated to serve the objectives of a balanced development program.[18]

For development planning in an open economy, it was also necessary to overcome the foreign exchange constraint. The writings of Nurkse, Lewis, and the structuralists emphasized the difficulty of increasing the exports of primary products and at the same time the difficulty of reducing imports when domestic output is to be expanded. In emerging countries, new governments would have to rely on government-to-government assistance from the more advanced economies. The latecomers to development ought to be able to tap the resources, technology, and skills of the early-comers to development.

The "two-gap" model of an open developing economy supported a policy of foreign aid to overcome the foreign exchange constraint on growth of output (Chenery and Bruno, 1962). The "two-gap model" is based on a structuralist concept of development and incorporates explicit limits on the rate of increase of domestic saving, investment, and exports. Focusing on the savings and foreign exchange constraints to development, the model states that while the shortage of domestic savings limits capital accumulation, the shortage of foreign exchange limits the country's capacity to import. If economic growth depends on the importation of goods that cannot be produced at home, then the country's growth rate will be constrained by its access to foreign exchange. These two gaps — the gap between required and available savings in a development program and the gap between required and available foreign exchange — can be filled by an inflow of foreign loans or grants from governments in the rich countries. By relaxing both the savings and foreign exchange constraints, the inflow of foreign capital can yield an increase in national income that is several times the cost of the foreign loan.[19] The two-gap model is analyzed in Little (1960), Chenery and Bruno (1962).

In sum, the early literature on economic development in the 1950s emphasized structural change for the latecomers through capital accumulation, industrialization via import substitution, a big push and balanced growth — all coordinated through central planning and supported with foreign assistance.

Although later in the 1970s and 1980s, the nature of development economics was to change markedly, the early post-war writings were notable in departing from the prewar views of colonial economics. Colonial "economics" may be a misnomer, for colonial studies before World War II were dominated by cultural anthropologists, sociologists, historians, political scientists, and public administrators. Economic analysis was slight. Indeed, national income statistics had not yet been produced.[20] The economic writings on the colonies that did exist tended to concentrate on topics of economic organization, commodity markets, and trade statistics. There were no grand models of development, and little concern with the analysis of surplus labor, capital accumulation, and industrialization as related to structural transformation of a colonial economy.

The early period of development economics attempted to remedy this deficiency for the emerging countries. It also put an end to what Myrdal called "the colonial theory" — namely, apologetic writing attempting to absolve the colonial regimes for the state of underdevelopment in colonies. Tropical climate, population pressure, lack of resources, or values and institutions that made the people unresponsive to opportunities for improving their incomes and living standards had been used by some as excuses for the lack of development in colonial economies. The post-war wave of de-colonization and the policy-oriented character of the early development economics changed all this. The classicists' concern with "the progressive state" came back. New analytical insights gave rise to a range of policy prescriptions. And optimism prevailed.

11.2 EARLY TEACHING

The enthusiasm conveyed in the post-war development writings carried over to the establishment of University courses and research in the new discipline of "development economics". At the University of Oxford, the successive changes from "colonial studies", to "commonwealth studies", and then to "development studies" provide a microcosm of what was happening generally.

Beginning in 1943, the Oxford Institute of Colonial Studies was active in sponsoring courses for members of the Colonial Service.[21] A leading member of the Institute was Margery Perham — Research Lecturer in Colonial Administration, 1935–39; Reader in Colonial Administration, 1939–48; and Director of the Institute of Colonial Studies, 1945–48. An expert on African administration, Miss Perham helped plan the courses for the Colonial Service in Oxford and taught courses in Colonial History and Administration.

For recruits in the pre-war period, the Colonial Service looked largely to Oxford and Cambridge graduates of the three-year undergraduate curriculum followed by an additional year's Colonial Service probationary course. This education was heavily weighted with English, classics, modern languages and modern history.[22] There was no teaching in any subject approaching development economics; the closest was "the Development of British Colonial Self-government since 1830", which covered mainly constitutional and political issues in Canada, Australia, New Zealand and South Africa.

Lecturing to the 1938 Summer School on Colonial Administration, Miss Perham observed that "of the three main agencies through which we have influenced the tropics, political, economic, and educational, the two last have largely escaped the control of the first. While we have been busy elaborating indirect administration, with its Authorities, Courts, and Treasuries, we have done little to relate them to the educational and economic forces which, operating in unofficial hands according to the laissez faire principle, have run upon different, and sometimes contrary, lines .... Economic maladjustments have been brought home to us in some recent reports, official and unofficial, upon economics and labor, by the riots in the copper belt, and by the West Indian disturbances."[23]

By the early 1940s, however, Miss Perham had recognized the growing complexity of colonial administration, the emerging needs of the colonies, and the necessity for relevant social science research. She also became devoted to the cause of training indigenous leaders in the colonies for self-government and independence. From 1943 to 1945, she worked closely with the Colonial Office and University officials on planning post-war training for the Colonial Service at Oxford.[24] She emphasized that the year 1938 marked a dividing line in colonial development. In that year there was the Royal Commission to the West Indies, leading to the Colonial Welfare and Development Act in 1940. This Act authorized expenditure of £5 million plus £500,000 in research over ten years. The need for a large expenditure on social services and economic development in the colonies was thereby recognized, and the responsibility devolved not on inadequate local resources but on the Imperial Exchequer. The responsibility for improving the standard of life in the colonies was now being interpreted in a new all-embracing way. Agriculture was being linked with education; social welfare was being linked with the fostering of local government; broadly all development and welfare schemes were being linked with the parallel growth of political institutions.[25]

In a series of six lectures by Miss Perham in 1941 and 1942 entitled "The Colonial Empire: Problems of Government and Economics," there finally came more attention to economics. One of the lectures was on "Finance and Economics", in which significant changes of the last five years were recognized — namely, the extension of state activity in the economic and social spheres and the change in state activity as something not only supervising and controlling but positive and constructive, originating as well as regulating human activity, and having as its objective the improvement of the standard of living (taken in the widest sense) of all citizens — now it has become impossible to divide constitutional (or political) from economic questions.[26]

The Colonial Office also began to recognize that Colonial Service training, colonial studies in the United Kingdom, and the support of colonial universities would together be post-war priorities for development in the overseas dependencies.[27] An application from Oxford for a comprehensive colonial studies program was granted from the Colonial Development Fund, and the Institute of Colonial Studies was initially supported in the belief that dependencies would continue to require Britain's guidance and management in the post-war era.

When recruitment and training resumed after the war, lectures and courses provided insights from new research not only in anthropology, law, and colonial administration — but also in economics. A lengthy forty-two page reading list on "Colonial Economics" was available in 1946 for "members of the Colonial Service who, in the circumstances of their profession, sometimes find it difficult to keep in touch with the literature upon colonial affairs".[28] After readings on " Introduction to Economic Theory" and "Colonial Economic History" the section on "Economics of Backward Areas" listed readings on production and distribution, land, labor and population, capital and investment, money and banking, international trade and commercial policy, public finance, and national income, economic progress and the trade cycle.

Transition from the teaching of "colonial economics" to the teaching of "development economics" occurred at Oxford in the early 1950s. In 1946, S. Herbert Frankel was appointed Professor of Colonial Economic Affairs; in 1956 his chair was renamed the Professorship of Commonwealth Economic Affairs; and it was eventually changed in 1963 to the Professorship of the Economics of Underdeveloped Countries.

Frankel's inaugural lecture (June 1949) focused on "the concept of colonization".[29] He stated that he wished

> to pay tribute to that small band of pioneers who developed colonial studies here [Oxford], and to the United Africa Company whose

generosity in endowing the Chair of Colonial Economic Affairs has made it possible for me to stand before you today. The development of these studies is based on a new appreciation of their significance, which I believe is greater than ever before. At no previous period in history have such large regions and vast populations found themselves drawn irresistibly into new orbits of economic activity, new spheres of conflicting political influence, and new social ideologies, which, disrupting old habit patterns, leave the peoples of the world bewildered and ill at ease. Mankind is once again on the march driven by the great disintegrating, but also formative, process of colonization which has always been the handmaid of civilization.

It is just one hundred and ten years since a Professor of Political Economy in the University of Oxford, Herman Merivale, devoted his attention exclusively to the economic aspects of colonization. Much of what he wrote is naturally no longer of relevance to-day, yet the spirit which inspired his *Lectures on Colonization and Colonies: Delivered before the University of Oxford in 1839, 1840 and 1841* was prophetic. He realized that his generation was witnessing the birth of yet another world economy which would dwarf in achievement all those of the past. He recognized the significance of the forces which were knitting together the economies bordering on the Atlantic, and were bursting forth to germinate new economic life across the seas: binding far-flung regions to form a new interdependent economic whole. Europe was its centre: an economic power-house from which great colonizing movements radiated outwards with irrepressible vigour of hope and expectation.[30]

Although Frankel began lecturing in 1947 on "Colonial Economics", his lectures in subsequent years were entitled: "The Criteria of Economic Development" (1954), "Population Growth and Economic Development" (1954), "Introduction to Problems of Economic Development" (1955), "Economic Growth and Structural Change" (1957), "Economics of Urbanization in Underdeveloped Countries" (1958).

In the 1950s, Frankel's writings distinguished his thinking from the "early analysis" discussed in Section 11.1. The contrast is especially evident in his critical review of the United Nations "Group of Experts" report on "Measures for the Economic Development of Under-Developed Countries" (1951),[31] and in his book *The Economic Impact on Under-Developed Societies*.[32]

Although his title was initially "Lecturer in Colonial Economics", Myint began lecturing at Oxford on economic development in 1951.[33] The Appendix provides a full outline for Myint's lectures in 1951–52 on "Introduction to the Economics of Underdeveloped Countries" Myint's choice of topics is instructive in showing the advance of the subject beyond colonial economics — with its focus on issues and concepts that are still of present concern to development economists: the very meaning of "development," the static and dynamic consequences of market imperfections, interplay of "macro-economic" forces and "structural" forces, trade and development, creation of suitable institutions, and the political economy of policymaking.[34]

Indicative of how the subject of development economics had expanded by 1954 is the bibliography compiled by Arthur Hazelwood.[35] In contrast to the limited list by Bower in 1946 and Frankel's supplement in 1949, Hazelwood's bibliography covered some six hundred books, articles and official publications related to the subject. A second edition in 1958 grew to 1,027 items, and an additional bibliography confined to English language publications of the period from 1958 to 1962 contained 732 listings.[36] The subject-matter of development economics had clearly become established, and its study ever more extensive.

APPENDIX
LECTURE OUTLINE BY HLA MYINT
Michaelmas and Hilary Terms 1952, Oxford

INTRODUCTION TO THE ECONOMICS OF UNDERDEVELOPED COUNTRIES

I What is an "underdeveloped" economy?

(i) Income per head definitions.
(ii) Definitions implying the causes of "underdevelopment":
  (a) "Underdeveloped resources", shortage of capital and technical backwardness.
  (b) "Overpopulation".
  (c) "Exploitation"?

II Some characteristics of the underdeveloped economies

(i) "Money" and "non-monetary" sectors of the economy; degrees of money economy; cash and credit transactions; international aspects of the subject.
(ii) Demand and supply of resources:
  (a) Proportion of labour and other resources employed in "Primary", "Secondary", and "Tertiary" industries.
  (b) Proportion employed in export and domestic industries.
  (c) Proportion of "land", "labour" and "capital" employed in producing the national product.
  (d) "Disguised unemployment" and surplus labour.
(iii) Proportion of income saved and spent; proportion of spending on imports and home produced goods.

III Structure of the market in the underdeveloped economies

(i) "Imperfections" of the product market; giant export-import corporations; middle men; retail trade; agricultural marketing boards and cooperative societies.
(ii) "Imperfections" in the factor market; imperfect mobility, and imperfect divisibility.
(iii) What is meant by "imperfect knowledge"?
(iv) The size of the market and division of labour.

(v) Specialization and structural rigidities: international specialization and "mono-culture".
(vi) Distinction between the static and dynamic consequences of market imperfections.

IV The instability of the underdeveloped economies

(i) Fluctuations in demand for primary products in international trade; the size of the outside impact.
(ii) The underdeveloped economy's reaction to a given impact: changes in output, employment and prices.
(iii) Institutional factors magnifying instability; distribution of the burden of readjustments between different sectors and types of incomes.
(iv) International measures of stability:
  (a) Commodity control schemes.
  (b) I.M.F.; Import-export bank; International Bank for Reconstruction and Development.
  (c) The sterling area and the sterling exchange system.
(v) Domestic measures for stability:
  (a) Marketing boards.
  (b) "Diversification of industries" and the trade cycle.
  (c) Difficulties of adopting "contra-cyclical" fiscal and monetary policy in an underdeveloped country.

V The problem of long-run economic development

(i) Limitations of the static theory of optimum allocation of resources: The Pigovian criterion of "social" marginal productivity and international investment programmes.
(ii) Some limitations of the short-term theory of employment.
(iii) Some beginnings of long-run theories of economic development: classical and modern theories of economic development.
(iv) The "stationary state".
(v) Determinants of the total demand and total supply of output and the flow-equilibrium of an expanding economy.
(vi) Interplay of the "macro-economic" forces and the "structural" forces.
(vii) "Bottlenecks" and the "stretching of the production frontier".
(viii) "Stretching" of the preference systems and propensities; the "educating" and "organising" demand for the "right" types of

goods; Shortage of technicians as an instance of lack of "effective" demand.

VI Some international aspects of the problem

- (i) "Leakage" of demand into imports; the concepts of multiplier and accelerator in underdeveloped economies.
- (ii) "Infant industries" or "infant economies"? The nature of cumulative process of economic development: analogy with the theory of location of industries.
- (iii) Distribution of gains from trade between advanced countries and underdeveloped countries:
  - (a) Price and income terms of trade.
  - (b) Distribution of "secondary rounds" of economic activity.
- (iv) A reconsideration of the theory of comparative costs.

VII Institutional requirements of economic policy

- (i) General requirements.
- (ii) Requirements for monetary policy.
- (iii) Requirements for fiscal policy.
- (iv) Requirements for direct controls.
- (v) The problem of *creating* suitable institutions as distinguished from the problem of working through existing institutions.

VIII Political economy of the underdeveloped countries

- (i) Absence of a coherent and clearly defined system of aims.
- (ii) Aims of the advanced countries.
  - (a) Political aims.
  - (b) Cheap raw materials; dollar earners.
  - (c) Market for manufactured products.
  - (d) Philanthropy.
- (iii) Aims of the underdeveloped economies.
  - (a) Economic nationalism and the new mercantilism.
  - (b) Distinction between individuals' preferences and the collective national aims of the governments.
  - (c) "Education" and the "stretching" of preference systems.
  - (d) Worship of economic witch doctors and imperfect realizations of the cost of economic development.

(iv) Need for a reconciliation of the divergent aims or at least a frank statement of the divergences: Illustration of this in terms of the conditions of demand and supply for international loans and grants.

(v) Are international transfers of resources to be made purely on a criterion of "productivity" or a criterion of "needs"? Are the possible dynamic repercussions of a more equal distribution of world incomes on world productivity overrated?

(vi) Difficulties of maintaining a position of ethical and political neutrality.

Notes

1. The leading neoclassical exception is Alfred Marshall; see W. W. Rostow, *Theorists of Economic Growth from David Hume to the Present* (New York: Oxford University Press, 1990), Ch. 6.
2. In post-war writings, a distinction was made between the formal optimal growth models derived for economically advanced countries and the economics of development relevant for "economically backward countries." The latter involved growth and change — modernization and structural transformation. Now the broader problems of growth have shaded into problems of development.
3. Lauchlin Currie directed the first World Bank country study mission to Colombia in 1949. He recalls that "there were no precedents for a mission of this sort and indeed nothing called development economics. I just assumed that it was a case of applying various branches of economics to the problems of a specific country, and accordingly I recruited a group of specialists in public finance, foreign exchange, transport, agriculture and so on." Lauchlin Currie, *Obstacles to Development* (East Lansing: Michigan State University Press, 1967) pp. 30–31. For an account of the mission, see Roger J. Sandilands, *The Life and Political Economy of Lauchlin Currie* (Durham and London: Duke University Press, 1990), Ch. 6.
4. This section overlaps with my "The Formative Period" in Gerald M. Meier and Dudley Seers, eds, *Pioneers in Development* (New York: Oxford University Press, 1984) pp. 3–21.
5. Kenneth J. Arrow, "General Economic Theory and the Emergence of Theories of Economic Development," in K. Arrow (ed.), *Balance between Industry and Agriculture in Economic Development, vol. 1: Basic Issues* (Basingstoke and London: Macmillan, 1988) pp. 22–32.
6. Paul N. Rosenstein-Rodan,"Problems of Industrialization of Eastern and Southeastern Europe," *Economic Journal*, vol. 53 (June–Sept. 1943) pp. 202–11.
7. See Paul N. Rosenstein-Rodan, "Natura Facit Saltum: Analysis of the Disequilibrium Growth Process," in Gerald M. Meier and Dudley Seers (eds.),

Pioneers in Development (New York: Oxford University Press, 1984), pp. 208–10.

8. Kurt Mandelbaum, *Industrialization of Backward Areas* (Oxford: Basil Blackwell, 1947). For a review of Mandelbaum's early study, see Hans Singer, "A Generation Later," *Development and Change*, vol. 10, 1979.
9. J. H. Boeke, *Economics and Economic Policy of Dual Societies* (Haarlem: Tjeenk Willnik, two volumes: 1942, 1946). Criticisms of Boeke's thesis and policy recommendations were offered by B. Higgins, "The 'Dualistic Theory' of Underdeveloped Areas," *Economic Development and Cultural Change*, vol. 4, 1956, pp. 99–115.
10. Following Lewis, significant dual economy models were presented by J. C. H. Fei and Gustav Ranis, *Development of the Labor Surplus Economy* (Homewood, IL: Irwin, 1964); Dale W. Jorgenson, "The Development of a Dual Economy," *Economic Journal* (June 1961), pp. 309–34. Ranis and Fei seek an understanding of transition growth through which societies endeavor to move between the sharply contrasting regimes of agrarian colonialism and modern economic growth. Jorgenson's analysis is more neoclassical in character.
11. Lewis expanded on his dual sector model in subsequent writings: "Unlimited Labor: Further Notes," *Manchester School* (January, 1958), pp. 132; "Reflections on Unlimited Labor," in L. E. Di Marco, ed. *International Economics and Development* (New York: Academic Press, 1972) pp. 75–96; "The Dual Economy Revisited," in *Selected Economic Writings of W. Arthur Lewis*, pp. 211 (New York: New York University Press, 1983). In the Preface to his *Theory of Economic Growth* (London: George Allen & Unwin, 1955), Lewis states "a book of this kind seemed to be necessary because the theory of economic growth once more engages world wide interest, and because no comprehensive treatise on the subject has been published for about a century. The last great book covering this wide range was John Stuart Mill's *Principles of Political Economy*, published in 1848."
12. Prebisch (1950), Myrdal–Singer (1956). Singer returned to this subject most recently in Singer, David Sapsford, and Prabirjit Sarkar, "The Prebisch–Singer Terms of Trade Controversy Revisited," *Journal of International Development*, 1992. See also United Nations, Department of Economic Affairs, *Relative Prices of Exports and Imports of Under-developed Countries* (New York: United Nations, 1949).
13. Haberler (1959) also indicated "the tremendous importance of trade for the underdeveloped countries" and emphasized dynamic benefits from international trade, in addition to the static gains resulting from the division of labor. So too did Hicks (1959).
14. Dependency theory is presented in Paul Baran, *The Political Economy of Growth* (New York: Monthly Review Press, 1957); André Gunder Frank, *Capitalism and Underdevelopment in Latin America* (New York: Monthly Review Press, 1967); Frank Agee, *Capitalism and Underdevelopment in Latin America* (New York: Monthly Review Press, 1967) For a more recent review of unequal exchange and international inequalities, see David Evans, "Alternative Perspectives on Trade and Development," in Hollis Chenery and T. N. Srinivasan, eds., *Handbook of Development Economics* (Amsterdam: North Holland 1989).

15. For discussions of the big push, see Fleming (1955) and Hirschman (1958).
16. Christopher Bliss, "Trade and Development," in Hollis Chenery and T. N. Srinivasan, eds., *Handbook of Development Economics*, (Amsterdam: North Holland, 1989) vol 2, p. 1193.
17. John P. Lewis cites a number of reasons in the 1950s for giving government the central role in promoting development. Among these were:

    an acceptance of the de facto primacy of government…
    At least in the early 1950s, reliable, socially efficient markets were not thought to be primordial institutions; they were considered creatures of government…
    There was a need to protect the economy's disadvantaged participants and to supply public goods…
    Many were impressed by the economic aggrandizement as well as the social restructuring that a command system had been able to achieve in the Soviet Union. In the West … wartime experience with extensive central planning and economic controls had been positive…
    In the developing countries themselves, many of their governments were descendants of independence movements; they were governments in a hurry. Because their institutions were weak, their private-sector entrepreneurial initiatives hesitant, their markets underdeveloped (and in former colonies suspect), and their traders in disrepute, the newly created states were seen as the only possible agency of large-scale development.
    Lewis, "Government and National Development." *Daedalus*, Winter 1989, pp. 71–72.
    See also Reynolds, below, Ch. XIV in this volume.

18. Although many of the early development economists rejected neoclassical economics, there were some who warned that the analysis of development should not be "price-less", that the functions of prices should not be ignored, that the economic responses to individual incentives should not be overlooked, and that the government should not intervene in the market price system. Such a view dominated the work by P. T. Bauer and B. S. Yamey, *The Economics of Underdeveloped Countries* (Chicago: University of Chicago Press, 1957). A strong case for the market mechanism as against detailed planning was also made by Harry G. Johnson, "Planning and the Market in Economic Development," *Pakistan Economic Journal* (June 1958).

    The literature on planning grew rapidly in the 1950s: for example, H. H. Aubrey, "The Role of the State in Economic Development," *American Economic Review Papers and Proceedings* (May 1951); S. H. Frankel, "United Nations Primer for Development," *Quarterly Journal of Economics* (August 1952); T. C. Mahalanobis, "The Approach of Operational Research to Planning in India," *Sankhya* 16 (1 and 2 December 1955), pp. 3–130; G. Myrdal, *Rich Lands and Poor* (New York 1957), Ch. VII; P. T. Bauer, *Economic Analysis and Policy in Underdeveloped Countries* (Durham 1957), Ch. 3; A. O. Hirschman, "Economic Policy in Underdeveloped Countries," *Economic Development and Cultural Change* (July 1957); E. S. Mason, *Economic Planning in Underdeveloped Areas* (New York 1958); Hugh G. J. Aitken (ed.) *The State and Economic Growth* (New York, 1959); Maurice Dobb, *An Essay on Economic Growth and Planning* (London, 1960), Ch. 1.

19. For later refinements and extensions of the two gap model, see Bliss (1989).
20. For the production of national income estimates, see F. C. Benham, *The National Income of Grenada 1942* (Barbados, 1943); Phyllis Deane, *The Measurement of Colonial National Income* (Cambridge: Cambridge University Press, 1948); A. R. Prest, *The Investigation of National Income in British Tropical Dependencies* (London: The Athlone Press, 1957).

    Colin Clark's influential *The Conditions of Economic Progress* (London: Macmillan, 1940) returned to the classical problem of long-term economic growth, supplied statistical evidence of the gap between rich and poor countries, and, as Heinz Arndt observes, "set the growth economics agenda for a generation of economists". Arndt, "Colin Clark as a Development Economist," *World Development*, vol. 18, no. 7, July 1990, pp. 1045–50.
21. For details on the Committee for Colonial Studies, see A. H. M. Kirk-Greene, "The Committee for Colonial Studies: The Minute Books of the First Quinquennium, 1943–1948," *Oxford*, vol. XL, no.1, 1988, pp. 84–90. In 1956, the Committee for Colonial Studies became the Committee for Commonwealth Studies.
22. For a detailed account, see Robert Heussler, *Yesterday's Rulers: The Making of the British Colonial Service* (Syracuse: Syracuse University Press, 1963), Ch. 5. For studies of colonial servants in an earlier period, see C. Jeffries, *The Colonial Empire and Its Civil Service* (Cambridge: Cambridge University Press 1938); Sir A. Burns, *Colonial Civil Servant* (London: Unwin).
23. M. Perham, *British Native Administration*, Oxford University Summer School on Colonial Administration (Oxford: printed at the University Press 1938) p. 103.
24. In July 1944, she wrote the University Registrar that the "Nuffield Colonial Research Centre and the embryonic Institute of Colonial Studies are at present, in default of the College building, situated in my flat." Perham manuscript archives, Rhodes House, MP 256/1/p.39.
25. Perham Archives, Rhodes House, 233–2.
26. Perham Archives, 231–39.
27. Colonial Office, *Postwar Training for the Colonial Service*; Report of a committee appointed by the Secretary of State for the Colonies, Colonial no. 198 (London: HMSO, 1946).
28. *Select Reading List for Colonial Studies*, II. *Colonial Economics*, prepared by P. A. Bower; preface by M. Perham. The series of reading lists were produced under the auspices of Nuffield College, of which Margery Perham was a Fellow. See also Philip Mayer, *Nuffield College Reading List on Rural Conditions and Betterment in the British Colonies* (London: Oxford University Press 1947); *Colonial Government: Annotated Reading List on British Colonial Government* (London: Oxford University Press, 1950).
29. S. Herbert Frankel, *The Concept of Colonization* (Oxford at the Clarendon Press, 1949).
30. *Ibid.*, pp. 3–4.
31. See S. Herbert Frankel, "United Nations Primer for Development," *Quarterly Journal of Economics*, August 1952, pp. 301–26. Compare the replies by W. Arthur Lewis, "United Nations Primer for Development: Comment,"

Quarterly Journal of Economics, May 1953, pp. 267–75; Anthony Y. C. Koo, "Further Comment," *Ibid.*, pp. 275–80; and Frankel, "Reply," *Ibid.*, pp. 280–85.

32. S. Herbert Frankel, *The Economic Impact on Under-Developed Societies: Essays on International Investment and Social Change* (Oxford: Basil Blackwell, 1953). See also, Frankel, *Some Conceptual Aspects of International Economic Development of Underdeveloped Territories*, International Finance Section, Princeton University (Princeton, May 1952).
33. In that year Myint had been a member of the "Group of Experts" who produced the Report on *Measures for International Economic Stability* (New York: United Nations, 1951).

    In the late 1940s and early 1950s, the Agricultural Economics Research Institute at Oxford also offered refresher courses in agricultural economics for students from the colonies and dominions. Colin Clark was Director of the Institute 1953–69. In 1950, W. Arthur Lewis presented a seminar at the Institute on "Industrialization of Backward Areas".

    Ursula Hicks was appointed in 1947 University Lecturer in Public Finance and was active in lecturing to the Colonial Service students and was influential through her writings on public finance for underdeveloped countries. In 1951 she published *Public Finance Survey of India* (New York: U.N. Department of Economic Affairs), and in 1961, *Development from Below* (Oxford: Clarendon Press)
34. Some topics from this outline were extensively analyzed and refined in a number of subsequent papers by Myint. For a collection of some of these papers, see H. Myint, *Economic Theory and the Underdeveloped Countries* (New York: Oxford University Press, 1971).
35. Arthur Hazelwood, *The Economics of 'Under-Developed' Areas* (London: Oxford University Press 1954).
36. Arthur Hazelwood, *The Economics of Development* (London: Oxford University Press, 1964).

References

Bliss, Christopher (1989) "Trade and Development" in Hollis Chenery and T. N. Srinivasan (eds.), *Handbook of Development Economics* (Amsterdam: North-Holland, 1989) vol. 2, p. 1188.

Chenery, H. B. and M. Bruno (1962) "Development Alternatives in an Open Economy," *Economic Journal*, vol. 72, pp. 79–103.

Chenery, Hollis and Srinivasan, T. N. (eds.) (1988–89) *Handbook of Development Economics* (Amsterdam: North-Holland) vols. 1 and 2.

Fleming, J. M. (1955) "External Economies and the Doctrine of Balanced Growth," *Economic Journal*, vol. 65, pp. 241–56.

Haberler, Gottfried. (1959) *International Trade and Economic Development* (Cairo: National Bank of Egypt).

Hicks, J. R. (1959) *Essays in World Economics* (Oxford: Clarendon Press).

Hirschman, A. O. (1958) *The Strategy of Economic Development* (New Haven, CT: Yale University Press).

Leibenstein, Harvey (1957) *Economic Backwardness and Economic Growth* (New York: Wiley).
Lewis, W. Arthur (1954) "Economic Development with Unlimited Supplies of Labour," *Manchester School*, vol. 22, no. 2, pp. 137–91.
Lewis, W. Arthur (1955) *The Theory of Economic Growth* (London: George Allen & Unwin, Ltd.).
Little, Ian M. D. (1960) "The Strategy of Indian Development," *National Institute Economic Review* (May), vol. 9, pp. 20–29.
Myint, Hla (1948) *Theories of Welfare Economics* (London: Longman)
Myint, Hla (1985) "Organizational Dualism and Economic Development," *Asian Development Review*, vol. 3, no. 1, pp. 24–43.
Myrdal, Gunnar (1956) *Development and Underdevelopment* (Cairo: National Bank of Egypt).
Nelson, Richard R. (1956) "A Theory of the Low-Level Equilibrium Trap in Underdeveloped Countries," *American Economic Review*, vol. 46, no. 5 (December), pp. 894–908.
Nurske, Ragnar (1953) *Problems of Capital Formation in Underdeveloped Countries* (Oxford: Blackwell).
Nurske, Ragnar (1958) "The Conflict between 'Balanced Growth' and International Specialization," *Lectures on Economic Development* (Faculty of Economics and Faculty of Political Sciences (Ankara University), Istanbul).
Prebisch, R. (1950) *The Economic Development of Latin America and its Principal Problems* (New York: United Nations).
Rosenstein-Rodan, Paul (1943) "Problems of Industrialization in Eastern and South-Eastern Europe," *Economic Journal* (June–Sept.), pp. 202–11.
Rosenstein-Rodan, Paul (1957) *The Objectives of United States Economic Assistance Programs* (Cambridge, MA: MIT Center for International Studies).
Rosenstein-Rodan, Paul (1984) "Natura Facit Saltum — Analysis of the Disequilibrium and Growth Process," in Gerald M. Meier and Dudley Seers (eds.), *Pioneers in Development* (New York: Oxford University Press), pp. 207–21.
Rostow, W. W. (1952) *The Process of Economic Growth* (New York: Norton, 1952; Oxford: Clarendon Press, 1953).
Rostow, W. W. (1960) *The Stages of Economic Growth* (Cambridge, England: Cambridge University Press).
Rostow, W. W. (1956) "The Take-off into Self-Sustained Growth," *Economic Journal*, vol. 66 (March).
Singer, H. W. (1950) "The Distribution of Gains Between Investing and Borrowing Countries," *American Economic Review*, 40, no. 2, pp. 377–82.
Viner, Jacob (1953) *International Trade and Economic Development* (Oxford: Clarendon Press).
Young, Allyn A. (1928) "Increasing Returns and Economic Progress," *Economic Journal*, vol. 38 (December), pp. 527–42.

12 Gamagori: In Retrospect

H. W. Arndt

In April 1960, the International Economic Association, urged by its Japanese members, held a conference at Gamagori, Japan. The proceedings, edited by Kenneth Berrill, were published four years later under the title *Economic Development: With Special Reference to East Asia* [Berrill, (1964)].

Making due allowance for the fact East Asia was to some of the participants, not least to the editor and to the distinguished President of the IEA, Professor E. A. G. Robinson, still the 'Far East", that is, east of Suez, it comes as a surprise to-day to find that the papers were almost entirely devoted to two countries, Japan and India. To Indonesia, Malaysia, the Philippines, Thailand, Hong Kong, and the two Chinas, there were a few passing references. The only one to Korea related to 1894. Singapore was never mentioned at all. The editor explained that India and Japan were "better known economies" and expressed the hope that the next conference on Asia would concentrate more on countries like the Philippines, Burma, and Indonesia. But that conference never eventuated.

The emphasis on Japan and India was also reflected in the composition of the conference. Of the 18 papers, 5 were given by Japanese, 3 by Indians, 9 by Westerners. Three of the authors (one of the Indians, one of the Japanese and a Taiwanese) were associated with the ECAFE Secretariat. Most of the other participants, 28 in all, were Japanese. Among other Asian countries, Indonesia, Hong Kong, the Philippines, Thailand and Burma had one representative each. Only three of these were academic economists, among them the Rector of the University of Rangoon, Professor Hla Myint.

The papers were divided into two parts, "Factors Affecting Growth" (land, labor, capital, entrepreneurship, foreign trade) and "Policies Affecting Growth" (price stability, fiscal policy, agricultural policy, choice of techniques, technical assistance). But the discussions, which the editor reported in extensive but inevitably condensed summaries, were dominated by Indian and ECAFE structuralism — in favor of national planning, direct controls over foreign trade, import substitution and priority for heavy industry. Contrary views were put, more or less forcefully, by several of the Western economists, especially John Adler and W. H. Nicholls. Among

Asian economists, the case for market and export oriented development was put most consistently by Hla Myint.

Re-reading the Gamagori volume now is a vivid reminder of how times have changed in the intervening thirty years. Hardly anyone in 1960 foresaw that not only Japan, but also the developing countries of east Asia which we now know as the northeast Asian newly industrialized economies (NIEs) and ASEAN would in the next thirty years become the outstanding growth area of the world. And few at Gamagori foresaw, or even favored, the trend in the next thirty years away from highly regulated inward-looking development. For economists, a retrospective review of the book is an exercise at once humbling and exhilarating.

12.1 EXPORT PESSIMISM

The staunchest proponent of structuralist views at the conference was the Director of the ECAFE Research Division, Professor Hiroshi Kitamura.

> World trade had changed since 1900 and this change meant poor prospects for development via expanded exports, especially in East Asia. Primary products were on the whole [facing] weak markets, [and] it was unlikely that advanced countries would be willing to import large quantities of manufactures from cheap labor countries. Economic growth must in today's conditions largely be developed in terms of a closed economy (231).

The contribution that foreign trade can make to economic development is marginal (198). Since for developing countries import needs inevitably outrun import capacity (202), "a broad range of government measures of encouragement and control will have to be advocated and sustained over a long period until the economy grows out of its infant status" (196). All unnecessary imports, including luxury goods, must be cut out; goods now imported must be replaced, if possible, by domestic production (209). "Exchange and trade control measures to deflect demand from imports to domestic production are much more subtle and flexible instruments than tariffs" (210). Only planned development, buttressed by a system of direct control of trade can correct "the bias against development that would have emerged if foreign trade had been left to market forces" (192).

Nothing illustrates more strikingly the export pessimism that underlay this structuralist view than a footnote to Professor Kitamura's paper. Having cited a Taiwanese study which suggested that, for Taiwan to attain a 6 per cent annual rate of growth of GDP, exports would need to grow at 15 per cent a year, he asked rhetorically: "Can we seriously count on such a high rate of growth of exports nowadays?"(199) He would have been astonished to be told that through the 1980s Taiwan's exports would grow at an average annual rate of 31 per cent, and those of all northeast and southeast Asian countries at 29 per cent [*Asian Development Bank* (1989, p. 187)].

The other participants were divided on this issue. Among the Asians, Dr Saburo Okita, pointing to the examples of Japan and Hong Kong, urged that "the possibilities of exporting more manufactures should not be underestimated" (229). Dr Amartya Sen, on the other hand, stressed the risk of large swings in the terms of trade to which countries with high foreign trade ratios are exposed and the possible adverse effects on the terms of trade of currency devaluation. Most of the Western economists stressed the static and dynamic gains from trade and deprecated undue export pessimism. "Adler preferred to be pessimistic about planners" (230). But Robinson was prepared to concede the case for an "infant industry" policy to escape from a situation in which failure to expand exports is limiting development. In line with the then current penchant for common markets and free trade areas, he adumbrated the idea — which he had recently incorporated in his UN team's design for ASEAN — of "a group of underdeveloped countries operating a combined 'infant industry' policy" (225). Hla Myint objected that Professor Robinson's paper was written in terms of India and Pakistan and did not apply to much of East Asia (231). Nicholls thought that India which possesses the fuel and ores needed for the metal trades, was in a relatively good position to capture a larger share of the world market for manufactures (361).

12.2 PLANNING AND STATE ENTERPRISE

The issues of planned versus market economy and state versus private enterprise were subjects of lively debate, especially in the sessions on entrepreneurship. Unsurprisingly, the Indian and ECAFE speakers strongly favored planning and state enterprise; the Western speakers favored a market economy and private enterprise, with reservations; the Japanese speakers came out for a judicious mixture. The strongest warnings about the weakness of public administration and public enterprise in developing countries came from Hla Myint.

The former Executive Secretary of ECAFE, Professor P. S. Lokanathan, had no doubt, in the light of Indian experience as he saw it, about the need for central planning and the merits of state enterprise. "The countries of Asia... must accomplish in a couple of decades what the Western countries did over more than a century. The State [therefore] has to assume the leading role which was undertaken by private entrepreneurs in Western capitalism" (184). Only the State could organize the expansion of heavy industry, leaving private enterprise to produce consumer goods (187). "In India today... the State itself is now the chief entrepreneur.... The economic activities of the State stimulate industrial entrepreneurship... by building the infrastructure and by developing the public sector of industry" (157). The Government was better than the private entrepreneur at appreciating new possibilities in the economy as a whole... In India today the supply of entrepreneurs was increasing at an astonishing rate" (190). "By the Third Plan the profits from public enterprises would be an important source of savings" (318).

Lokanathan was strongly supported by Kitamura — "planning is nothing but the rational principle of resource allocation" (191) — and by C. N. Vakil, who explained that in the Indian steel industry "the biggest part of the expansion was to come from Government plants managed by civil servants" (190). Sen claimed that in developing countries, because of the prestige of civil service jobs, public corporations attracted better people than private firms (188). Some of the Western economists agreed with the Indians on some points. Thus Chenery argued that Government was good at deciding which type of industry should be started (189) and Robinson that government planners should be "safeguarders of economic common sense" (232).

The French economist, Professor Fauvel, expressed cautious dissent: There is no doubt that public entrepreneurship was possible, but he was by no means sure it was the best. "The moment a government gives up the market economy, it assumes in effect the responsibility for investment planning, and that is one of the most tricky problems in the world" (139). John Adler proclaimed a "rule of reluctance" for the Government to expand the scope of its operations into pursuits which can be left to the private sector. He questioned "the assumption that somehow Government can acquire the missing competence more readily than a private firm" (219). Howard Ellis agreed (189). Dr Okita thought most Asian countries should follow the experience of Western countries but should speed up their development by government leadership and planning (403). According to Professor Nakayama, Japanese history showed the advantage of the State starting enterprises and later handing them over to private enterprise (189).

Adler's "rule of reluctance" was strongly supported by Hla Myint. "If the Government cannot do the basic jobs well it should not move into new sectors, even though they seem necessary and attractive. In Burma there was a great shortage of good people in the government service, and the attempt to have a welfare state at the same time as trying to re-establish law and order had meant that they had failed to provide either. The unit cost of all government activity was very high and the Government continually failed to put first things first" (318).

In the background to much of the discussion were the Soviet model of industrial development and the Soviet challenge to the West. India's Second Plan (1956–61), designed by Mahalanobis, consciously followed the Soviet model with its emphasis on heavy industry. Kitamura echoed Mahalanobis in advocating autarkic development as the only way of ensuring an adequate supply of capital goods (201). Lokanathan also echoed Mahalanobis in insisting that only the State could organise the necessary expansion of heavy industry (187).

Nicholls and others urged the Asian developing countries to follow the Japanese rather than the Soviet model. Asian leaders tend "to overlook the extent to which Japan, Malaya, and Hong Kong offer alternative models involving much less direct government control" (358). But, three years after Sputnik, some of the Western economists were mesmerized by the Soviet challenge. The Swedish economist Svennilson accepted without a murmur a recent statement by the chairman of Gosplan, Kosigin, that the Soviet Union, within the near future, "will build 400 complete factories in 22 developing countries" (406) and no one questioned Lokanathan's assertion that "India had set up three steel plants by the package method. The Russians had proved exceptionally good at transferring their know-how, the British reasonable, and the Germans poor" (426).

Twenty years later, the Indian economist, Raj Krishna, summed up Indian experience very differently. "The basic cause of India's dismal growth record is the extreme inefficiency with which capital has been utilized. Between the first and the fifth Plan, India has managed to double her investment ratio, but the capital–output ratio had also doubled. The vast investment funds, extracted from the people through heavy taxation, inflation and the transfer of people's funds in the financial institutions to the government, have been used with steadily declining productivity by an unholy combine of politicians and government servants."

"The reasons for this extraordinary inefficiency lie in the established framework of economic policy and administration. There is no competitive or coercive pressure for efficient performance either in the state monopolies run by a callous babu-class, nor in the overprotected and overcontrolled private monopolies. Competition is ruled out because we are socialists; coercion is ruled out because we are democrats!.... The maintenance of capacity is extremely poor, so that precious public capital is rapidly depreciated or sabotaged. And the chronic unrest of the unionized working class keeps physical productivity at a pitiably low level by international standards" (Krishna, 1980).

12.3 DIMINISHING RETURNS

As Nicholls pointed out, the Soviet model had been widely influential in encouraging in Asia a strong emphasis on the uneconomic development of heavy industry and... neglect of agriculture" (358f). Sen still thought that fears of what would happen if Indian agricultural output failed to expand at the planned rate were much exaggerated. Countries which were short of land should concentrate on industrial output (374).

The problem, as Kitamura explained, was the old Malthusian one of diminishing returns. He drew on Hla Myint's recent article on "'The 'Classical Theory' of International Trade and the Underdeveloped Countries" (Myint 1958) to distinguish between two types of primary producing countries in Asia. For one of these, exemplified by Burma or Thailand, where population was sparse in relation to natural resources, the opening of trade created "vent for surplus". Here agriculture showed only "gently diminishing returns", although here, too, as rapid population growth sets in, export capacity will taper off (203f). For the second type, the export-oriented plantation economy, illustrated by Ceylon or the Federation of Malaya, high population density threatens sharply diminishing returns. In both cases, more urgently in the second than in the first, the remedy is increase in productivity through capital accumulation and technical progress. But as an ECAFE study of Ceylon shows, "the productivity gains that are expected from investment of a given unit of resources will be relatively higher in the non-export sectors" (208).

Such pessimism was strongly contested by Nicholls. He castigated India for following the Communist model, criticized Western economists, such as Benjamin Higgins and in lesser degree even Arthur Lewis, for supporting the emphasis on heavy capital-intensive industry, and marvelled at the "relative confidence" Wilfred Malenbaum placed on Chinese claims about growth of agricultural output during the Great Leap Forward (357). "The appeal of the Soviet (and now Chinese) model lies in part in the apparent rapidity of Chinese economic development and, perhaps in greater part, in the ceaseless propaganda barrage which has exaggerated the gains and concealed the costs and shortcomings of the Communist experience" (358).

He argued that Japan had demonstrated the importance of increased agricultural productivity as a precondition of industrial development and asserted confidently that "India has tremendous opportunities for increasing yields per hectare by modest capital expenditures on land-saving techniques, such as fertilizer, improved seeds, insecticides and pesticides, and better cultivation and irrigation practices" (363, 366). "Like Japan, India can earn very high returns on investments in the discovery, propagation, and financing of land-saving methods through agricultural research and extension services" (366).

Oddly, in retrospect, on the eve of the Green Revolution in rice, there was little support for Nicholls's views in the discussion. Even the Japanese agricultural economist, Professor Henmi, was pessimistic about prospects for Asian agriculture. He doubted "whether it was possible to get a good increase in agricultural yields in East Asian countries in the next few years" (372). Adler said that agriculture was resistant to technical change (375). Chenery agreed with Swan in disliking the concept that food was a very special commodity (374). Moh. Sadli said it was not much use devoting all one's attention to increasing food output if the only result was increased food consumption in the country without any switch of activity towards investment (374).

12.4 CONCLUSION

The IEA volume was reviewed in the *Economic Journal* by Henry Rosovsky and in the *American Economic Review* by Gustav Ranis.

Rosovsky criticized the contributors for what he thought was extravagant admiration of Japan and for their failure to mention a most important lesson taught by Japan: patience. He complained that there was not a single paper on China and that "Korea has, once again, been entirely neglected". Somewhat surprisingly, he complimented Lokanathan on "a most valuable discussion of Indian problems with the entrepreneurial sector" (Rosovsky 994f).

Ranis patted Kitamura on the back with one hand — "Kitamura rightly emphasizes the dethroning of trade as the major engine of growth" — and slapped him with the other: "His conclusion that the foreign exchange problem is best solved by import substitution is difficult to accept, and… his faith in government planning as a resource allocator and growth promoter seems a bit ex cathedra… Kitamura should be reminded that the failure of the price structure to reflect real costs correctly is as often the consequence of planning via overvalued exchange rates and direct controls" (Ranis 207).

Ranis did not mention Myint by name but referred to "vent for surplus" though in rather a different context from the Burmese one that Myint had in mind: "Even when trade cannot serve as the major stimulus to development it is likely to play a major role in relieving the over-all resources tightness by providing a vent for its (embodied) surplus labor: in the presence of a necessarily narrow domestic market". He also used a concept which the profession some years later came to associate with Hla Myint's overall report in the Asian Development Bank's volume on *Southeast Asia's Economies in the 1970s*: '"Export substitution', that is the shift to exports incorporating relatively more labor and human ingenuity and relatively less natural resources" (Ranis, 207).

The purpose of the foregoing post mortern on Gamagori has not been to throw brickbats at the exponents of what was then still the conventional wisdom in much of the less developed world — a practice not to be recommended to anyone sitting in a glasshouse — but to demonstrate how easy it is for intelligent men of goodwill to follow false trails on major issues of economic policy and to express quiet satisfaction at the almost worldwide spread since 1960 of the "free market and free trade policies" that Hla Myint rightly claims to have advocated "for much of the time" (Myint, 1987).

References

Asian Development Bank (1983) *Asian Development Outlook* (Manila).

Berrill, K. (ed.) (1964) *Economic Development: With Special Reference to East Asia* (London: Macmillan).

Krishna, Raj (1980) in *Indian Express*, 7 August.

Myint, H. (1958) "The 'Classical Theory' of International Trade and the Underdeveloped Countries," *Economic Journal*, June; reprinted in *Economic Theory and the Underdeveloped Countries* (Oxford University Press, 1971).

Myint, H. (1971) "Overall Report" in Asian Development Bank, *Southeast Asia's Economy in the 1970s* (London: Longman).

Myint, H. (1987) "Neoclassical Development Analysis: Its Strengths and Limitations" in G. M. Meier (ed.), *Pioneers in Development*, Second Series (New York: Oxford University Press).

Ranis, G. (1965) Review of Berrill 1964, *American Economic Review*, March.

Rosovsky, H. (1964) Review of Berrill 1964, *Economic Journal*, December.

13 Structural Adjustment Policy: Asian Experience*

Shigeru Ishikawa

13.1 *DIRIGISME* AND STRUCTURAL ADJUSTMENT POLICIES: INTRODUCTION

In recent years the transition to the market economy system in the former Soviet Union and East European countries has become a world-wide concern. Yet, it is not so widely recognized that waves of transformation in the economic and social system of a similar nature and with a similar world-wide significance have been taking place since the end of the 1970s in many developing countries, as a result of protracted balance of payment crises and the ensuing adherence to the proposed World Bank-IMF structural adjustment policies.

The economic regimes of these countries, most of which acquired independence during and after World War II, could be loosely termed as *dirigiste.*[1] For, while the content of policies varies widely, there is a common presumption that the visible hand of the state is needed to supplement the weak, underdeveloped hand of the market mechanism. Typical instruments of *dirigisme* are two: one is establishment of the state-owned enterprises on the basis of which important economic activities of the country are conducted directly by the state; and two, setting up a system of licensing and other controls and thereby regulating the economic activities that are left to the private sectors. The loosest form of *dirigisme* is found in those countries, such as in Southeast Asia, which appear to have adopted a market-economy regime after World War II, but in various aspects of the economy and depending upon the period, state enterprises exist and state control systems operate. At the opposite extreme, there is a regime of

*This paper is a reconstructed and revised version of my public lectures made, under somewhat different titles, at the Economic Research Institute, Hitotsubashi University and School of Oriental and African Studies, University of London in May and June 1991, respectively. I wish to thank Professor Hideki Esho, Dr Kazumi Goto, Professor Christopher Howe, Mr Seiji Kojima, Dr Johannes Linn, Professor Hla Myint, Professor Kazushi Ohkawa, Dr Saburo Okita, Professors Gustav Ranis, John Toye, Juro Teranishi, Toru Yanagihara, and Dr Oktay Yanel for their valuable comments on the draft.

"centralized, physical planning" like that of China before the recent economic reform, where almost all important economic activities are carried on by the state enterprises under the directives of the state plans.

Even the motives behind adoption of *dirigisme* are not confined to the usual one of supplementing weak market mechanisms and thereby promoting economic development. One special case may be pointed out: *Dirigisme* sometimes accompanies a motive of traditional, "patrimonial bureaucracy", namely the motive to consider state property as identical to one's own private property and to utilize it, for example, to provide jobs and incomes to family members and followers.[2] Moreover, in those countries with a stricter form of *dirigisme*, a kind of "social welfare" system is often in practice, to provide security of lifetime employment and living wages to workers. Each work unit there is turned more or less into a village-like community.

The IMF and World Bank are, of course, the central world organizations, together with GATT, assuming the responsibility of maintaining postwar world economic order. Since the late 1970s, a large number of *dirigiste* countries have fallen into protracted balance of payment crises and requested the assistance of the IMF and World Bank. Accordingly, the IMF and World Bank attempted a major change in their lending facilities, and the traditional division of labor of the two organizations in lending to the developing countries has begun gradually — and since 1986 rapidly — receding. The new facilities of the World Bank are Structural Adjustment Lending (SAL) and Sectoral Adjustment Lending (SECAL) introduced in 1980; those for the IMF are Structural Adjustment Facilities (SAF) introduced in 1986, and Extended Structural Adjustment Facilities (ESAF) introduced in 1987, in addition to Extended Fund Facilities (EFF) already in operation since 1977. These facilities, by imposing "conditionality", require countries to enforce, in addition to the familiar IMF stabilization measures, programs of reform to replace *dirigisme* by market-oriented institutions and policies.

The rationale behind SA policies is the IMF and World Bank's contention that *dirigisme* measures are the basic cause of various distortions in the economy, thereby significantly contributing to the protracted balance of payment crises. It is believed that the crises can be overcome only when conventional stabilization measures are supplemented by powerful SA measures.

The prescribed measures are quite comprehensive and, despite great variations in the recipient country economies, fairly uniform in policy orientation, thus presenting a kind of prototype prescription.

On the macro-economic side, the reform program stipulates fiscal and monetary policies to reduce overall demand, and exchange rate and import/export taxes and subsidies to alter the relative incentives between tradables and non-tradables. On the micro-economic side, the program requires the removal of price distortions, and the opening up of more competition and dismantling administrative controls ("deregulation"), thereby improving the efficiency of resource use. In the domain of non-market activities, rationalization of government expenditures and public enterprise management and even privatization are required.[3]

The purpose of this paper is to investigate the rationale of the IMF and World Bank's SA policy as well as its effectiveness in replacing post-World War II developing countries' *dirigisme* by market-oriented institutions and policies and, side-by-side, to achieve stabilization and growth, according to the original policy aims. With regard to the performance of the SA policy, a variety of studies for evaluation have so far been published, revealing a number of cases in which the policy aims were not achieved.[4] To the extent that this was the case, one has to inquire how to revise the SA programs. For this inquiry, it is essential to prepare a consistent method of evaluating the effectiveness of the SA policy.

Throughout this chapter, I rely only upon the experience of the countries of East and Southeast Asia, not only for a broad testing of our hypothesis on the feasibility of the SA policy, but also for obtaining insights into the relationship between *dirigisme* and the SA policy.

In the following, Section 13.2 deals with an an analytical history background of *dirigisme* and the SA policy, or the rivalry between so-called "structuralism" and "neoclassical resurgence". Certain remaining difficulties with the latter as a framework for the analysis of developing economies are discussed, and are related to the practical difficulties of the SA policy.

In Section 13.3, the effectiveness of the fairly uniform programs of the SA policy is evaluated mainly in terms of their congruence to certain important initial conditions that are specific to the individual developing countries concerned. The initial conditions selected are of four categories: (1) resource endowments (and the development models specific to particular types of resource endowment), (2) *per capita* income level, (3) degree of development of the market economy and administrative systems, and (4) economic institutions, policies, and political culture. Findings of the effectiveness of the SA policy in this evaluation are examined on the basis of country-by-country analysis of empirical data.

In Section 13.4, the effectiveness of the SA policy is further evaluated by focusing on initial conditions (3) and (4) and interpreting the congruence relations in rather dynamic terms. Certain new concepts of analytical importance are introduced: "adaptation" of the SA policy to the initial condition and the "reconfiguration" of the socio-economic forces such that this adaptation is made possible.

Section 13.5 shows that "adaptation" of the major aid policy was in fact made in the past even by the World Bank itself. In the last section, some conclusions are made regarding the future effectiveness of SA policy.

13.2 THEORETICAL FOUNDATIONS OF SA POLICIES — "NEOCLASSICAL RESURGENCE" AND ITS LIMITATIONS

The theoretical background to structural adjustment policies is the so-called "neoclassical resurgence" in development economics that took place in the 1960s and 70s.[5] This line of thinking was in reaction to the "structuralist" approach of the 1950s. Many authors during the 1950s were brought up with the training of Keynesian, Neo-Keynesian, or Marxist economics, and without sufficient personal knowledge or available research data on the developing countries, which was inevitable at that time. They therefore constructed many hypotheses about the developing economies on the bases mostly of conjectured assumptions of domestic structural rigidity or export difficulties. The "structuralist approach" is a generic name referring to these authors. Neoclassical authors, on the other hand, have benefited from the newly available empirical data and the research opportunities in the field, criticizing effectively the unrealistic assumptions and ensuing results.

It is not necessarily practical, however, to take these two approaches as definite alternatives. Also it would be a great loss if a number of still useful hypotheses grasping the underdevelopment or dynamics of the development process were denied altogether owing to their rigidity assumptions. But, more importantly, I wish to note that common to both approaches is a failure to observe some essential features of developing economies of which two relate closely to the theme of this essay:

(1) Such economies are marked not only by the underdevelopment of productive forces but also by underdevelopment of the market institutions. Economic development should be explained in some way or other as the process of development of an underdeveloped market economy.

(2) Developing economies vary considerably in the pattern of their resource endowment, and hence in terms of which factors of production are scarce, abundant, or underutilized, and which factors are not. Growth is thus often a process of bringing into use, or fuller use, resources that are underutilized. The pattern of growth will hence vary according to the pattern of resource endowments.[6]

As the neoclassical economists, and some structuralists too, assume the existence of a fully developed market economy and full employment their failure to observe these two aspects was a logical result. This, in turn, makes the theoretical relevance of SA policy weakly based.

13.3 FEASIBILITY OF SA POLICIES

The feasibility or effectiveness of structural adjustment depends largely on two factors. First, the principle of market competition that is advocated by the SA policy conforms to the general spirit of the contemporary international economic order, represented by the IMF, World Bank, and GATT. Therefore, any developing country that intends to develop its economy continually (that is, even after the developing phase is over) as a partner in international trade, should adhere to it sooner or later. The same principle also conforms to the general direction of progress that the domestic economic system in the dirigiste countries should take whenever any positive element of *dirigisme* diminishes and the inefficiency aspect of *dirigisme* comes to the fore. This is a strong point in favor of the feasibility of SA programs.

Secondly, in terms of the relevance to the immediate domestic economic and social conditions of individual developing countries, however, the uniformity of the policy prescriptions means that the SA policy may not necessarily be appropriate, and its feasibility is likely to vary depending upon initial conditions of the individual developing countries concerned.

Investigations of the performances of the SA programs applied in Asian countries broadly confirm the validity of the hypothesis that a few common factors determine the program's feasibility:[7]

(1) The most successful tend to be those in which *per capita* incomes are already in the middle-income country range and in which the market economy and administrative systems are fairly well developed. In contrast, the less successful are usually among those in which incomes are low and the market economy and administrative mechanisms are very underdeveloped.

(2) Feasibility tends to be greatest in economies that are rich in natural resources and small in population, and tends to be less successful in economies where the reverse holds.

(3) A decisive role is often played by institutions and policies and the underlying political culture of the economy. Sometimes they play the role of denying feasibility, despite favorable conditions in the above factors

(1) and (2). There are other cases in which unfavorable conditions in those factors are overcome and turned to favorable ones.

Some of these findings may be even obvious logically. As for finding (1), we may note that because SA policies presuppose at least a fair degree of development of the market economy, including the existence of capable entrepreneurs and bureaucratic technocrats, a low degree of development of a market economy places a definite constraint upon the acceptance of the usual measures of SA policies.

As for finding (2), the more favorable position of the resource-rich countries can be explained by the fact that these countries are usually developed as primary export economies in which a high rate of "natural rent" is easily captured at the stage of primary product export. The "natural rent" is potentially capable of being used as "primitive accumulation capital" for sustaining non-primary economic development, unless that capital is dissipated unproductively by the yet inexperienced national governments.[8] Once efforts at increasing the productivity of the export goods are neglected, the "natural rent" declines gradually and their comparative advantage will be lost.

In contrast, resource poor and densely populated economies are mostly poor, and their savings are also low. For these economies, economic development probably means industrialization, requiring the transference to the emerging industrial sector of both part of the agricultural labor force and the surplus agricultural produce to feed it. This is not an easy thing to accomplish, as it certainly necessitates a substantial increase in both land and labor productivity in agriculture; but the agricultural sector usually does not have sufficient resources to accommodate it.[9]

As for finding (3) a few cases may be mentioned. Under a certain type of political culture, the high rate of "natural rent" tends easily to be dissipated for unproductive constructions and leisure consumption and even to cause suspension of the previous effort for economic self-reliance (for example, by a campaign for increasing food-grain production or for establishing certain new branches of manufacturing industry.) The latter is a phenomenon similar to "Dutch disease" or "oil syndrome". Under certain other types of political culture, dutch diseases are skilfully avoided, and resource-poor, overpopulated countries are capable of fully utilizing whatever opportunities happen to emerge for industrialization.

Perhaps more importantly, the differences in the degree of development in the market economy and administrative systems, and even in the productivity level, in factor (1), are not inflexible constants. The length of time required for advancing from one development stage to another could be compressed or stretched depending upon the human effort, which in turn depends significantly on the type of political culture.[10]

In the following, these findings are elaborated with respect to two broad groups of Asian countries classified according to factor (1). Descriptions of an individual country's case are preceded by a short account of the nature of balance of payment difficulties and the related IMF and World Bank actions.

A. The Republic of Korea, Thailand, Malaysia, and Indonesia are selected for elaboration. Among those countries in which a market economy has developed to a fair extent, the level of *per capita* income is not low, and performance in stabilization and liberalization are in general good.

In Korea, serious balance of payment crises occurred in 1979 side by side with domestic inflation. The impact of the rapid worsening of the international economic environment in that year and after was especially serious as Korea undertook ambitious heavy and chemical industrialization after the mid-1970s, relying upon private foreign borrowing.

To tide over the post 1979 crisis, Korea obtained stand-by credits from the IMF in 1980 and 1983, and Structural Adjustment Loans from the World Bank in 1981 and 1982. As for "conditionalities" for these credits and loans, only stabilization measures by way of fiscal, financial, and income policies were in fact implemented. By 1986, the stabilization measures achieved a significant success and the economy regained a high rate of growth. Meanwhile, the Korean government enacted an Anti-Trust Law (1981) on its own initiative, and the role of economic planning was turned to that of indicating guide-posts. Liberalization of imports, abolition of the preferential interest rates formerly applied to export firms, and discontinuance of the policy to promote specified industries (1986) also occurred on Korea's initiative.

Thailand suffered also from similar macro-economic crises after 1979. The World Bank supported Thailand by two SALs in 1982 and 1983. The conditionality covered many areas for reform and policy changes, following its prototype. By 1986, stabilization measures achieved substantial success. For Thailand, structural adjustment was of special interest in relation to the agricultural sector. The conditionality required a reform of the agricultural incentive system, recognizing that further agricultural development through continuous opening-up of the cultivated area was no longer possible. As a major component of the reform, the export taxes on rice, rubber and other main export products were reduced, so that the income of producer farm households was increased. Thus, the proportion of the export tax on rice to the f.o.b. Bangkok price of rice declined from 30 per cent in 1981 to only 4 per cent in 1985. In addition, the minimum price guarantee program for producers was abolished. These reforms were, however, made possible by the fact that Thailand mobilized a high rate of "natural rents" arising from traditional rice exports quite effectively and allocated them first for *switching* among major export products, (namely from rice to corn, kenaf, and tapioca), and then for *restructuring* the economy for export industrialization (namely, by developing agricultural resource-based as well as final demand-based manufactured products, like plywood and textiles.) *Per capita* personal disposable income thereby increased considerably.

As for Indonesia, macro-economic crises occurred after the reverse oil-shock of 1982. The World Bank SA lending took the form of a series of SECALs, focusing on trade policy and private sector development (1987, 88 and 89). Although no conditionality was attached, the Indonesian government, starting from 1983, quite effectively implemented stabilization and structural adjustment policies along the line of the World Bank's prototype. The outcome is generally considered a success: Indonesia is now able to move on again toward long-term economic development. As an underlying factor, the success of *switching* of export primary products in the outer-islands (to rubber and palm) and *restructuring* toward both resource-based and final demand-based industrialization in Java might be mentioned. Also, Indonesia did not suffer from Dutch disease, although she is a big oil exporting country. The current amount of accumulated foreign debt, however, is more than 53 billion US dollars, and both the foreign debt-service and the foreign currency support for the above *restructuring* require continuation of the current-level ODA commitment of over 4 billion US dollars per year.

Malaysia did not receive any aid from the IMF or World Bank. However, when it suffered from balance of payment difficulties in the early 1980s, it formulated a stabilization-cum-structural adjustment policy similar to the IMF and World Bank prototype. The outcome was a significant success. Switching and restructuring with the prudent use of a high rate of "natural rents" (obtained from rubber and tin) was also similarly effective.

B. Turning now to the group of countries in which the market economy is still underdeveloped and where stabilization and/or liberalization have been lagging behind, we shall focus on Bangladesh and Sri Lanka.

First, Bangladesh is a country with dense population and very poor resources; even the infrastructure for a minimal required standard to sustain people's life does not yet exist. The market economy is compartmentalized and is at a very low development stage. The rate of saving is low, the budget is in deficit, and it is only because of the continual provision of large aid from the World Bank, the United States, and other donors has it been able to sustain a chronic current account deficit. The SA policy has been enforced since 1980 by the strong advice of the IMF and World Bank, although the IMF's SAF and World Bank's SECAL (in manufacturing, energy and finance) were not formally introduced until after 1986. An outcome of the application of the uniform SA prescription is illustrated by the conditionality for the agricultural sector. It follows a prototype consisting of (1) reduction of the export tax rate, (2) discontinuance of producers' and consumers' subsidies on food grains, (3) reduction of the price subsidies to the agricultural input goods, (4) discontinuance of the low-interest-rate agricultural credit through institutional finance, and (5) elimination of the state enterprises in the marketing sector. The outcome has been to throw into extreme difficulty all the lower-strata peasants with only tiny land holdings and hence with their main income coming from engagement in casual wage-labor.

Sri Lanka received the IMF's EFF and SAF supports in 1977 and again in 1988. The macro-economic difficulty still remains. This is related to the fact that the *dirigiste* regimes throughout the post-war years transformed the country into a "social welfare state" of a high degree, financially relying upon the high rate of "natural rents" obtained from tea exports. On the other hand, measures for productivity increase in the nationalized tea plantations were neglected. Therefore, the rate of "natural rent" declined, and the chances to use it for switching and restructuring were largely lost.

13.4 ADAPTATION OF THE DEVELOPING ECONOMIES TO THE "DOMINANT STRATEGY"

Much room still remains for investigating the feasibility issues in connection with factor (3). This investigation would be facilitated by extending the scope of our analysis to cover the whole post-war period in which the same Asian countries reacted to the IMF, World Bank, and United States aid strategies. These aid strategies we may call "dominant strategies", although they were subject to change from time to time.

When we do this investigation, we first find that the crucial feasibility factor has usually been the existence or non-existence of the will and capability in recipients to adapt to the requirements of the "dominant strategy". "Adaptation" is defined here not necessarily as a willingness to follow rigidly the prescriptions of the dominant strategies, but rather, in terms of the ability to select from the proposed regimes those elements in it that are congruent with the recipient economy's policies and institutions.

The second finding is that the success of such adaptation depends upon whether it is possible to reconfigure domestic socio-economic forces in a way that allows those with the will and ability for change to exercise effective influence on economic development.

The first finding may be elaborated by referring to the experience of Korean development since the 1950s. Leaving aside the "land reform" enforced by the military government of the Allied Forces, the dominant strategy over Korea of the major donor, the United States government was, until the mid-1960s, economic recovery and reconstruction. The aid was extended under generous terms. In the early 1960s, foreign trade sector reform was required, but only a downward revision of the exchange rate was implemented. After the mid-1960s, the donors wanted the government to reduce controls over the private sector activities and to adopt a liberalization policy. The policy stance of South Korea to this dominant strategy was summarized in a well-known aid-effectiveness study of 1986 commissioned jointly by the IMF and World Bank. The study says that "overall, policy advice was followed if it supported the distribution of power and the national directions already determined by government" and that since the early 1960s Korea has been an effective user of concessional assistance.[11] However, this does not mean that Korea sidestepped the necessary reforms. In fact, Korean strategy was to go forward in accord with the objectives of the dominant strategies, but not through the prescribed channel; instead, "adaptation" and maintenance of Korea's own priorities and method were followed.

Four comments are in order:

(1) As is becoming more widely known, South Korean foreign trade policy has never chosen either import-substitution or export-promotion as sole alternatives. In fact, the choice has been made in a composite and parallel manner, with the priority changing according to the necessity of industrialization in each period — namely, from the period of import-substitution before the mid-1960s with the aim of becoming exporters of textiles and other light-industry goods, to the period until the mid-1970s with relative emphasis on an export-drive of the same categories of goods, and thereafter to the period with relative emphasis again turned to import-substitution of heavy and chemical industry goods with the aim of becoming an exporter of machinery and other engineering goods.

(2) A characteristic aspect of South Korean policy has been an "industrial policy" of the Japanese type, which may be defined as a policy for industrial development by using industry-specific instruments of public finance,

money and banking, foreign trade, and even direct administrative means. In Korea, such a policy was enforced more vigorously than in Japan, with particular use of selective credit extensions. Many laws and regulations for the policy were transplanted from Japan even to the extent of having the same titles. But despite the formal similarity, the contents and aims of the policy were essentially different. Whereas the industrial policy in Japan after World War II was undertaken on the basis of industries and enterprises already established, in Korea there existed no manufacturing industries and firms of any significant strength. In fact, it was the aim of the industrial policy to initiate and establish them with sufficient international competitive power.

(3) Economic development in South Korea started with the strong leadership of the late President Park, but not only with that. The organization of the ministries and agencies has been functionally efficient, and the supporting bureaucrats, especially the economic technocrats, have been highly capable. After 1961, a few hundred government officials who passed the upper-class civil service examinations were annually sent to the United States for graduate study for one or two years. When they returned, they were assigned to posts of economic policy making. Also a large number of Korean students who obtained Ph. D. degrees in the United States returned to Korea to work at important think-tanks like the Korean Development Institute.

(4) Once the aims of establishing competitive industries and firms and of promoting the export and import trade were achieved, Korea started the policy of liberalization in various fields of the economy. The upshot was that in November, 1988 Korea was made an Article 8 country of the IMF, and in January, 1990 an Article 11 country of the GATT. This implies that while the destination of Korean economic development has been the same as that of IMF-World Bank aid strategy, the route to that destination was largely chosen by the Koreans themselves.

In contrast to the case of Korea, adaptation in Thailand occurred under the donors' rigorous requirement of following "dominant strategies". But it was made in fact very prudently and effectively. The starting event was the Thai government's request to the United States government and the World Bank, soon after the end of World War II for economic aid to tide over both the fiscal and balance of payment difficulties. As conditionality to such aid, the United States government and the World Bank required policy reform. In a more formal and systematic form, this requirement is spelled out in a recommendation of the World Bank Mission Report prepared in 1957–58.

The Thai Government under Prime Minister General Sarit, which emerged as a result of the 1958 coup d'etat, accepted that recommendation. Its stipulations were (1) to discontinue the existing policy of industrialization through establishment and operation of state enterprises, and to entrust the direct productive activities to the private sector, (2) to confine the scope of direct government intervention to the infrastructure construction, (3) to liberalize fully direct investment by foreign private capital, and (4) with these confirmed as basic principles, to design national economic plans and thereby to provide an orientation to national development.

Adaptation to these requirements had two main aspects. One aspect is that while the rationale of the discontinuance of industrialization policy based upon establishment of the state enterprises is debatable in the early stage of economic development when entrepreneurs, capable managers, and capital are all considered insufficient, the acceptance of this policy would be rational if in actuality it would eliminate the prevailing mode of management by "patrimonial bureaucracy" that characterized Thai state enterprise.

A patrimonial bureaucracy or state relates to Max Weber's concept of "patrimonialism". It is a sub-type of "traditional authority", one of the societal relationships between domination and obedience classified according to the pattern of legitimacy for domination. (Traditional authority precedes age-wise modern, "legal authority".)[12] The patrimonial bureaucracy in the Thai context involved the loyal families, aristocrats, or top government bureaucrats who were bestowed part of the administrative power from the king and who had a common tendency to maximize their own net private benefit instead of the net public benefit. Moreover, each of the patrimonial bureaucrats maintained a large group of followers and subordinates under a patron-client relationship. As the jobs and incomes of the followers had to be secured by the patrimonial bureaucrats the so-called state enterprises had to be established not to serve some public purposes, but as their private assets to fulfill their private purposes.

The absolute monarchy of Thailand was transformed into a constitutional monarchy by a "constitutional revolution" in 1932. However, leaders of the revolution, that is, the military and civil bureaucrats of middle-class origin, soon degenerated into traditional, patrimonial bureaucrats. Side by side with the previously existing state enterprises, controlled or possessed by the royal family members and aristocrats, a large number of the new state enterprises were established to secure the interest of the followers of these patrimonial bureaucrats.

The 1950s has been described as the period in which establishment of such state enterprises reached its apex. The fact that the Prime Minister, who accepted World Bank conditionality in 1956, was himself considered to be one of the top patrimonial leaders, may suggest that his acceptance of the conditionality was motivated by his strategy *vis-à-vis* inter-group struggles. Regardless of the motivations behind his acceptance, it certainly led to diminution of the importance of the patrimonial state enterprise. Moreover, this policy shift was buttressed by the Investment Promotion Law of 1962. Since then the role of creating new industries and new modern enterprises, including joint ventures with foreign manufactures, has been played increasingly by the private sector.

A second aspect of adaptation relates to the requirement to formulate and implement the national economic plans. The United States government and the World Bank advised the government as a means of aid administration to strengthen the market economy regime. Following the advice, the First Five- Year Development Plan was started in 1961. Since then the economic aid of the United States AID and the World Bank, in particular their aid to development projects, has been determined according to the plans. Side by side, a National Economic and Social Development Board has been established as the central government agency chiefly responsible for the Five Year Plans. The budget system of the central government has also been rationalized. A series of these administrative reforms were closely related to the recent emergence of a modern technocrat bureaucracy in Thailand.[13]

In Indonesia, the patrimonial bureaucracy had flourished particularly with the expansion of foreign trade control. After the enforcement of "deregulation" in 1982, however, state corporations began disappearing. This, together with the establishment of the system of modern economic administration, are two main forms of "adaptation" in Indonesia. However, the adaptation was accomplished much earlier in Thailand than in Indonesia, and this seems to be an important reason why development is much better in Thailand than in Indonesia. In the Philippines during the Marcos government, the rule of "patrimonial bureaucracy" was the worst; hence, the present economic performance is the poorest among the ASEAN countries.

To elaborate our second finding on the reconfiguration of power to make such adaptation realizable, we may first designate five major actors of domestic socio-economic forces common to the Asian countries:

(1) bureaucrats (including military officers), who are, in turn, classified into (i) patrimonial bureaucrats, (ii) nationalists, and (iii) technocrats,
(2) landlords, rich farmers, and merchants,
(3) industrialists and urban middle class people,
(4) urban workers, and

(5) peasants.

A typical configuration of power in traditional East and Southeast Asian economies was that the patrimonial bureaucrats coalesced with land-owning elites to become a ruling class, which, in turn, exploited both peasants and merchants and suppressed the emerging industrialists. Modern reconfiguration means that coalitions between patrimonial bureaucrats and land-owning elites give ground to coalitions of bureaucratic nationalists, technocrats, and industrialists. Where such changes in the power structure materialize, adaptation is made possible and dominant strategies are likely to be successful. On the other hand, the countries where such adaptation is not observable are often those in which the traditional coalition of patrimonial bureaucrats and landlords remains as strong as before, or those in which even though new classes are emerging, their coalition is not yet strong enough to replace the traditional coalition.

In South Korea (and Taiwan) this modern change has taken place. Toward the end of the 1980s even an entire new class of the organized urban workers had emerged. In Thailand, a similar change has been going on, though more slowly. Initial postwar change was undertaken by a rivaling patrimonial bureaucrat who utilized the World Bank pressure in favor of himself. But later, with the emergence of bureaucratic technocrats, the change really became a modern one. In Indonesia, it was remarkable that the coalition of technocrats with the World Bank has become strong enough in the 1980s to compete with the ruling patrimonial bureaucrats. A weak point is that most of the emerging industrialists are non-Indonesians.

In the Philippines, the ruling class is traditionally represented by the landlord elites of the Spanish type who have been also sugar-plantation and sugar cane-factory owners. Later they were active in import-substitution industrialization. However, an excessive protection of both sugar production for export (through preferential taxes and quotas awarded by the United States in the Laurel-Rangley Agreement of 1955) and import-substitution industries weakened their international competitive position, although internally it strengthened their position as the single dominant socio-economic force of the country. Although the late President Marcos wanted at first to reform this situation, he was not successful and instead he himself became the most powerful patrimonial bureaucrat. The Philippines case represents those countries in which adaptation was not possible because of the difficulties in reconfigurating socio-economic classes.

13.5 THE EVOLUTION OF DOMINANT STRATEGIES VIA ADAPTATION

The reality of "adaptation" can be observed in terms of the dominant strategies as well as in domestic arrangements. We observe that at least in South-East Asia until the end of the 1960s, the prototype dominant strategy consisted of the following prescriptions:

(1) industrial development financing by means of government disbursements and deliberate allocation;
(2) investment promotion of specified industries through Boards of Investment (BOI);
(3) import substitution in selected industries through quotas and protective tariffs;
(4) formulation of comprehensive economic plans.[14]

Since the 1970s, each of these prescriptions has been modified by the IMF and World Bank in pragmatic ways. In the case of Thailand, the shift to the export-promotion industrialization took place in 1970 when the Thai government accepted a World Bank recommendation to that effect. This recommendation culminated from the finding of a comprehensive economic survey conducted for the same year by the World Bank that the import-substitution industrialization in Thailand had been pursued in final consumer goods without leaving room for additional development; it was about to enter high-cost fields such as automotive assembly, electric appliances, and petro-chemicals.[15]

The policy shift accompanied the gradual modifications of the above prototype prescriptions, such as a reorganization of the BOI (reduction of its investment allocation function and conversion to a research organization) and the diminution of the scope of planning in the national economic plan and its conversion to a program of public investment. The Structural Adjustment program of the 1980s represents a crystalization of attempts at these modifications. It is to be hoped that Structural Adjustment will be subject to a similar process of pragmatic adaptation.

13.6 CONCLUSION

On the basis of the above studies of the countries of Asia, what can we say about the formulation of the IMF–World Bank SA Policy in the future? Since these studies are still tentative and the analysis is still very broad the following comments must necessarily be also tentative.

1. Most important for the improvement of the SA Policy is the need to study and comprehend the initial conditions of each individual economy of the applicants for the SAF, ESAF, and SAL more systematically according to a common analytical framework. This study must essentially be of long-term forces and has to be made in addition to analysis of the current state of IMF type fundamentals. Once these studies are done, it will become possible to investigate the congruence of individual policy items in the SA conditionality program with the initial conditions. Moreover, they will facilitate the designing of development scenarios (possibly optional), comprising both a stabilization-structural adjustment state and a long-term development stage.

2. Feasibility of individual items of the SA conditionality is to be assessed essentially by investigating whether development of the market economy framework as well as of the administrative systems are such that they conform to what the items of SA conditionality assume. For countries in which the actual institutional development is relatively low (as is more often the case with the low-income countries), the conditionality should accompany substantial measures to help improve and even create the market and administrative framework. In countries in which institutional development is relatively advanced, the scope of the items of the SA conditionality might be more or less narrowed down, and/or the demand for their enforcement be made more flexible. Overall, the developing countries' own devices and efforts to overcome the institutional deficiency (that is, the "adaptation" in the sense of section 4) should be encouraged.

3. At the same time, the measures to prevent the cases of moral hazard from occurring should be enforced much more strictly.

4. Effectiveness of the SA policy is in the final analysis facilitated by creating the environment where "adaptation" as well as the will and capability to adapt are promoted. In terms of international aid policy, this will be done by identifying and enforcing prudently the appropriate items of aid forms that are classified as investment projects and technical assistance and that relate to the construction of infrastructure for the development of a market economy and human capital formation. The latter, essentially consisting of formal and informal education and training, is vital for the development of the will and capability of adaptation. The capability and hence social influence of one of the core forces for adaptation — namely, the technocrat bureaucrats — may then be strengthened more immediately by extending various kinds of technical cooperation in the field of economic policy making.

APPENDIX: A FRAMEWORK OF ANALYSIS FOR DESIGNING BY-COUNTRY ECONOMIC DEVELOPMENT SCENARIOS

Basic Model	Elements determining variants of the basic models			Variants of the basic models	
① Growth process which varies depending upon types of factor endowments, incl. human capital	② Growth stage in terms of levels of an average *per capita* GNP	③ Growth stage in terms of levels of development in market economy and administration systems	④ Types of economic institutions and organizations, political culture and economic policy	⑤ By-region variants which are broadly formulated	⑥ By-country variants to be specified
1. Countries with abundant natural resources and scarce population - A "Vent-for-Surplus" Theory (H. Myint) 1-a An industrialization phase to getting over a V-S trap	1. very low income 2. low income	1. very under-developed 2. under developed	1. Centrally planed type 1-a Transitory to market-oriented reform 2. *Dirigiste* type	(Example 1) Sub-Saharan developmental crisis type	
2. Countries with scarce natural resources and abundant population - A "Unlimited Supplies of Labour" Model (W. A. Lewis) 2-a A period of falling into a "Lewis" trap	3. lower middle income	3. mediumly developed	3. Market-oriented but government intervention type -Developmental Autocracy	(Example 2) East Asian type	
3. Countries with abundant land and scarce but educated population - A Staple Theory (M. H. Watkins) -a An industrialization phase to getting over a staple trap	4. upper middle income 5.	4.	4. Populist type 5. Patrimonial State type	(Example 3) Latin American type	
4. ....(yet to be formed)	6.	5.	6.		
5. ....(yet to be formed)		7.			

Notes

1. Among the literature which deals with the *dirigiste* regimes of the post-World War II developing countries comprehensively, the following three may be referred to: (1) Gunnar Myrdal, *Asian Drama*, vol II., New York, Twentieth Century Fund, 1971, which covers the issues in South and Southeast Asian countries; (2) Ian Little, Tibor Scitovsky and Maurice Scott, *Industry and Trade in Some Developing Countries; A Comparative Study*, London, Oxford University Press, 1970, which summarizes seven comparative developing country studies sponsored by the OECD Development Center: Brazil, India, Mexico, Pakistan, Philippines, Taiwan and Argentine. (3) J.N. Bhagwati and Padma Desai, *India: Planning for Industrialization*, London: Oxford University Press, 1970, which constitutes part of the above OECD comparative studies but which is probably the most comprehensive and systematic analysis of state controls over private sector activities.
2. A further description of the concept "Patrimonial bureaucracy" is made in the text, pp. 217–18.
3. World Bank (OED), *Report on Adjustment Lending*, August 1, 1988 p. 83.
4. According to *Ibid.*, pp. 2–3, of the 30 sample countries that received 100 per cent of the adjustment loans before 1985, 12 countries achieved a reduction of the resource gap, but at the cost of growth. In five countries, the GDP growth rate increased, but the resource gap also increased. Only 12 countries exhibited both an increase in GDP growth and a reduction in the resource gap. In *Ibid.*, pp. 85 and 90, the results of a detailed examination of implementation of conditionality in 51 adjustment loans in 15 developing countries are shown: on the average 60.3 per cent of all items of conditionality were fully implemented during the loan period. If the evaluation is made as of 1988, the percentage increases to 67.5 per cent. This means that the rate of slippage was about 40 per cent and 32 per cent respectively.
5. The naming is probably made first in Ian M. D. Little, *Economic Development*, New York: Basic Books, 1982, pp. 19–21. See further Gerald M. Meier, "The Formative Period," in Gerald M. Meier and Dudley Seers (eds). *Pioneers in Development*, New York: Oxford University Press, 1984.
6. I have argued that the two features described in (1) and (2) should be among the central themes of any study on development economics, in Shigeru Ishikawa, "Problems of Late Industrialization: An Asian Perspective," in K. Arrow ed., The *Balance between Industry and Agriculture in Economic Development: Volume 1, Basic Issues*, London, Macmillan, 1988. This and other articles making the same argument are reproduced in my collected essays entitled Kaihatsu Keizaigaku no Kihon Mondai (Basic Issues of Development Economics), Tokyo: Iwanami Co., 1990. My approach is very similar to Professor Hla Myint's emphases on "organizational dualism" and on the development process with at least one of the factors of production un- or under-employed, for example, his own "Vent-for-Surplus" theory. See his paper "The Neo-classical Resurgence in Development Economics: Its Strength and Limitations." in Gerald M. Meier (ed.), *Pioneers in Development*, Second Series, New York: Oxford University Press, 1987.

7. Regarding the method for evaluating the feasibility (or effectiveness) of the IMF–World Bank's structural adjustment policy, the following comments are in order.

   This evaluation should, primarily, be made in two steps:
   (1) To derive qualitatively and as a hypothesis the mechanism by which the SA policy does or does not bring about the effects that it originally aims at, and
   (2) To test the validity of that hypothesis with the use of either individual country or international-cross-section data on aggregative economic performances. Given the practical difficulties of conducting a rigorous test according to step (2), most studies have had to be satisfied with a rough checking of the hypothesis on the SA effects derived from step (1) with very crude and partial data showing aggregative economic performances. The difficulty in testing comes largely from the difficulty of isolating statistically the available economic performance data from the effect of non-SA policy factors, so that the effect solely of the SA policy factors can be identified. Naturally, an important reservation is made in these studies regarding the resulting lack of precision in the evaluation. Two examples are: (1) In two important documents for the World Bank's self-evaluation of the SA policy effect, namely The World Bank (OED) *Report on Adjustment Lending* (*op. cit.*) p. 2 and The World Bank (CED), *Adjustment Lending Policies for Sustainable Growth*, 1990, p. 2, the similar reservation was explicitly made about their conclusions. (2) In an independent study by Paul Mosley, Jane Harrigan, and John Toye, *Aid and Power: The World Bank and Policy-based Lending, vol. I, Analysis and Policy Proposals*, Routledge, London, 1991, Part III, similar difficulties were explicitly set out. And, while attempts were made to separate out the effects of non-SA policy factors, relying on multi-country regression analyses and a few single-country simulation analyses, the outcomes so far may not be considered fully satisfactory.

   Perhaps a more important issue in the effectiveness study of this stage lies in the difference among the studies in the perception of the mechanism in the domain of step (1) — the mechanism in which the SA policy may or may not bring about effective outcomes. The perception by the World Bank is that although there remain problems in the total performance of the SA policy as implemented and in the ease of realizing the objectives of individual elements of policy, the program design itself is valid, and the SA policy scheme has now become a firmly established form of World Bank lending activities. The evaluation of Mosley, Harrigan and Toye, *op. cit.* is somewhat different. As criticism of the World Bank's SA policy, they argue that between two essential components of the SA program, that is, (i) a quick-disbursal of lending for the support of the balance of payments and (ii) enforcement of the SA policy as conditional to that lending, there exist intrinsic conflicts and practical dilemmas. With regard to the SA policy itself, while it concerns solely the market failure that arises from inappropriate state intervention into the economy, it overlooks the "endogenous" market failure that tends to occur due to the weakness of the market forces in operation, and hence requires appropriate state intervention to supplement them.

Gustav Ranis argues for the importance of formulating for each individual recipient an aid policy of "a genuine credible adjustment-with-growth-and-equity package": the IMF–World Bank should overcome the routine, stylized fashion of forming policy packages by "picking from a checklist of short-term IMF demand side adjustments in fiscal, monetary, and exchange-rate policy, with the World Bank throwing in additional concerns, such as privatization, agricultural prices, tax reform, and the import regime, chosen from a supply-side checklist." (G. Ranis, *Adjustment, Growth and Debt Fatigue: Can the Case-by-Case and Global Approaches be Combined?*, International Center for Economic Growth, Occasional Paper No. 17, Panama City, 1989.)

My approach is similar to the above studies in putting a major reservation on the difficulty of pursuing step (2). The uniqueness of it, however, may lie in the method taken in step (1) to establish the appropriateness or inappropriateness of the uniform SA programs applied to specific economic and social conditions of the individual developing country. I have utilized for this purpose a framework of analysis that I developed in S. Ishikawa, "Effective Measures of Economic Cooperation for Japan Amidst Diversifying International Economic Environments," *op. cit.* This framework consists of alternative economic development models, as *basic models*, each of which is applicable to particular developing countries with different types of resource endowment (such as Myint's Vent-for-Surplus model or Lewis's model of dualistic economic development) and additional factors that tend further to condition the working of the above basic models, namely differences among countries according to the stage of productivity growth, differences in the stage of development in market economy and administrative systems, and different types of economic institutions and organizations, political culture, and economic policy. Basic features of individual developing countries are thus captured in terms of the variants of the individual basic models. An illustrative map of this framework is shown in the Appendix.

8. The process by which countries with rich natural resources and sparse population were developed as primary export economies is analyzed by Myint in his well-known Vent-for-Surplus Theory: Hla Myint, "The Classical Theory of International Trade and the Under-Developed Countries," *Economic Journal*, June 1958. With regard to the analysis of the process for further economic development of these economies after full employment of the existing natural resources (especially land resources), Myint later suggested the importance of natural resource-based industrialization ("export substitution") and a "green revolution", Myint, *Southeast Asia's Economy, Development Policies in the 1970s*, London, Penguin Books, 1972, Chs. 2 and 3. A more comprehensive and systematic analysis of the development issues of this type of the economy is made in the African context by R. H. Bates, *Market*

and States in Tropical Africa: The Political Bases of Agricultural Polices, Berkeley: University of California Press, 1981. See further S. Ishikawa "Industrialization in Primary Export Economies: Introduction to part IV," in Nural Islam (ed.), *The Balance between Industry and Agriculture in Economic Development, vol. 5, Factors Influencing Change*, London: Macmillan 1989.

9. Economic development of the economies in this resource pattern is usually congenial to the analysis relying on Lewis's dualistic development model with unlimited supplies of labor to the emerging industrial sector. Regarding the issue of financing industrialization, see the cases of China and India in my "Patterns and Processes of Intersectoral Resource Flow: Comparison of Cases in Asia," in G. Ranis and T. P. Schultz (eds.), *The State of Development Economics: Progress and Perspective*, Oxford, Basil Blackwell, 1988.
10. In the Appendix, a few different types of the economies according to the difference in political culture are shown: a centrally planned type, a *dirigiste* type, developmental autocracy, populist, and patrimonial state.
11. Robert Cassen and Associates, *Does Aid Work, Report to an Intergovernmental Task Force*, Oxford: Clarendon Press, 1986, pp. 356–7.
12. Max Weber, *Economy and Society: An Outline of Interpretative Sociology*, ed. by Guenther Roth and Clause Wittich, New York, Bedminister Press, 1968, Part one, Ch. III particularly pp. 212–41.
13. In writing this section on Thailand, I have drawn heavily from two excellent studies: J. Alexander Caldwell, *American Economic Aid to Thailand*, Lexington, Mass., Lexington Books, 1974, and Oey Meesook, "The Political Economy of Poverty, Equity and Growth: Thailand," March 1987, Washington D.C.
14. In ASEAN countries, the time period in which laws for investment promotion of specified industries were enacted and a Board of Investment established was for Thailand 1954 (the first law), and 1959; for Malaysia, 1958 (the first law), 1968 (the second law) and 1967 (Federal Industrial Development Board); for Indonesia, 1967; and for the Philippines, 1968 (both a law and BOI). A comprehensive economic plan started in 1960 in Thailand; 1966 in Malaysia; 1969 in Indonesia; and 1974 in the Philippines. The fact that the priority industry for promotion by the BOI was the import-substituting consumer goods industry (especially textiles) by joint-Thai-foreign ventures is well documented in Akira Suehiro, *Capital Accumulation in Thailand 1855–1985*, Tokyo: Center for East Asian cultural Studies, 1988, pp. 179–181.
15. Meesook, *op. cit.*

14 Government and Economic Growth

Lloyd G. Reynolds

This ambitious title suggests two questions, distinct but readily confused. First, what is the role of government in the decades surrounding the turning point from extensive to intensive growth? What part does government play in *initiating* intensive growth? Second, once a country has embarked on intensive growth, how does the policy stance of government influence its *growth rate* in subsequent decades? These are perhaps the most important questions that can be asked about the development process. They have called forth an enormous theoretical and empirical literature. In what follows we shall attempt a brief summary of this literature, at the risk of oversimplifying complex events.

14.1 GOVERNMENT AT THE TURNING POINT

Although our main concern is with the second question, we cannot forgo a brief comment on the first. The growth history of a country can be divided into two stages. In most countries, during the nineteenth and early twentieth centuries, one observes that population is increasing slowly and that national income is growing at about the same rate. Any increase in output *per capita* is so small as to fall within the margin of error in the data. Such a situation I define as *extensive growth*. I follow Kuznets in accepting this as genuine growth, deserving of study. One reason is that some of the developments during the era, if not strictly prerequisite to a later rise in *per capita* output, are at least helpful in facilitating such a rise.

Again, in most though not all less developed countries (LDCs), at various points in time since about 1849, we see the beginnings of a sustained rise in *per capita* output. Sustained means that, although the growth rate fluctuates from year to year, *per capita* output does not fall back to its initial level. Such a sustained rise in *per capita* output I define as *intensive growth*. In a recent book[1] I surveyed the historical record of all less developed countries with a 1980 population in excess of ten million. These countries, with the turning-point dates assigned to each, were as follows:[2]

A Chronology of Turning Points

1840	Chile	1900	Uganda
1850	Malaysia	1900	Zimbabwe
1850	Thailand	1910	Korea
1860	Argentina	1920	Morocco
1870	Burma	1925	Venezuela
1876	Mexico	1925	Zambia
1880	Algeria	1947	India
1880	Brazil	1947	Pakistan
1880	Japan	1949	China
1880	Peru	1950	Iran
1880	Sri Lanka	1950	Iraq
1885	Colombia	1950	Turkey
1890	Nigeria	1952	Egypt
1895	Ghana	1965	Indonesia
1895	Ivory Coast	—	Afghanistan
1895	Kenya	—	Bangladesh
1895	Taiwan	—	Ethiopia
1900	Cuba	—	Mozambique
1900	Philippines	—	Nepal
1900	Tanzania	—	Sudan
		—	Zaire

These dates should be interpreted with caution. The turning point is actually a period of a decade or two around the cited year, during which one observes a significant and continuing rise in *per capita* income.

These turning-point dates are earlier, frequently much earlier, than the "take-off" dates popularized by Rostow.[3] The reason, I think, is a misperception of the development process that was common in the 1950s and 1960s. The take-off was (wrongly) associated with the appearance of large-scale factory industry. Actually, this is a late stage in the development process. Most countries reached the turning point *before* 1940. In these countries the beginning of intensive growth was usually associated with a sharp rise in primary exports, in absolute terms and as a percentage of GDP. The resulting rise in national income gradually broadened the market for manufactures. For a long time, however, this demand was met mainly from an increase in domestic handicraft production supplemented by imports. As demand continues to grow, and as the market is confirmed and mapped out by imports, domestic factory production eventually makes its appearance. But this happens with a long lag, and should not be identified with the turning point itself, which usually lies well in the past.

The evidence for this world view, together with some consideration of conflicting views is presented in the work cited above and need not be repeated. Accepting it as valid, some 23 of our forty-one countries reached the turning point during the long economic boom of 1850–1914; only three did so during the depressed period 1914–1945; and eight newcomers have joined the growth procession since 1945. Seven countries still show no sign of intensive growth. The fact that the eight new developers include the large countries of India, Pakistan, China and Indonesia has no doubt contributed to the illusion that intensive growth began in the post-war period.

What part did government play in the timing of turning points? Note first that the turning point is almost always associated with some significant political event. In only four cases (Ceylon, Brazil, Venezuela, Peru) was this not true. The political events were of several sorts. The most interesting cases, though not the largest in number, involve a transfer of power within the country from a less progressive to a more progressive regime. Cases that fall under this heading include: (1) installation of the modernizing ruler Rama IV as king of Thailand (1851); (2) the Meiji Restoration in Japan (1868); (3) collapse of the Ottoman Empire and emergence of Kemal Ataturk as ruler of Turkey (early 1920s); (4) emergence of Iraq as an independent state under British tutelage (1925); (5) the communist-led revolution in China (1949); (6) overthrow of the monarchy and installation of President Nasser in Egypt (1956); (7) overthrow of Sukarno and installation of President Suharto in Indonesia (1967).

In Latin America the key event was declaration of independence from colonial rule by Spain and (in the case of Brazil) by Portugal. This was followed by a prolonged period of recurring civil war, lasting as late as 1876 in Mexico and 1885 in Colombia. The turning point typically dates from the emergence at long last of a stable government capable of exercising effective control over the country.

Most numerous are the cases in which intensive growth can be dated from the time of colonization by a foreign power: the ten European-created African countries plus Burma and Malaysia (Britain), Taiwan and Korea (Japan), Cuba and the Philippines (United States), which replaced prior colonial rule by Spain. Japan was especially growth-minded and set about systematically to develop Taiwan and Korea as "rice baskets" for Japan. But Britain and the United States also took steps to increase exports from their new colonies. No doubt the increments in national income thus created accrued disproportionately to citizens of the colonial powers and to an elite of local residents. The fact of increased capacity to produce, however, is confirmed by an upturn of export (and usually import) volume, an upturn typically associated with the date of colonization.

A half-dozen countries failed to reach the turning point during the colonial era: India, Indonesia, Egypt, Sudan, Mozambique, and Zaire. The fact that several very large countries appear in this group has no doubt contributed to an impression that colonial rule was hostile to economic growth, a conclusion that does not seem to be generally true.

In the success cases, early intensive growth was along capitalist lines. The role of government in the century before 1940 was largely to provide the physical infrastructure needed to move products to points of export. The necessary financing came from tax systems that were typically proportionate or even regressive. Profits were lightly taxed and income taxation was usually absent (or not effectively enforced). Trade policies were increasingly liberal, at least until the Great Depression of the 1930s. The policy stance of government was typically to accelerate development, or at any rate to stand out of the way of private producers.

It is worth noting that governments in less developed countries of this period were typically *not* under popular control. In the case of colonial regimes, this follows by definition. But even the independent countries were typically governed by a small oligarchy of the political elite, often in alliance with leading business families. As we shall see, democratic institutions pose serious obstacles to the growth process and can even be regarded as antithetical to growth.

14.2 INTENSIVE GROWTH SINCE 1945: THE LIBERAL PRESCRIPTION

Since 1945 the theory and practice of economic development has followed a parabolic course. First came a strong revolt against neoclassical liberalism, and the general adoption of an "economic planning" approach to the subject. Later, beginning around 1970, there was growing disillusionment with planning and government intervention in the economy accompanied by gradual reversion to more traditional growth prescriptions. During the late 1980s this movement was accelerated by the collapse of communism in Eastern Europe and the Soviet Union, and by the fumbling efforts in those countries to re-create a market economy. Today's conventional wisdom is that growth is best promoted by following a (modified) capitalist course.

Let us be clear, first, about what the traditional view of the role of government in the economy amounted to. There is still nothing superior to the early formulation by John Stuart Mill.[4] Mill was a man of broad human sympathies, a reformer concerned with economic progress and with improving the welfare of "the laboring classes". He paid little attention to disciplinary boundaries, and although he was capable of rigorous economic analysis he had no hesitation in discussing government and other topics that would now be considered the province of sociology.

Mill regarded economic growth as a natural, organic (under British and American conditions, almost inevitable) process. It is not propelled particularly by government, though perhaps requiring a certain kind of government. He thought that "all other nations will successively return upon the same course" as those presently developed. The institutional requirements for economic development he summarized as follows:

"The desideratum for such a [less developed] country, economically considered, is an increase of industry and of the effective desire of accumulation. The means are, first, a better government; more complete security of property; moderate taxes, and freedom from arbitrary exaction under the name of taxes; a more permanent and advantageous tenure of land, securing to the cultivator as far as possible the undivided benefits of the industry, skill, and economy he may exert. Secondly, improvement of the public intelligence....Third, the introduction of foreign arts, which raise the returns derivable from additional capital....and the importations of foreign capital, which renders the increase of production no longer exclusively dependent on the thrift or providence of the inhabitants themselves...and by installing new ideas and breaking the chain of habit....tends to create in them new wants, increased ambitions, and greater thought for the future. These considerations apply more or less to all the Asiatic populations and to the less civilized and industrial parts of Europe, as Russia, Turkey, Spain and Ireland...."[5]

Almost 200 pages of Mill's thousand-page treatise are devoted to "The Influence of Government". The discussion is very modest, a nice example of British understatement. The *necessary* functions of government are limited largely to institution-building, including a certain amount of economic infrastructure. But government often goes beyond this to engage in "interferences of government grounded in erroneous theories". Mill is especially severe on interference with prices — such as usury laws or efforts to depress food prices — which he regards as harmful or ineffective. There is an extended discussion of tax theory. Taxes of an objectionable character include taxes on profits, which "necessarily reduce the incentives to saving".

Most interesting is a concluding chapter, "Of the Grounds and Limits of the *Laissez-faire* or Non-interference Principle." Mill starts from the premise that "there is a circle around every human being which no government ...ought to be permitted to overstep". Intervention by government in private decision-making is always suspect, for several reasons: it consumes resources and thus has to be financed by taxation; it enlarges the power of government; it overloads the administrative capacity of government, so that "most things are ill-done or not done at all"; and it reduces the ability of people to make mistakes, to learn by doing. *Laissez-faire*, then, should be the general rule: "every departure from it, unless required by some great good, is a certain evil".

He admits, however, of certain exceptions. Individuals may be myopic about the future, and on this ground he makes a strong cases for public education. Or, legislation may be required, not to override individual judgments but to give effect to them. People cannot choose voluntarily to replace a ten-hour day by a nine-hour day, even if daily productivity were equal. The last page of Mill's book has LDC overtones. In some times and places nothing will be done unless government does it, because of a wide gap between the capacity of the rulers and the ruled. Even here, however, "a good government will give its aid so as to encourage individual exertion ...government aid, when given in default of private enterprise, should be so given as to be as far as possible a course of education for the people in the art of accomplishing great objects by individual energy and voluntary cooperation".[6]

It is surprising that in the economic writings of the next century we find nothing comparable to Mill's analysis of government and its functions. There is very little of this in Marshall or Schumpeter or Keynes. Only when we come to W. Arthur Lewis's *Theory of Economic Growth*[7] is Mill's discussion resumed, this time in a growth context. The outlook of the two authors is basically similar. Writing a century later, Lewis expands the functions of government beyond institution-building to include such modern topics as "influencing the distribution of income, controlling the quantity of money, controlling fluctuations, ensuring full employment, and influencing the level of investment". But in essentials, the two works show a strong family resemblance. Like Mill, Lewis ignores the conventional disciplinary boundaries and roams freely across the social sciences and beyond. He not only surveys systems of belief and institutions but also the ways in which these change over time in ways favorable (or unfavorable) to growth. And how does growth react on institutions? Is growth cumulative, or self-arresting? He does not, incidentally, believe that "there are stages of development through which every society must pass"; the economic growth story is open-ended.

The key to economic growth is capital formation, which depends on the rate of saving. "The central problem in the theory of economic growth is to understand the process by which a community is converted from being a five per cent saver to a twelve per cent saver, with all the changes in attitudes, in institutions, and in techniques which accompany this conversion."[8] The key to this, in turn, is the rise of an entrepreneurial class and an increase in the share of profits in national income. Like Mill, Lewis believed that profit recipients would save while others would not. "It follows that the correct explanation of why poor countries save so little is not because they are poor, but because their capitalistic sectors are so small. No country is so poor that it could not save twelve per cent of its national income if it wanted to."[9]

He recognizes the possibly benign influence on the growth rate of an authoritarian and right-minded government: "Given a government which sets itself to promote economic growth, and which has a reasonably competent understanding of the issues involved, a backward society on an authoritarian basis is almost certain to grow more rapidly than a backward society on an individualistic basis. The rub is in the premises: governments can be intelligent, and they can be authoritarian, and they can have the interests of the common people primarily at heart; but to find these three features in combination seems to be the exception rather than the rule."[10]

"Much depends also on how much the particular community has learned of the art of public administration. Most governments are, and always have been inefficient and corrupt...In countries where government is corrupt and inefficient, *laissez-faire, laissez-passer* is the best recipe for economic growth. It is only as an efficient administration is built up that the relative merits of private entrepreneurship and of public ownership or control merit serious debate."[11]

This theme of not overloading the administrative machine recurs throughout Lewis's writings. In another essay he declares, "Now a strong and incorrupt administration is just what no backward country possesses, and in the absence of such an administration it is often much better that governments should be laissez-faire than that they should pretend to plan...the first objective of planners must be to create an administrative machine that can do the work of planning...in the meantime, no administration should be loaded with tasks more numerous or more delicate than it can handle."[12]

14.3 REVOLT AGAINST LIBERALISM

Almost simultaneously with Lewis's reaffirmation of the neoclassical tradition, there set in a groundswell of opposition to it. The new wisdom was that economic development is the inescapable responsibility of government. Private entrepreneurship was thought to be lacking in the LDCs. Rather than waiting for it, or trying to stimulate it, government should simply supplant it. Only government has the vision, the long-range planning capacity, which would make it possible to accumulate resources and to launch the nation into self-sustained growth.

This view, which dominated development thinking from 1945 until the early 1970s and subsided gradually thereafter, is at first glance difficult to understand. How could so many of the best and the brightest have been so misguided? It is necessary to reconstruct the atmosphere of the period to arrive at a sympathetic understanding of the planning movement.

14.4 POLITICAL INFLUENCES

Although economists may have thought that they were in charge of events, the decisive developments of the period were undoubtedly political. Pride of place must go, first, to decolonization. The British Empire was replaced in the short period 1945–60 by a commonwealth of supposedly equal independent nations, although many continued to receive British tutelage and financial aid. The French withdrew almost as suddenly and completely, their departure from North Africa being hastened by the Algerian War. The Dutch were ousted from their Indonesian base by a civil war. Belgium gave up the Congo without a struggle and with minimal preparations for independence. By 1960 only the Portuguese enclaves of Angola and Mozambique remained of the great empires that had occupied Africa and half of Asia.

The new governments varied widely in stability and administrative competence. Best situated was India, where the British had developed a strong army and a Civil Service with British traditions of performance. Pakistan and Malaya were some distance behind. From there the ranking runs downward to many, especially in Africa, which were governments in name only, presiding over a motley array of tribal groupings and subject to frequent coups and civil strife.

But able or not, these governments were determinedly independent, resolved to make a 180-degree turn from the policies of the colonial past. Since these policies had been supportive of private economic activity, the new regimes embraced statism, which in practice meant control of the economy by the urban elites who had succeeded to power to the neglect of the ninety per cent of the population who remained in rural areas. Policies that resembled those of the past — advocacy of free trade, free pricing, free markets, private economic initiative — were portrayed as an effort by the former rulers to regain their power. In political debate the argument that a line of policy was "neocolonial" told decisively against it.

A second factor, especially in the aid-giving countries, was misleading conclusions drawn from the success of the Marshall Plan in Europe. This success was due, not so much to the transfer of capital from the United States as to the fact that the human capital of the war-torn countries — skills, habits, institutions, organizing ability — had survived the war. The conclusion should have been that, where human capital remains intact, physical capital can be reconstituted rapidly. Instead, a misplaced emphasis on physical capital created the impression that money can do everything. This made it plausible to assume a constant incremental capital-output ratio (ICOR). Pour a certain amount of capital into a less-developed country and there will automatically be a proportionate increase in GNP.

Nor should we minimize the influence of Cold War competition between the USSR and the Western powers for the allegiance of third-world countries. For decades the charge that a national leader was venal or incompetent was countered by the argument that "he's on our side", and this was thought to justify a continuing flow of economic aid. Waste of resources was interpreted as a contribution to global political stability.

A third factor was a drastic change in the nature of international capital movements. Before 1940 capital had flowed largely through private channels and in support of private economic activities. After 1945 government-to-government transfers came to dominate the scene. There was debate over how far these should be bilateral or multi-lateral, through agencies such as the World Bank, the United Nations, or regional development banks. But the *destination* of the flows toward governments in the recipient nations was rarely challenged. Private capital movements continued, especially in Latin America, but they no longer occupied the center of the stage.

14.5 INTELLECTUAL CURRENTS

We should note first the appearance in the post-war period of new streams of thought — structuralism in Latin America, Marxism in many parts of the world — which either ignored neoclassical economics or directly opposed it. To structuralists, the neoclassical policy prescriptions were irrelevant because they overlooked what were thought to be distinctive structural features of the Latin American economies. To Marxists, the neoclassical framework was not merely irrelevant but pernicious. Countries should develop their resources with minimal interaction with the developed capitalist world, drawing such aid as they might need from other socialist countries. In the United States these doctrines circulated largely as "underground economics", and received little attention in development courses. But in many other countries, they dominated economic research and teaching as well as advice to governments. Equally influential were the socialist doctrines developed by the Fabian Society and espoused by the British Labour Party, which came to power in Britain in 1945. Government — an idealized, British-style government — was to "capture the commanding heights of the economy". In Britain this meant nationalization of coal, steel, and other heavy industries to deprive the capitalists of their power base. In the LDCs, it was thought to mean development of large-scale industries under public ownership from the beginning. Nehru, a socialist by conviction, set out to build a socialist society in India. Nyerere and other African leaders espoused creation of "African socialism".

Both the political leaders and their economic advisers had an image of government, not as it actually was, but as it might be. There was a gross exaggeration of the authority, the right-mindedness, and the administrative competence of the small urban elites who had come to power in these nascent countries. So Arthur Lewis's strictures were ignored in the rush to get something done, and the weak administrative structures of the new states were overloaded far beyond capacity.

On the technical side, a prominent feature was the emergence of growth models. The Harrod–Domar model had in fact been developed for a quite different purpose. It was oriented toward mature industrial economies with an aggregate demand problem. It tried to answer the question: in such an economy, what are the requirements for stable growth with full employment?

It is ironic that early writers on economic development seized on the Harrod–Domar model and converted it from the original demand orientation to an emphasis on growth of output capacity under highly simplified conditions. But it is understandable in that, as of 1950, it was the *only* model of long-term growth lying ready to hand. And it was readily fortified with data from national income accounts. During the 1940s and 1950s the methods of national income measurement pioneered by Kuznets in the United States and by Stone in England were widely adopted throughout the world. The United Nations decreed that every country must measure its national income and the key components thereof, and blank tables were distributed to be filled in by all member nations. The members responded as best they could, though their statistical staffs and data sources were often minimal. The return flow of data was enshrined in the *UN Yearbook of National Accounts Statistics*, and was thereafter graven in stone.

Thus the building blocks were in place for planning models, which among other things served the useful purpose of fortifying foreign aid requests. Consider the following arithmetic: Country *X* wishes to increase its output at, say, five per cent per year. Assume that the ICOR is constant at, say, 3:1 (which somehow emerged as a magic ratio during the 1950s). Thus gross investment must amount to fifteen per cent of GNP if the growth target is to be attained. Unfortunately, the projected gross domestic savings rate is only ten per cent. So, dear IBRD or AID, kindly remit. When a model of this sort for Pakistan was being presented to a Yale seminar, Tjalling Koopmans remarked perceptively, "Ah, an aid-getting model."

This approach was often combined with the Rostow hypothesis of a quick "takeoff" into self-sustained growth. If, with the help of foreign aid transfers, the investment rate could be held at the desired level for a decade or so, the growth of output would raise domestic saving (via a Keynesian savings function) to a level at which foreign aid would no longer be necessary. Paul Rosenstein-Rodan, in a remarkable article, used this mixture of Harrod-Domar, Rostow, and Keynes to predict the amount of foreign aid required to launch every one of the world's LDC's into self-sustained growth.[13] In the donor countries too, economic planning seemed to serve a useful purpose. No longer would foreign aid requests come in in piecemeal fashion. Instead, there would be an internally consistent macroeconomic framework for the requested aid. So recipient governments were advised, or even required, to plan — by the World Bank, AID, Ministry of Overseas Development, or whatever. Planning became the fashion of the day; governments hastened to create planning commissions or similar agencies, alongside or superior to the traditional budget-making bodies such as the Ministry of Finance. Since the amount of foreign aid received depended partly on the quality of the plan document, there was a premium on turning out superior pieces of paper. Local economists were sent abroad for schooling in planning and related techniques. And local staffs were reinforced with advisers from the developed countries. The rising generation of development economists in the United States and other developed countries was able to benefit and to learn from direct immersion in policy problems.

In practice, "planning" turned out to mean many different things in different countries. Some plans were no more than macroeconomic skeletons, while others were fleshed out in considerable detail. Their control over the private sector, which in most countries embraced most economic activity, was usually very limited. Even in the public sector, the new agencies had difficulty in replacing traditional budget-making. In the most successful cases the planning board had strong political support and was located close to the office of the President or Prime Minister. There it succeeded in creating a multiyear budget, embracing current as well as capital expenditures, which served as a guide for preparation of annual budgets. The requirement that each department document its requests more fully, and relate each year's budget systematically to past and future years, could scarcely fail to improve resource allocation in the public sector. But the planning movement had other less fortunate effects. It reinforced the widespread belief that "government knows best", and that new economic ventures should be assigned automatically to the public sector. Control boards and commissions multiplied throughout the economy. Aid funds were channeled into government investment in infrastructure, industry, and other activities. Government intervened in particular markets to fix prices and wages, often far from market-clearing levels, and frequently took direct responsibility for commodity distribution. This was true especially in the agricultural sector, where a maze of controls served to depress rural incomes for the benefit of the urban elite. In their totality these controls far outweighed the favorable effects of economic planning.

Recall that all this was occurring during the long economic upswing of 1945–73, when capital supplies often seemed unlimited and economic growth seemed inevitable. Average growth rates in both developed and less developed countries rose well above pre-1945 levels. What passed almost unnoticed was the wide dispersion of growth rates in the less developed world. A few countries grew rapidly, while a larger number grew moderately; but in some countries the growth rate was imperceptible, while in still others *per capita* income clearly declined. As these differences became glaring, and as the reasons for them were more thoroughly explored, the conventional wisdom of development theory in the 1950s and 1960s was called into question.

14.6 RESURGENCE OF ECONOMIC LIBERALISM

Signs of a reverse movement toward freer markets were first noticeable in East Asia, and they appeared first in international economic policy. Even in the 1960s Taiwan and South Korea were turning from import substitution to export promotion and were opening their economies to the outside world. Policies affecting exchange rates, tariff rates, and tax structures were coordinated to this end, and the output response was dramatic. From 1965 to 1975 exports from both Taiwan and South Korea rose at much above world levels, and exports moved in a more capital-intensive direction. By the early 1970s the pool of surplus labor was substantially exhausted in both countries, which grew thereafter along developed-country lines.

From East Asia the movement toward trade liberalization spread gradually to Southeast Asia, and eventually to Latin America. Two notable series of country studies, one sponsored by the OECD and the other by the National Bureau of Economic Research, were highly critical of the trade-restricting policies in most countries. The drum fire of criticism, combined with pressure from the International Monetary Fund, gradually had its effect. One country after another readjusted its exchange rate, adjusted or abandoned its exchange controls, and revised tariffs downward. Among major countries only India remained aloof from this general movement.

Microliberalization — the freeing of particular prices, and transfer of activities from public to private hands — set in somewhat later. This was an extremely complex process, moving faster in some economies than in others, and at different speeds even within the same country. In some countries there were sharp breaking points, involving adoption of a wholesale reform program; in other cases there was merely a gradual erosion of government intervention. The direction of movement, however, was consistently toward a loosening of controls.

By 1980 free markets and realistic prices were well established in Malaysia and Indonesia, though less so in the Philippines. During the 1980s changes of regime in Chile, Mexico, Argentina and Brazil led to a series of package agreements with the IMF. In return for transitional assistance these countries pledged themselves to reform programs that included budgetary controls as well as freer micro policies. Colombia and Venezuela had already embraced such measures in piecemeal fashion. In Africa controls were slower to erode, but even there some progress was visible.

In the late 1980s the collapse of communist regimes and the shift to greater reliance on private markets in the countries of Eastern Europe gave additional momentum to the movement. The Soviet model of growth was thoroughly discredited. The largest remaining communist-led economy, China, had a curiously old-fashioned air. It continued to grow, owing to the vigor of private activity in the special economic zones in southern China, plus the peculiar Chinese ability to evade awkward regulations. But communism as a faith was clearly in decline and seemed destined to pass away with the ageing Party leadership.

Outside influences were undoubtedly important. A policy of international economic liberalism does not fit well with tight internal controls. Pressure from foreign competitors impinges on markets and prices within the country. In the end these pressures are likely to prevail, leading to a closer alignment of the domestic price structure with international norms. The IBRD and the IMF consistently favored reform of government-dominated economies, and their advice was supported by lending power.

There was also a marked shift in the intellectual climate from the 1950s to the 1980s. Structuralists ceased to have appreciable influence. Marxist economists were viewed increasingly as oddities, out of touch with reality. Mainstream economics, and particularly micro-economics, was revitalized and directed toward a detailed critique of government intervention in the economy. Economists like Ian Little and Hla Myint in Britain, or Arnold Harberger and Theodore Schultz in the United States, were listened to increasingly. "Socialism" was no longer a good word and leftist economists who had dominated early discussions of development strategy were thrown on the defensive. Advocates of market guidance predominated increasingly in policy discussion.

14.7 PROSPECTS FOR THE NINETIES

So where do we now stand? What will the reformed economies toward which both Eastern Europe and the less developed countries are groping look like? Will the trend toward reliance on markets continue or has it perhaps run its course?

Those who predict that other countries will converge toward post-Thatcher Britain or Reagan-Bush America are likely to be disappointed. For one thing, few countries have the devotion to competitive markets that prevails — at least in theory — in the United States. They tend rather to follow a Schumpeterian line. In an age of giant enterprises, monopoly is not only normal but also vulnerable and transitory. Particularly is this true when boundaries around national economies are being greatly weakened, so that a monopoly based in one country is open to competition from monopolies based elsewhere.

As footloose industries are diffused more widely around the world, national economies will come to resemble each other more closely than at any other time in modern history. Each economy will be dominated by large enterprises — industrial, service, financial — some of domestic and others of foreign origin. Governments will also be larger and more consequential than in Mill's day. But instead of being critical of, or hostile to, private economic activity they will be generally supportive of it, while at the same time trying to steer it in profitable directions.

In these modernized capitalist economies, government will serve several functions. It will continue to be the main focus of institution-building, a task especially important in countries where socialist structures have been dismantled and some kind of capitalist replacement must be built from the ground up. In most LDCs too, economic institutions are evolving at a rate much higher than in older industrial countries. Debate over the proper directions for such evolution will be the central political issue for a long time.

Government ownership of industry may be in disrepute; but government guidance of the economy is alive and well. Only government can establish the macro-economic equilibrium that is a necessary ingredient of economic success. This requires careful and coordinated attention to government budgets, the price level, interest rates, money supply, and other macro-variables. At a micro level, governments will wish to nudge some industries forward in the international competitive race. The model in this respect is Japan which, by methods too subtle to be readily categorized, has managed to shift its industrial base while maintaining its competitive edge. Taiwan and South Korea also, leaders in the growth race among the LDCs, did not succeed by simply relying on market guidance. In both countries government played a major role in steering the economy and in aiding enterprises to become active and respond to market signals.

Successful governments will pay particular attention to national rates of saving and investment. Japan's high savings rate may owe something to cultural factors; but it also owes much to intelligently pro-capitalist policies of government, to encouragement of profit making combined with light taxation of profits. In this respect Japan is much closer to Mill's prescription than is present-day Britain or the United States.

Government's share of national income will continue to be much larger than it was in the nineteenth century. Governments have become inextricably involved in the game of redistributing income shares. Entitlement programs will continue to grow throughout the world. So too will ambitious programs of education and health care, whose cost is bound to rise faster than GNP. These trends will certainly outweigh the (probable) continued retreat from public ownership, and transfer programs will come to dominate government budgets.

In this effort to generalize we should not overlook the great variety of governments throughout the world. There are still countries whose ability to govern themselves is minimal. In other countries an authoritarian leadership attaches low priority to economic growth. All this in addition to wide variations in the resource base. So national growth rates will continue to vary widely, as they have in the past, and countries will continue to re-rank themselves in the *per capita* income tables. Success will be apparent only after it has been achieved.

Notes

1. *Economic Growth in the Third World, 1850–1980* (New Haven: Yale University Press, 1985).
2. *Op. cit.*, p. 32.
3. W. W. Rostow, "The Take-off into Self-sustained Growth," *Economic Journal* 66 (March 1956) 25–48. Perhaps because of its optimistic connotations expressed in a catchy phrase, the term passed rapidly into the literature.
4. John Stuart Mill, *Principles of Political Economy* (London: Parker and Company, 1848), 2 vols. Reprinted in many later editions. Page references herein are to the 1909 edition, edited by W. J. Ashley.
5. *Ibid.*, pp. 189–90.
6. *Ibid.*, p. 978.
7. W. Arthur Lewis, *The Theory of Economic Growth* (London: Allen & Unwin, 1952).
8. *Ibid.*, pp. 225–26.
9. *Ibid.*, p. 236.
10. *Ibid.*, p. 83.
11. *Ibid.*, p. 80.
12. W. Arthur Lewis, *The Principles of Economic Planning* (London: Unwin University Books, 1949), pp. 121–22.
13. P. N. Rosenstein-Rodan, "International Aid for Underdeveloped Countries," *Review of Economics and Statistics* (May 1961), pp. 107–38.

15 The Future in Perspective

Gerald M. Meier

Even though the subject of this book cannot be encapsulated in a set of neat conclusions, this final chapter does summarize some of the ways in which classical economics remains relevant for development economics, examines the present state of the subject, and attempts to place future research in perspective.

Although far from being comprehensive, preceding chapters have demonstrated that modern development economics has strong roots in classical economics (or perhaps more precisely, classical political economy). At the same time, the subject has in recent decades applied techniques of neoclassical analysis to development problems that were unexamined by the classicists.

15.1 LEGACY OF CLASSICAL ECONOMICS

From classical analysis, we still rely on a number of insights:

(1) The classical variables of capital accumulation, population, and technology remain the "heavy" variables in development analysis,
(2) If not for the current fashion of micro analytic (or micro-micro) maximizing models, classical analysis does remain relevant for the "magnificent dynamics" and the "grand issues" of the development process. Some may consider this analysis too soft, but it remains indispensable for identifying the "why" questions (recall Lal, Chapter 3) and for placing micro studies in their broader context.
(3) The classical variables are central in models of long run growth — whether in dual sector models or the "new growth theory" that allows for dynamic externalities and Smith-Young increasing returns due to specialization.
(4) For the classicists, sectoral analysis was important — in order to consider the rural-urban divide and to investigate "balance" in the growth process. At bottom, it is the larger analysis of structural transformation — with its emphasis on relationships among sectors — that gives development economics its differentiated quality.

(5) A classical emphasis on agriculture now remains central for many developing countries.
(6) Smith's "productivity" theory and "vent-for-surplus" theory of international trade are both relevant in analyzing the export sector as the leading sector in development. The classical attention to relationships between trade, economies of scale, and growth is echoed in current research on trade and development.
(7) In their analysis of the growth process, the classicists did not identify the process with simply better resource allocation, but rather with the mobilization of additional resources and the dynamic gains from trade.
(8) Savings, profits and capital accumulation, demand, and income distribution were of prime importance to the classicists. And they still matter now for development economics in both its theoretical and policy dimensions. "Instead of steady state growth, the appropriate view, even over the long term, is one of continuous displacement along successive traverses with accompanying sectoral transformation" (Fishlow, 1991, p. 1731).
(9) Classical concerns about how to expand the supply of entrepreneurship — and realize the superior quality of private over public entrepreneurship — are now reappearing in liberalization efforts.
(10) In general, the classical support of a system of economic freedom and the advocacy of a minimalist state conform to much of the current thought on market-friendly policies. This is understandable insofar as Smith was reacting against mercantilism, and the current reaction is also against excessive and distortionary government interventions in neo-mercantilist regimes. Economists are by nature reformers. To promote the "progressive state", the classicists formulated their agenda and non-agenda for state action. In similar fashion, modern development economists seek an improvement in development performance by their criticism of policy errors and advocacy of policy reform. Whether they will be as influential as were the classicists remains to be seen.

15.2 PRESENT STATE OF DEVELOPMENT ECONOMICS

While the roots of the subject lie in classical economics, development economics has continually evolved in the post-war period. The greatest change has resulted from the neoclassical resurgence since the 1970s (Little, 1982, p. 209). It is to neoclassical economics — with its refined techniques of analysis and emphasis on micro studies — that we now look for answers to the "how" questions of development policy. Gone, or certainly fewer, are the grand models of earlier days. As Kenneth Arrow (1988) notes, "There are fewer and fewer of these grand theories and more and more highly specific applications. The neoclassical insight lends itself to this kind of analysis of specific situations, for example, the effects of a change in tariffs or agricultural subsidies. Indeed, the tendency to be specific is one of the advantages of the neoclassical approach. Grand visions do not lend themselves to useful policy."

Although some refinements in neoclassical analysis give a new basis for government correction of market failure, the main thrust of development economics now is that governments should use markets more effectively, supplementing but not supplanting the market.[1]

Two fundamental theorems of modern welfare economics underlie the dominant neoclassical paradigm. First, under a set of mild restrictions on production technology and individual preferences, the equilibrium of a *laissez-faire* market economy is Pareto efficient. Second, given a set of rather restrictive assumptions including the absence of technological externalities and increasing returns to scale and production, any situation of Pareto efficiency is also a competitive equilibrium (Srinivasan, 1988, pp. 3–4). In part, early development economists supported state intervention on the basis of exceptions to the validity of the static version of the second theorem. Now exceptions to the extended version of the second theorem are emphasized because of the absence of a complete set of contingent markets and asymmetries in information and strategic behavior (Srinivasan, 1988, p. 4). Recent research in development economics incorporates the phenomena of incomplete markets, imperfect information, transaction costs, and imperfect competition.

The neoclassical resurgence has led some to speak of the death of development economics and to assert that there is only a single economics discipline, a "mono-economics" (Hirschman, 1981). Major surveys of the present state of development economics, however, still stake a claim to an independent existence for the subject. Thus, Bell (1987, p. 825) notes that development economics also contributes to knowledge of the more mature economies. For example, analysis of the macro-economic problems of Latin America has influenced writing on the more advanced economies. Similarly, the more diverse contractual arrangements found in the markets for labor tenancies and credit in agrarian economies have provided a basis for new work in micro-economic theory, especially risk sharing incentives and the economics of information. Moreover, there is still a special role for government in LDCs in which insurance and forward markets are conspicuously thin and incomplete.

Bliss (1989, p. 1188) argues that general economic principles are precisely too general to give us insights into applications for less developed economies. Alone, the parts of economic theory and method that apply more or less universally "tell us less than we need in a particular application. To give them life they have to be enlarged and translated. When this is done a specialty is created. Development economics consists in part of the refinement of general economics to deal with questions which arise in the context of development, and partly of certain special ideas which have proved useful in studying developing countries."

Stern (1989, p. 597) also addresses his survey to "economists and students of economics who do know the tools of their trade but not necessarily how they have been applied to and fashioned for the analysis of the economics of developing countries".

Although many characteristics of the discipline of development economics now differ from the earlier post-war period, the classical variables of capital accumulation, population growth, and technological progress remain of major concern in growth theory. Moreover, the classical emphasis on increasing returns now provides an endogenous explanation for economic growth. The "new theories of growth" model production functions that show increasing returns because of specialization and investment in knowledge.[2] The idea that specialization could lead to increasing returns is a return to Adam Smith. So too are the notions of widening the market and entrepreneurship. Alfred Marshall also emphasized that the role of nature in production may be subject to diminishing returns, but the role of man is subject to increasing returns. And again, in an earlier period, J. M. Clark observed that "knowledge is the only instrument of production that is not subject to diminishing returns".[3] The "new growth theory" now endogenizes technological progress and human capital formation within general equilibrium models of long run growth. In the context of an imperfectly competitive economy, aggregate demand spillovers may cause aggregate investment in knowledge to exhibit increasing returns to scale and thereby allow investment in knowledge capital to be a sustainable process.[4]

This emphasis on removing the constraint on the adoption of increasing returns technologies has revived Rosenstein-Rodan's "big push argument". It has done so with models that have the common feature that complementarities between industrializing sectors work through market size effects to make it possible for a firm to "help foster a mutually profitable big push even when it would lose money industrializing alone".[5]

Indeed, Paul Krugman has submitted that "in the light of new developments of industrial organization, international economics, and growth theory, the old development economics now looks much more sensible than it seemed during the 'counter-revolution' against interventionist development models".[6] Krugman contends that although development theorists in the 1950s stressed "the importance of increasing returns and pecuniary external economies arising from the effects of market size," they were "at first unable, and later unwilling, to codify them in clear, internally consistent models. At the same time the expected standard of rigor in economic thinking was steadily rising. The result was that developmental economics as a distinctive field was crowded out of the mainstream of economics. Indeed, the ideas of 'high development theory' [of the 1950s] came to seem not so much wrong as incomprehensible."[7] But now, with rigorous analytical refinements of imperfect competition, external economies, and strategic complementarity, Krugman concludes that "intellectual credibility" can be restored to a useful set of core ideas from the early analysis of the 1950s. "What was ironic was that a competitive neoclassical orthodoxy settled in on the development front just as the orthodoxy was breaking up in other fields. We can now see that whatever bad policies may have been implemented in the name of high development theory, the theory itself makes quite a lot of sense. Indeed, in some ways it was a remarkable anticipation of ideas that would come to analytical fruition thirty years later in the fields, for example, of international trade and economic growth."[8]

The new growth theory indicates that public policies and incentives for the accumulation of physical and human capital become extremely significant for continued capital accumulation and an increase in productivity. So, too, do new refinements in macro-economics — especially the attention to limited information and missing markets — provide a higher and broader understanding of conditions leading to market failure.[9] But although these additional considerations indicate a potential role for government intervention, problems of imperfect information and incomplete markets are now deemed to be also at least as pervasive in the public sector as the private sector. This raises questions whether the government could or would remedy the problems.[10] Moreover, the new (positive) political economy casts doubt on whether development economists can influence governmental policies in the direction of the economists' prescribed second best policies to bring about a Pareto-preferred pattern of development.

Both welfare economics and the new growth theory now give more emphasis to the micro-foundations of the development process than did the early writings in development. Increasingly, there are more empirical micro-studies of topics as diverse as markets, industrial organization, innovations, human capital. The information-theoretic approach to development economics is notable in explaining some conditions of unemployment in imperfect labor markets, sharecropping, credit contracts, interlinked factor markets. Agricultural household models are also being applied in numerous empirical studies, especially as related to the efficiency of farmer decision-making and empirical studies of supply functions and price responsiveness. Moreover, large micro-data sets are being increasingly utilized, particularly for labor markets and problems of human resource development.

Human resource development is also receiving much more attention through studies of nutrition, health, and education. Indeed, the content of economic development now proceeds beyond monetary indicators of GDP *per capita* to numerous non-monetary indicators selected to reflect quality of life and to emphasize that development is fundamentally concerned with the well-being of people and the eradication of poverty. The construction of a "human development index" is a step in this direction.[11]

15.3 FUTURE RESEARCH

Looking to the future evolution of development economics, we may agree with Stern (1991, p. 132) that "there will be a much broader view of advancement of development than consumption or income as conventionally measured. The perspective of standard of living will include health, education, political liberties, and environment .... The positive analysis of the determinants of the standard of living, and its improvement, of individuals in society will go hand-in-hand with an appraisal of what governments can do to protect individuals through social programs, and in other ways."

Future research will also continue to seek more inclusive explanations of the sources of growth, particularly the long-run growth of total factor productivity. Again, we may agree with Stern that "we seem to have too many theories claiming 'property rights' in the unexplained 'residual,' and have no reassurance that any of them, separately or together, really capture what is going on. Just as worrying is that they omit many issues which are probably crucial to growth in the medium run, including economic organization and the social and physical infrastructure. We still have a great deal to learn about the six factors which we have identified as contributing to growth and about the role of the state in improving their contribution" (Stern, 1991, p. 131).

The six factors on the agenda for understanding the determinants of growth in output per head are capital accumulation; human capital (including learning); research, development and innovation; management, and organization, infrastructure; and the allocation of output across directly productive sectors (Stern, 1991, p. 128). Future analysis of these factors should help to reduce the mystery of the unexplained residual.

To help analyze these factors, it would be desirable to return to historical studies such as were prominent in the 1950s and 1960s (Gerschenkron, Habakkuk, Kuznets, Rostow).[12] With Jeffrey Williamson (1991, pp. 2–3), we may lament that

> caught up in the urgency of contemporary crises, development economists today seem to be less interested in the big questions informed by economic history than was an older generation who eagerly read Kuznets when he began publishing his articles in *Economic Development and Cultural Change* in the 1950s. Indeed, there seems to be a growing gap between contemporary development economics and economic history. What a great irony this is since we now know far more about past industrial revolutions than we did three decades ago. To put it quite bluntly, economic history is far better equipped to educate contemporary debate in the less developed world than it was back in the 1950s and 1960s.

The process of policymaking — both in substance and implementation — should also command more attention in the future. Even though development economics has refined the formal technical theory of policy in imperfect economies, we must still agree with Fishlow (1991, p. 1736) that "what development economics lacks is an adequate theory of government policy".

Development economists cannot view the giving of economic advice as merely a technical exercise; instead, they must integrate it with knowledge of the country's political process. To determine the feasibility and desirability of various policies, economists first need to learn the underlying reasons for government failure. If early writings on development focused on market failure, future writings will give more consideration to government failure and its remedies. In doing so, development economics will incorporate more insights from public choice theory and the new (neoclassical or positive) political economy.[13]

In their knowledge of the policy-making process, development economists — like other economists — are still limited to situations of incremental policy changes involving what Albert Hirschman calls "chosen" problems — those that decision makers "have picked out of thin air" as a result of their own preferences and perceptions. In contrast, "pressing" problems are those "that are forced on the policymakers through pressure from injured or interested outside parties" (Hirschman, 1963). Incremental policy changes are to be contrasted with large, innovative changes.

Figure 15.1 Development analysis in different policy situations

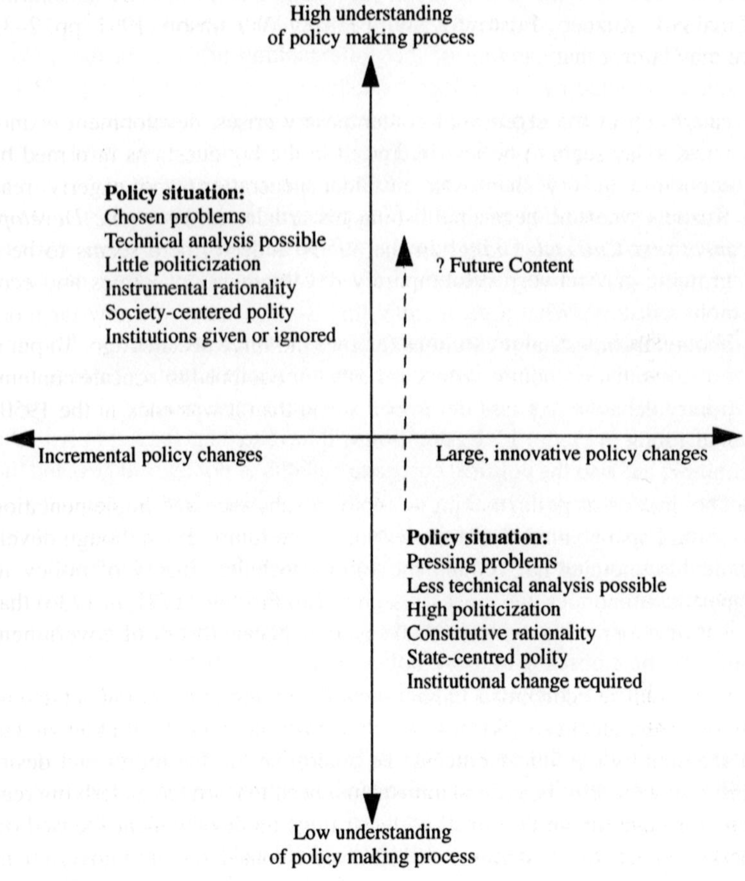

Source: Meier (1991), p. 315.

The incremental policy change involving a chosen problem is amenable to considerable technical analysis and hence a low degree of politicization (that is, politics as usual). It also relies on instrumental rationality: the economist identifies technical policy instruments to be used to achieve policy objectives. The perspective is from a society-centered polity, with government acting as a clearinghouse or broker among interest groups. Moreover, institutions are given or ignored. This type of policy space is represented by the northwest quadrant in Figure 15.1, characterized as the application of ordinary economic analysis with a high understanding of the policymaking process on the part of economists.

In contrast, in situations involving large, innovative policy changes — such as those that characterize problems of development — economists are called upon to advise in a political economy context in which they have a lower understanding of the policymaking process. In this policy space represented by the southeast quadrant in Figure 15.1, the problems are usually pressing. They are not amenable to as much technical analysis but instead are highly politicized. The type of rationality called for is constitutive — that is, decisions have to be made about how decisions are to be made: a constitution is needed. The policymaking process is also more state-centered, influenced by bureaucratic politics and forces that relate to state interests. And an institutional context for decisionmaking has to be established.

If development economists are to attain a better understanding of how to correct non-market failures and overcome resistance to policy reform, they will have to focus more on the policy situations represented by the southeast quadrant in Figure 15.1. Attention will have to be given not only to the economic but also the political costs and benefits of policy changes, and the gainers and losers will have to be identified. It will then be necessary to examine possible ways to compensate the losers, discover the possibilities for building supportive coalitions, and consider the scope for alternative arrangements.

If the evolution of development thought proceeds in these new directions it may become possible to move policy problems represented by the southeast quadrant in Figure 15.1 to the northeast quadrant where understanding of the policymaking process is greater. Thus, a research agenda of the future may follow the broken line in Figure 15.1, requiring development economists to achieve greater understanding of pressing problems that are less amenable to technical analysis, more politicized, involve issues of constitutive rationality, and require institutional change.

Although we can only speculate on the future content of development economics, we can be assured that as long as there is concern for what Smith called the "progressive state" and his objective of "universal" opulence, there will continue to be evolution in development thought. And believing with Smith that "no society can surely be flourishing and happy of which the far greater part of the members are poor and miserable", economists will continue to enjoin the "statesman or legislator" to adopt their policy prescriptions for accelerated development.

Notes

1. World Bank, *World Development Report 1991* (New York: Oxford University Press, 1991) Chs. 7–8.
2. Paul M. Romer, "Increasing Returns and Long-Run Growth, "*Journal of Political Economy*, 94, October 1986, pp. 1002–37; "Growth Based on Increasing Returns to Specialization," *American Economic Review*, vol. 77, no. 2, May 1987, pp. 56–62; "Endogenous Technological Change," *Journal of Political Economy*, vol. 98, no. 5, part 2, Oct. 1990, pp. S71-S99; "Are Non-convexities Important for Understanding Growth?" *American Economic Review*, vol. 80, no. 2, May 1990, pp. 97–103. See also Robert E. Lucas, Jr., "On the Mechanics of Economic Development," *Journal of Monetary Economics*, XXII, July 1988, pp. 3–42. The new endogenous growth models conform better to the evidence on diversity in growth rates among countries over the past three or four decades than does the neoclassical growth model. See Isaac Ehrlich, "The Problem of Development: Introduction," *Journal of Political Economy*, vol. 98, no. 5, part II, Oct. 1990, pp. S2-S3, S7. See also Jati K. Sengupta, "Growth in NICs in Asia: Some Tests of New Growth Theory," *Journal of Development Studies*, January 1993, pp. 342–57.
3. J. Maurice Clark, *Studies in the Economics of Overhead Costs* (Chicago: University of Chicago Press, 1923), p. 120.
4. See Kevin M. Murphy, Andrei Shleifer, and Robert W. Vishny, "Industrialization and the Big Push," *Journal of Political Economy*, vol. 97, no. 5, 1989, pp. 1003–26.
5. *Ibid.*, pp. 1004–06, 1024, Cf. H. W. Arndt, "External Economies in Economic Growth," *Economic Record*, November 1955; Arndt, "Sorting out Externalities," *Malaysian Journal of Economic Studies*, vol. XXVII, nos. 1 & 2, (1990).
6. Paul Krugman, "Towards a Counter-Counterrevolution in Development Theory," Proceedings of the World Bank Annual Conference on Development Economics, Supplement to *World Bank Economic Review* (1992).
7. *Ibid.*, p. 15.
8. *Ibid.*, p. 29.
9. Joseph Stiglitz, "The New Development Economics," *World Development*, 14 (2), Feb. 1986, pp. 257–62.
10. *Ibid.*, pp. 257–59.
11. UNDP, *Human Development Report 1992* (New York: Oxford University Press, 1992) Ch. 1.
12. For excerpts, see Gerald M. Meier, *Leading Issues in Development Economics* (New York: Oxford University Press, 1964) Ch. I. cf. also, Chs. II, IX, above.
13. For a fuller discussion, see Meier (1991). Also instructive for the remainder of this chapter is the analysis by Merilee Grindle and John Thomas, *Public Choices and Policy Change* (Baltimore: Johns Hopkins, 1991) pp. 86ff. Some of their insights are duplicated here.

References

Arrow, Kenneth (1988) "General Economic Theory and the Emergence of Theories of Economic Development," in *The Balance Between Industry and Agriculture in Economic Development*, vol. 1 (London: Macmillan).

Bell, Clive (1987) "Development Economics" in *The New Palgrave* (London: Macmillan) pp. 819–26.

Bliss, Christopher (1989) "Trade and Development" in Hollis Chenery and T. N. Srinivasan (eds.), *Handbook of Development Economics*, vol. 2 (Amsterdam: North-Holland).

Fishlow, Albert (1991) "Review of *Handbook of Development Economics*," *Journal of Economic Literature*, vol. XXIX, no. 4 (December) pp. 1728–37.

Grindle, Merilee and John Thomas (1991) *Public Choices and Policy Change* (Baltimore: Johns Hopkins University Press).

Hirschman, A. O. (1963) *Journeys Toward Progress* (New York: Twentieth Century Fund).

Hirschman, A. O. (1981) "The Rise and Decline of Development Economics" in *Essays In Trespassing: Economics to Politics and Beyond* (New York: Cambridge University Press, 1981).

Little, Ian M. D. (1982) *Economic Development* (New York: Basic Books).

Meier, Gerald M. (1991) *Politics and Policymaking in Developing Countries* (San Francisco: ICS Press).

Srinivasan, T. N. (1988) "Introduction" in Hollis Chenery and T. N. Srinivasan (eds), *Handbook of Development Economics*, vol. 1 (Amsterdam: North Holland).

Stern, Nicholas (1989) "The Economics of Development," *Economic Journal*, vol. 99, no. 397, September, pp. 597–685.

Stern, Nicholas (1991) "The Determinants of Growth," *Economic Journal*, vol. 101, no. 404, January, pp. 122–33.

Williamson, Jeffrey G. (1991) *Inequality, Poverty and History* (Cambridge, MA: Blackwell).

Index